Short Plays
For Young Actors

Smith and Kraus *Books For Actors*

YOUNG ACTORS SERIES

Great Scenes and Monologues for Children
Great Scenes for Young Actors from the Stage
Great Monologues for Young Actors
Multicultural Monologues for Young Actors
Multicultural Scenes for Young Actors
Monologues from Classic Plays 468 BC to 1960 AD
Scenes from Classic Plays 468 BC to 1970 AD
New Plays from A.C.T.'s Young Conservatory Vol. I
New Plays from A.C.T.'s Young Conservatory Vol. II
Plays of America from American Folklore for Children K-6
Plays of America from American Folklore for Young Actors 7-12
Seattle Children's Theatre: Six Plays for Young Actors
Villeggiature: A Trilogy by Carlo Goldoni, *condenced for Young Actors*
Loving to Audition: The Audition Workbook for Young Actors
Movement Stories for Children
An Index of Plays for Young Actors
Discovering Shakespeare: **A Midsummer Night's Dream**, *a workbook for students*
Discovering Shakespeare: **Romeo and Juliet**, *a workbook for students*
Discovering Shakespeare: **The Taming of the Shrew,** *a workbook for students*

CAREER DEVELOPMENT SERIES

The Job Book: 100 Acting Jobs for Actors
The Job Book II: 100 Day Jobs for Actors
The Smith and Kraus Monologue Index
The Great Acting Teachers and Their Methods
The Actor's Guide to Qualified Acting Coaches: New York
The Actor's Guide to Qualified Acting Coaches: Los Angeles
The Camera Smart Actor
The Sanford Meisner Approach
Cold Readings: Some Do's and Don'ts for Actors at Auditions

If you require pre-publication information about upcoming Smith and Kraus books, you may receive our semi-annual catalogue, free of charge, by sending your name and address to Smith and Kraus Catalogue, P.O. Box 127, One Main Street, Lyme, NH 03768. Or call us at (800) 895-4331, fax (603) 795-4427.

Short Plays
For Young Actors

Craig Slaight and Jack Sharrar, Editors

Young Actors Series

SK

A Smith and Kraus Book

A Smith and Kraus Book
Published by Smith and Kraus, Inc.
One Main Street, PO Box 127, Lyme, NH 03768

Copyright © 1996 by Smith and Kraus
All rights reserved

Manufactured in the United States of America
Cover and Text Design by Julia Hill

First Edition: March 1996
10 9 8 7 6 5 4 3 2 1

Library of Congress Cataloging-in-Publication Data

Short plays for young actors / edited by Craig Slaight and Jack Sharrar.
p. cm. --(Young actors series)
Summary: A collection of fourteen short plays for young adults including works
by Thornton Wilder, Edna St. Vincent Millay, and Mac Wellman.
ISBN 1-880399-74-1
1. Young adult drama, American. 2. One-act plays, American. [1. Plays.]
I. Slaight, Craig. II. Sharrar, Jack F., 1949- III. Series.
PS625.5.S.S56   1995
812'.041089283--dc20   95-26295
CIP
AC

For Mary and Alva Gregory

CRAIG SLAIGHT is the Director of the Young Conservatory at American Conservatory Theater. During the past seven years in this position, Craig has worked passionately to provide a creative and dynamic place for young people to learn and grow in theater arts. With a particular commitment to expanding the body of dramatic literature available to young people, Craig has published five volumes, *Great Scenes from the Stage for Young Actors, Great Monologues for Young Actors, Great Scenes and Monologues for Children, Multicultural Scenes for Young Actors,* and *Multicultural Monologues for Young Actors,* co-edited by A.C.T.'s Jack Sharrar. *Great Monologues for Young Actors* was selected by the New York Public Library as one of the outstanding books of 1993 for teenagers. Additionally, Craig began the New Plays Program at the Young Conservatory in 1989 with the mission to develop plays by professional playwrights that view the world through the eyes of the young. The first five are collected in a publication by Smith and Kraus publishers, *New Plays from the A.C.T. Young Conservatory Volume I.* Educated in Michigan in Theater and English, Craig taught at the junior and senior high school, college, and university levels, prior to moving to Los Angeles, where he spent ten years as a professional director (directing such notables as Julie Harris, Linda Purl, Betty Garrett, Harold Gould, Patrick Duffey, and Robert Foxworth). Since joining A.C.T., Craig has often served as Associate Director for main stage productions. In addition to the work at A.C.T., Craig is a consultant to the Educational Theater Association, a panel member for the National Foundation for Advancement in the Arts, and is a frequent guest artist, speaker, workshop leader, and adjudicator for festivals and conferences throughout the country. In August of 1994, Slaight received the President's Award from The Educational Theater Association for outstanding contributions to youth theater.

Jack Sharrar is Registrar and Director of the M.F.A. program for the American Conservatory Theater, where he also teaches a variety of classes in studio A.C.T. and the Young Conservatory. Mr. Sharrar is a graduate of the University of Michigan, and holds a Ph.D. in theater history and dramatic literature from the University of Utah. At Utah he taught performance workshop, teaching methods for secondary school teachers, administered the Utah State Drama Festival, and supervised student teachers. Among his professional theater credits are roles at Michigan Repertory Theater, Mountainside Theater, the BoarsHead Theatre, Theatre 40, and the Pioneer Theatre Company. He has directed over 50 plays and musicals, and is a member of Actor's Equity and the Screen Actor's Guild. He is author of *Avery Hopwood, His Life and Plays;* contributor to Oxford University Press's *The American National Biography;* and coeditor (with Craig Straight) of *Great Scenes for Young actors from the Stage, Great Monologues for Young actors* (which the New York Public Library selected as one of the Best Books for the Teenage 1993), *Great Scenes and Monologues for Children, Multicultural Monologues for Young Actors* and *Multicultural Scenes for Young Actors.*

Preface

The idea of assembling a collection of short plays for young actors presented itself with an equal mix of excitement and trepidation. We were excited because there are few collections of short plays in existence that deal with a young person's point of view. The trepidation entered when we considered the wide range of possibilities that might compose such a book—nothing short of the great body of dramatic literature. Nonetheless we believed that a collection of short plays for young actors was essential, partly because in our own work with young actors we had a great need for accessible plays that didn't take two to three hours to perform; so we started digging.

Early on, we felt that this collection should appeal to a wide variety of theatrical tastes and that it should embrace a variety of styles and themes. Although the unifying factor here is a youthful perspective and the length of the play, the stories told, as well as the ways in which they are presented, are decidedly different. The hope is that young actors, directors, and teachers will have before them a treasure of diverse life—journeys that can serve for many years. In no way do we feel that this is a definitive collection. Rather, we have chosen short plays that we believe are compelling in their writing and passionate in their delivery. If anything we have intended to stretch the "usual" with alternatives that challenge and inform. By design, the look at the world offered here is one that embraces the past and the present: it is universal in ideas, yet diverse in language and style.

Here then is your opportunity to explore short plays that offer a youthful viewpoint. From the neo-classic LA DISPUTE of Marivaux and the classical and poetic Harlequinade of Edna St. Vincent Millay's ARIA DA CAPO, to the vaudeville antics of THE POT BOILER, to the contemporary theatrical dream world of Mac Wellman's CLEVELAND, your journey can yield new dimensions in your acting. Brad Slaight's OPEN ROAD mixes contemporary with classical language, when a young man who is so inspired by the passions of Walt Whitman's poetry decides to impersonate him. Lynne Alvarez dispenses with verbal language altogether and employs physical expression as the sole form of communication in WHO IS CHASING WHOM! From the small-town Texas of 1947 in Horton Foote's THE DANCERS to a remote village in Japan in the 1600s in Velina Hasu Houston's telling of a Japanese myth, THE MATSUYAMA MIRROR, the dramatic road map in this collection allows for exciting adventures in worlds perhaps yet untraveled in your life.

As you study these plays during your actor training, we urge you to consider producing them as well. Taking the full journey from page to stage holds an exciting promise for any actor. Just as Thornton Wilder asked us to consider "the grand and the particular" in our world, so do we challenge you to do the same in your artistic life; for it is through our appreciation and creation of art that the world somehow seems a better place.

Craig Slaight
Jack Sharrar
San Francisco

Contents

Introduction
Lean Forward
An Orientation to Professionalism For the Student Actor

by Jack Sharrar

There is a vitality, a life force, an energy, a quickening that is translated through you into action and because there is only one of you in all of time this expression is unique and if you block it, it will never exist through any other medium and be lost, the world will not have it.

—Martha Graham

The words of Martha Graham speak to us as actors as well as to dancers. If we are to express ourselves completely and share the uniqueness of our creative energy, we must remove the obstacles that inhibit our creativity. Achieving this freedom is no easy task, however. In order for us to achieve our creative potential, we must not only study the techniques of our craft, we must also develop in ourselves a standard of professionalism that shows we respect our art and the other people who practice it. Indeed, the attitude and manner with which we approach our training and performance is as important to our art as the techniques and skills with which we perform.

Professionalism is learning the skills and aims of one's profession, and then striving to uphold those ideals to the best of one's ability. Professionalism is excellence, commitment, and personal integrity. Professionalism is respect for one's self, respect for one's work, and respect for the work of others. Professionalism has to do with one's attitude and approach to work rather than the fame or financial rewards achieved.

Cultivating a professional attitude is an essential component to actor training. As actors, we must continually strive to commit ourselves to our art—our work—to grab hold and reach for the highest standards of excellence in all that we are called upon to do. We must establish training and craft goals for ourselves. If we approach our art in this way, we elevate ourselves and our profession.

PROFESSIONALISM BEGINS OFFSTAGE

As actors, we should work to reflect the image of the world we want to see; have a vision of what mankind can be. We must strive to be people of substance, people who are informed and have a point of view about life and art, for it is through theater and the other arts that we can investigate the mysteries of living and express the truths we feel.

> *I regard the theater as the greatest of all art forms, the most immediate way in which a human being can share with another the sense of what it is to be a human being.*
> —Thornton Wilder

Taking a class or accepting a role in a production is a contractual obligation. We must be prepared to meet the requirements and demands of the process, realizing that others have also entered into this contract—we have entered a partnership. We must show respect for the work, ourselves, and our fellows.

Once cast in a production or enrolled in a class, we must honor that commitment. We must never miss rehearsals or expect others to work around our personal schedule. We must always arrive on time and ready to work. This means arriving early in order to warm up and prepare for class or rehearsal. Remember, in the professional theater, time is money. But also realize: a paycheck doesn't make a professional.

Since we have chosen this profession and training, we should also choose to make the process positive. Our attitude makes a difference. We must learn how to work with our fellow artists—to be attentive, supportive, and cooperative. Such an atmosphere enhances the ensemble, develops camaraderie, encourages spontaneity, and allows the most exciting discoveries to happen. We should exhibit this creative attitude in training, rehearsal, and production. As Stanislavski said, "Love the art in you, not yourself in the art."

> *Actors have to come to a play with creative energy, instead of defensive energy about proving themselves worthy.*
> —Robert Joy

We must strive to keep our minds and bodies alert during rehearsal and class work. We have to "lean forward," as Harold Clurman said, and actively pay attention and observe rather than lie back and drift off, for there is something to be learned from every experience.

> *Acting provides the fulfillment of never being fulfilled. You're never as good as you'd like to be. So there's always something to hope for.*
> —Glenda Jackson

We must cultivate self-motivation, and not expect the instructor or director to be a cheerleader. We must work to make ourselves interested, choosing to listen to everything in the studio and rehearsal, asking how we might benefit from the direction. Often the advice given to other actors is applicable to us and is most useful.

We shouldn't always depend upon teachers, stage managers, and directors to maintain control or enforce discipline. We must be our own disciplinarians, for each artist must be free to focus his or her energy on the creative process.

> *I sometimes think that if professional actors reflected a little more on how we all learn acceptable social manners, it would be a valuable guide to many of the techniques of their craft.*
> —Tyrone Guthrie

We must be aware of the impact we have upon the dynamics of the group, conscientiously working to strengthen the ensemble: sharing and giving our energy to others rather than taking and sapping; always giving focus to the work of others and not stealing it. We must never forget that training with others is a privilege, and that the process and the work is larger than ourselves.

> *The actors must understand each other, help each other, absolutely love each other. They absolutely must.*
> —Laurence Olivier

Actors learn through observation. We must always concentrate and focus our energy on our fellow artists during class work and rehearsal. We should keep notes on all class work and rehearsals—study them, and review them before our next session. Keeping a journal can be both an enjoyable time for reflection and a valuable aid in evaluating our progress, assessing our strengths, weaknesses, and growth as people and as artists.

> *In the studio you learn to conform—to submit yourself to the demands of your craft—so that you may finally be free.*
> —Martha Graham

PROFESSIONAL TRAINING AND REHEARSAL ETHICS

Please note: the following precepts, and those throughout, should not be thought of as hard-and-fast "rules"; they are mutually agreed upon principles that should not be violated casually, unthinkingly, or without good reason.

Make it a point to read all handbooks for the school or production company of which you may be a part. Reading about the history and philosophy of a company is also helpful in better understanding its aims and goals.

Be early in order to warm up.

Avoid personal activities that interfere with concentration and energy:

- eat beforehand, not in the studio or in the theater

- do not read newspapers during rehearsal or class; it's rude and can be demoralizing to your associates; do this reading during breaks outside the space
- do not chew gum; it may be distracting to others
- always wear clothing that the instructor or director has requested
- learn and follow all smoking rules; you are responsible for the health and safety of others
- do not wear dangling or jangling jewelry; it may be distracting to others

Take responsibility to do your own research and analysis—this is part of your process.

Memorize all lines accurately and on schedule as directed.

I can't understand actors who learn their lines approximately. If it's a good script, the writer has sweated over every part of it and a single word can throw everything.
—Katharine Hepburn

Never interrupt the teacher/director and the actors during rehearsal.

Avoid walking between the director/teacher and the actors during rehearsal.

Do not direct or coach your fellow actors; if you have suggestions, channel them through the director/teacher.

Control impulses to recite fellow actors' lines while they rehearse or to cue them if they forget a line.

Avoid the temptation to proffer opinions about scene work or attempt to "fix" the work of others.

In discussion, think as an investigator, not as a director or a critic.

Accept criticism without defensiveness; use what works and discard the rest.

Apply observations of others to your own work.

Be open to new methods and techniques; there is no one "right" way to successful acting.

Create your own method. Don't depend slavishly on mine (or someone else's). Make up something that will work for you! But keep breaking traditions, I beg you.
—Constantin Stanislavski

Avoid talking and whispering during class work and rehearsal. Many times the actors perceive such talk as negative criticism. We must work to remove obstacles, not create them.

Never invite guests to attend class or rehearsal unless you have secured permission from the stage manager/instructor in advance.

Take responsibility to keep the studios and rehearsal rooms clean.

We should show enthusiasm for the work of our fellow artists: actors, designers, technicians, directors, and teachers alike, giving praise when it is justified, and offering constructive criticism when it is appropriate. When discussing the work of our colleagues, we must strive to be open and honest while avoiding negative, destructive comments which may serve to mask our own insecurity; pettiness and selfish defensiveness produce negative energy.

We must aim for "character" in the moral and ethical sense of the word, compounded of the virtues of mutual respect, courtesy, kindness, generosity, trust, attention to the others, seriousness, loyalty, as well as those necessary attributes of diligence and dedication.
—Uta Hagen

We must be loyal to our fellow artists and the projects we are creating, choosing to contribute positively to the work rather than finding fault. A supportive atmosphere is essential so that the group feels secure; not in a cozy, comfortable sense that encourages complacency, but in an atmosphere of nurturing that encourages actors to take risks and stretch themselves.

> *An actor has no right to mold his partner so as to provide greater possibilities for his own performance. Nor has he the right to correct his partner...Intimate or drastic elements in the work of others are untouchable and should not be commented upon even in their absence. Private conflicts, quarrels, sentiments, animosities are unavoidable in any human group. It is our duty towards creation to keep these in check in so far as they might deform and wreck the work process.*
> —Jerzy Grotowski

We must create an environment away from the studio where we can explore and develop: channel our energy and make it work for us rather than against us by structuring our time so that we are able to bring our full creative power to the artistic process.

> *Let someone explain to me why the violinist who plays in an orchestra on the tenth violin must daily perform hour-long exercises or lose his power to play? Why does the dancer work daily over every muscle in his body? Why do the painter, the sculptor, the writer practice their art each day and count that day lost when they do not work? And why may the dramatic artist do nothing, spend his day in coffee houses and hope for the gift of (inspiration) in the evening? There is no art that does not demand virtuosity.*
> —Constantin Stanislavski

Actor training is a demanding, lifelong process. We must continuously work to improve our bodies, voices, imaginations, and knowledge; we are our own instruments. We must cherish our health the most and take care of ourselves, especially avoiding substance abuse and unsafe sexual activity. If substance abuse is a problem, we must seek help and commit our energy to our art.

Like it or not, we must accept acting as a competitive profession. We will be constantly competing with other actors for roles. And, like it or not, we are constantly auditioning and presenting ourselves to others. Yet we won't get every role we seek. Therefore, a sense of self-worth and self-esteem are essential if we are to keep our careers in perspective. We must persevere and be self-assertive without being pushy or cutthroat. Negative energy backfires.

AUDITION PROCEDURE AND BEHAVIOR

Read the play.

Find out as much information as you can about the director, the play, and the type of audition.

Find out if there will be cold readings or prepared pieces.

Find out if all roles are open, or have some been precast.

Check out the audition space, if possible.

Wear clothing that seems to be in the spirit of the play, but not a costume or theatrical makeup.

Assess your previous commitments and time conflicts.

Arrive early enough to warm up.

Carefully read all written instructions and accurately fill out all forms.

Bring a resume and quality head shot.

Make certain your resume *accurately* and *honestly* reflects your acting experience.

Don't try to second-guess the director; make your choices and present them to the best of your ability.

It should be a cardinal rule of an actor's life: Always audition. You may find out something about the role you haven't gleaned from the written page; you may find the director has a concept totally unlike the writing. Half the actor's life is auditioning, half is performing. Why stint on the auditioning half?
—Michael Shurtleff

When performing, we must build our day around that event, preparing ourselves so that we can give full energy to the work we have helped create.

Performance schedules vary and change; check your assumptions.

Be on time; lateness can be equivalent to absence.

Always enter and exit through the stage door, never through the lobby and house.

Leave personal problems at the stage door.

Always sign yourself in; telephone the stage manager if you are going to be late.

Check the call board every day for information.

Do not smoke, eat, chew gum, or drink in costume or in the wings unless required by performance.

Check on your own props at half hour.

Do not sit on prop furniture backstage.

Place only props on the prop tables.

Remember, backstage energy affects onstage energy.

Respect the warm-up and pre-entrance preparation of your fellow actors.

Always be ready in the wings for your entrance; missing an entrance is betraying the trust of your fellow artists. Always be thinking ahead.

Be aware of sightlines; if you can see the audience, they can see you.

Play every role to the best of your ability, no matter how small or how large.

Always respect the audience, regardless of size; the audience is a partner, not an adversary.

Do not break the illusion of the theater by appearing in costume and makeup offstage or outside the theater.

Never allow the comments of outsiders to change any aspect of your characterization; always consult with the director about your work.

One mustn't allow acting to be like stockbroking—you must not take it just as a means of earning a living, to go down every day to do a job of work. The big thing is to combine punctuality, efficiency, good nature, obedience, intelligence, and concentration with an unawareness of what is going to happen next, thus keeping yourself available for excitement.

—John Gielgud

There are no shortcuts to solid artistic work as an actor. The cultivation of a self-disciplined, professional attitude in our training and production work is a commitment we must all be prepared to make. We must have patience and strive together, supporting one another in our development. This kind of attitude strengthens and enriches the technical skills we learn to communicate a character effectively to an audience, and leads us closer to an invigorating, successful life in the theater.

Painted Rain
A Play In One Act
By Janet Allard

JANET MALIA ALLARD is originally from Hawaii where she began playwriting. She has since studied at Trinity College, Dublin Ireland and interned with the Mark Taper Forum in Los Angeles. *Painted Rain*, Allard's first play was produced at Playwright's Horizons as part of the Young Playwright's Festival (1989). *Painted Rain* received subsequent productions including an International production in Australia (at the Gipsland Art Center) and publication by Dell (an anthology entitled *Hey Little Walter*) and by Smith and Kraus in 1994 (*Scenes and Monologues for Children*). Allard's other plays *Sand Dragons, Anything Nice At All, Waiting for Mu'u Mu'us,* and *Salivate* have all received productions and/or staged readings at venues in America and abroad. Her latest play *The Fattest Man In The World Lives Upstairs* was most recently produced at the Yale Cabaret theater as part of their 1995 summer season. Janet is currently in her second year as a playwright at the Yale School of Drama, where she recently received the Truman Capote Fellowship for Dramatic Writing.

ORIGINAL PRODUCTION
Painted Rain was originally produced at The Kennedy Center, with the following cast:
> Laura Kenyon
> Jerome McGill
> DeMarco Boone

CHARACTERS
> Teddy
> Dustin
> Barbara

PAINTED RAIN

SCENE ONE

The lights rise to reveal the bedroom of two foster children. There are two beds situated to the side of a rather large window, which is separated into squares of glass by a thin wooden frame. There are a few personal items, a couple of old-looking pictures and painting tools scattered about Dustin's side of the room. Teddy's side is mostly bare. As the lights rise to a dim, early morning, we find Dustin, a boy of sixteen, lying in bed asleep. Behind the bed, and barely visible, are a wheelchair, a pair of long leg braces and a pair of crutches. Teddy, a boy of about eleven, is sitting on his bed singing a simple, childlike song, or humming and playing absentmindedly with his bed sheets. He quiets down and pauses, then looks over at Dustin.

TEDDY: (*Softly.*) Dustin? (*Pause.*) Hey, Dustin? (*Teddy gets up, wanders over to Dustin's bed, and stands looking down on him.*) Dustin, are you awake?
(*Dustin remains still, and there is silence. Teddy stands looking down on him for another minute, then begins his singing again. He walks softly back to the area between the two beds and sits in the middle of the floor. Leaning over, Teddy reaches under his bed and pulls out a large bag filled with many interesting items he's collected over the years. One by one he pulls these things out and places them on the floor. As he does this, he begins talking. The sound of rain hitting against the windowpane can be heard softly in the background.*)
TEDDY: Look, Dustin, it's raining. (*Dustin remains asleep.*) Not very hard, though. I guess whoever's making the rain doesn't want to wake you up. (*He looks over at Dustin.*) Dustin? (*Pause.*) Dustin? You awake yet?
DUSTIN: (*Groggily.*) Yeah.
TEDDY: Want to go out and play?
DUSTIN: I want to go back to sleep. It's two o'clock in the morning.
TEDDY: No, it's not. It's three.
DUSTIN: Who the hell cares? Just shut up and go to sleep.
TEDDY: (*Softly.*) I care. (*Teddy goes back to the floor and, singing softly, puts his stuff back in his bag. He comes across a pair of dark glasses,*

which he examines with interest, then puts on. He puts his stuff back under the bed, keeping the glasses on. He starts feeling around in front of him as if he were blind. He gets up and walks forward, still pretending he's blind, and runs into the furniture.) Dustin? (*No response.*) Dustin, I'm blind. (*Still pretending, Teddy walks over to Dustin's bed and looks down on him.*) Dustin, I can't see.

(*After getting no response, Teddy reaches down and touches Dustin's face. Dustin bolts to a sitting position.*)

DUSTIN: What are you doing?

TEDDY: I'm blind, Dustin.

DUSTIN: Would you take off those stupid dark glasses and quit playing around?

TEDDY: No. Dustin, come play with me. You could lead me around.

DUSTIN: I don't want to. I want to sleep.

TEDDY: Then I guess I'm just going to run into things, huh? (*Teddy starts walking around, hits Dustin's bed, and falls on top of him.*)

DUSTIN: Hey, cut it out! Get off of me!

TEDDY: That's what happens when nobody leads blind people around.

DUSTIN: You're not blind, stupid. Now, let me sleep.

TEDDY: But, Dustin ...

DUSTIN: Teddy, I mean it!

(*Teddy goes back over to his bed and lies down on his back. Keeping the dark glasses on, he feels in the air, still pretending he's blind. Teddy begins singing softly again and slowly raises his voice. Dustin turns over and looks at Teddy.*)

DUSTIN: I can't even go back to sleep now.

TEDDY: Why not?

DUSTIN: Because I'm mad, that's why.

TEDDY: I didn't do anything. I only wanted you to lead me around.

DUSTIN: (*Pays little attention to Teddy. He sits up, brings the wheelchair around from behind his bed, and drags himself into it with his arms as Teddy is saying his line. As soon as Dustin is in his chair, the lights brighten.*) Well I'm not going to.

TEDDY: Then I'll lead you around. Now that you're up, we can play.

DUSTIN: No. Now that I'm up, I can paint.

TEDDY: Dustin, you're my brother. You're supposed to play with me.

DUSTIN: I am not your brother.

TEDDY: Well, we're almost brothers

DUSTIN: You can't almost be brothers with someone.

TEDDY: Yes, you can. We've lived together for a long time and that makes us almost brothers.

DUSTIN: It hasn't been more than a year.

TEDDY: That's a long time.

DUSTIN: That's relative.

TEDDY: Barbara says that I could think of you as my brother if I wanted.

DUSTIN: Well, don't.

TEDDY: Why not?

DUSTIN: Just don't.

TEDDY: She says that I could think of you as my brother as long as I know that if you get adopted, you can belong to someone else too.

DUSTIN: Yeah, well, I'm not going to get adopted.

TEDDY: Okay. I won't either.

(*Teddy turns away and begins singing again. Dustin pulls out his paints and starts painting. Teddy's singing gets louder and louder until Dustin interrupts.*)

DUSTIN: Will you shut up!

TEDDY: Yeah. I think I will.

(*Dustin goes back to painting, ignoring Teddy.*)

TEDDY: I didn't have anything to sing anyway. I'm running out of songs. Help me pick one, Dustin.

DUSTIN: How would I know what you want to sing?

TEDDY: I don't know. You could help me make one up.

DUSTIN: Teddy –

TEDDY: We could sing a song about painting if you want.

DUSTIN: Shut up! I'm trying to work.

TEDDY: A true artist could paint with me talking. But that's okay. We'll make the room very quiet so you can concentrate.

(*Both of them are silent. Then they look over at each other at the same time.*)

DUSTIN: Teddy!

TEDDY: Shhh! You're trying to concentrate.

(*Dustin throws a pillow at Teddy.*)

TEDDY: Okay, okay, you win! (*Silence. Then Teddy looks over at the painting.*) What are you painting?

DUSTIN: Come over here and take a look.

TEDDY: No.

DUSTIN: If you took off those stupid dark glasses, you could see it from there.

TEDDY: I want you to tell me about it.

DUSTIN: Teddy, paintings are meant to be looked at, not told about.

TEDDY: Who says?

DUSTIN: Everybody says. That's just the way it is.

TEDDY: Aw, com'on, Dustin. Any artist could show their painting. It takes a really good one to describe it.

DUSTIN: Where did you hear that one?

TEDDY: I made it up. It's just that I've never heard anyone describe a painting before.

DUSTIN: Well, I'm not going to describe it.

TEDDY: Then I'm going back to sleep.

DUSTIN: Good.

TEDDY: Why is that good?

DUSTIN: Because it's three o'clock in the morning.

TEDDY: No, it's not. I bet it's almost four.

(*Lights fade to black.*)

SCENE TWO

Teddy bends over backward from his bed, reaches under it, and pulls out a bottle of orange juice. He then flips over onto the floor and opens the lid. Dustin keeps painting.

TEDDY: Hey, Dustin?

DUSTIN: What?

TEDDY: Want some orange juice?

DUSTIN: Where did you get that?

TEDDY: Under the bed.

DUSTIN: You can't keep orange juice under the bed, stupid. It'll spoil.

TEDDY: I'm going to drink it before it spoils, so I can keep it wherever I want.

(*He takes a long sip, then offers it to Dustin, who turns away.*)

DUSTIN: At least drink it out of a glass.

TEDDY: Why?

DUSTIN: Because everybody drinks out of glasses.

TEDDY: Well, I don't. Maybe everyone else should drink like I do.

DUSTIN: (*Absentmindedly.*) Maybe.

TEDDY: Adults always say you should drink out of glasses and paint the sky blue and the trees green. Why?

DUSTIN: What are you asking me for? I'm not an adult.

TEDDY: If everyone else jumped off a cliff, would you do it too?

DUSTIN: Of course I wouldn't. Would you?

TEDDY: Maybe I would, but it would be a *different* cliff.

DUSTIN: Teddy, just leave me alone for a while.

TEDDY: (*Moves over to Dustin.*) Dustin, why is it all sort of blue?

DUSTIN: Why is what blue?

TEDDY: Your painting.

DUSTIN: I don't know. It just is.

TEDDY: What time is it?

DUSTIN: Time?

TEDDY: In the painting.

DUSTIN: (*As if he's picking a time at random.*) It's two o'clock in the morning.

TEDDY: And it's *blue?*

DUSTIN: Yeah. What's wrong with blue?

TEDDY: Never mind, you don't care.

DUSTIN: You're right.

TEDDY: It's just that it's yellow at two o'clock in the morning.

DUSTIN: The sun's not up yet. It's blue.

TEDDY: If you wanted to do it right, you'd paint it yellow. That's the color it is at that time.

DUSTIN: I told you it doesn't matter. Besides, yellow wouldn't look right anyway.

TEDDY: How about red?

DUSTIN: Red?

TEDDY: Yeah, a big red splash.

DUSTIN: It would look out of place.

TEDDY: Not if you were the red splash.

DUSTIN: Teddy, you can't be a red splash.

TEDDY: I can be whatever I want to. Maybe you couldn't pretend you're one. But I could.

DUSTIN: That's stupid, Teddy.

TEDDY: Splash.

DUSTIN: What?

TEDDY: From now on I want you to call me Red Splash.

DUSTIN: Teddy –

TEDDY: Splash.

DUSTIN: You're being stupid, Theodore.

TEDDY: Teddy!

DUSTIN: I thought you wanted me to call you Splash.

TEDDY: I changed my mind. I don't like it.

DUSTIN: Good.

(*Teddy gets up, moves over to the window and stands looking out. Dustin begins to look over at Teddy and take an interest in what he's doing.*)

DUSTIN: You like what you see out there, Teddy?

TEDDY: Yeah, you can just look straight out into the trees and grass. At home I used to just look out the window and watch the rain.

DUSTIN: Did it rain a lot?

TEDDY: Yeah, all the time. I used to sit with my face right up against the glass and try and see if I could find one raindrop and follow it all the way until it hit the ground.

DUSTIN: Could you?

TEDDY: Naw, they always moved too fast. It works with snow, though. Snow just kinda floats.

DUSTIN: You like snow, Teddy?

TEDDY: (*Nods.*) I like rain better. Raindrops are more fun to watch. Did you ever watch 'em?

DUSTIN: I guess I must've.

TEDDY: Do you like rain?

DUSTIN: It's okay.

TEDDY: Do you like it to go out in?

DUSTIN: I did when I was a little kid.

TEDDY: Not that it matters, but I just thought I'd tell you that I would have followed you out into the rain, Dustin.

DUSTIN: What are you talking about?

TEDDY: About that one time when you were really mad at me and I went out into the rain and you didn't follow me. Remember that time?

DUSTIN: No, not really.

TEDDY: Dustin?

DUSTIN: What?

TEDDY: Never mind. (*Pause.*) Dustin?

DUSTIN: What?

TEDDY: Would you follow me out into the pouring rain?

DUSTIN: It's not pouring, Teddy.

TEDDY: If it was.

(*Dustin doesn't answer.*)

TEDDY: We could jump out through the window if you wanted.

DUSTIN: What?

TEDDY: If we go out through the window, then you're out in the rain right away. We'd have more time to play. We wouldn't have to walk down the hall and go through lots of doors.

DUSTIN: That's stupid.

TEDDY: No, it's not. I could help you through the window.

DUSTIN: I don't think so. You're being childish.

TEDDY: Child*like*. It would be fun. Come on.

DUSTIN: Teddy, I'm busy.

TEDDY: You could stop painting and we could go out and climb trees and play in the mud. We could just splash around in the puddles if you wanted.

DUSTIN: Naw, I don't feel like it.

TEDDY: Why not?

DUSTIN: I'm not in the mood to splash around.

TEDDY: You would be when we got out there. You could probably make bigger splashes than I could.

DUSTIN: (*Motioning to his wheelchair.*) Not in this thing.

TEDDY: Dustin.

DUSTIN: Forget it, Teddy. It's hardly raining anymore. It wouldn't be much fun. (*He goes back to painting.*)

TEDDY: I guess. Rain is always more fun when it's coming down hard. (*Dustin looks away, frustrated by Teddy's childlike way of thinking. There is a sound of a doorbell.*)

TEDDY: It's probably Barbara.

DUSTIN: Barbara?

TEDDY: Yeah, she was going to stop by to talk to us sometime.

DUSTIN: When?

TEDDY: I thought you didn't care about time.

DUSTIN: Teddy – just go let her in.

TEDDY: Why can't you?

DUSTIN: Because I'm *painting*.

TEDDY: Okay!

(*Teddy exits. Dustin waits until he's gone, then wheels to the corner of the room, where his braces are resting. He picks them up, wheels back to the bed, and leans down, shoving the braces under the bed. Dustin returns to painting. Teddy bounds into the room, jumps on the bed, then collapses, and lies down on his back with his hands behind his head. Barbara enters. She is a social worker in her early thirties. Other than being noticeably overweight, she is relatively pretty.*)

BARBARA: Hi, guys!

TEDDY: Barbie! What a surprise. Look, Dustin, Barbara stopped by to see us.

DUSTIN: I can see her, Teddy.

BARBARA: How do you think I look?

DUSTIN: Fine.

BARBARA: I lost a few pounds last week.

TEDDY: It looks like you found them again this week.

BARBARA: (*Laughs.*) What's that supposed to mean?

TEDDY: It means that I *didn't* lose any weight last week, and I'm still skinnier than you.

BARBARA: Aw, come on. I'm not that fat.

TEDDY: Well, you have something to bug us about, so we have to bug you about something too.

BARBARA: The only reason you say I'm overweight is because other than a couple pounds, you can't find anything wrong with me.

TEDDY: Oh, yeah?

BARBARA: Yeah! You can't even see straight with those dark glasses on. So I shouldn't even listen to you.

TEDDY: I don't have to see straight. I can tell you're fat anyway.

BARBARA: How?

TEDDY: You sound fat.

BARBARA: Why don't you take them off, Teddy?

TEDDY: 'Cause I like them on.

BARBARA: Come on now. This game was fun for a little while, but it's time to take off the glasses.

TEDDY: I can't. I'm blind.

BARBARA: You are not blind, honey.

TEDDY: I am too.

BARBARA: Two weeks ago you were pretending you were deaf.

TEDDY: So what?

BARBARA: So you can't keep pretending there's something wrong with you.

TEDDY: There's nothing wrong with me. I'm just blind, that's all.

DUSTIN: Cut it out, Teddy.

TEDDY: Why?

DUSTIN: 'Cause Barbara's not here to play games with you.

TEDDY: Yeah, she's here to bug me about being blind.

BARBARA: We do have some things we should talk about, Ted.

TEDDY: I just want to play right now.

DUSTIN: Didn't you hear her? She said she wants to talk to you.

TEDDY: I want you to come.

DUSTIN: No. We just can't go outside and play and leave Barbara here.

TEDDY: (*Walks to the door frame and looks at Dustin.*) Are you coming or not?

DUSTIN: No. Now, come back here and sit down.
(*Teddy exits.*)

DUSTIN: Teddy! (*Dustin jerks his wheelchair toward the door and looks as if he's going to go after him. He stops himself, slowly turns back, and begins painting again.*)

BARBARA: That's all right. Let him go. I wanted to talk to you a little too.

DUSTIN: Anything special, or you just want to talk about whatever comes to mind?

BARBARA: How about Teddy?

DUSTIN: He's been acting real weird lately.

BARBARA: (*Making both beds.*) Weird? How?

DUSTIN: I mean, he's been acting like he's a little kid. I can't even carry on a conversation with him.

BARBARA: Could you ever?

DUSTIN: (*Laughs.*) He also asked me to go out and play with him when it was raining really hard. I mean, it just came out of nowhere. All of a sudden he wanted me to go climb trees in the rain.

BARBARA: Did you go play with him?

DUSTIN: I'm too old to play his stupid little games.

BARBARA: Is that all?

DUSTIN: Well, the wheelchair doesn't help any. And I really wanted to paint. I mean, look at this. (*He holds up his painting for Barbara.*) It's a lot more fun to create something like this than to try and climb a tree in a wheelchair.

BARBARA: What about using your braces?

DUSTIN: You think I could climb a tree with *them* on?

BARBARA: No. But I do think you could walk with them on.

DUSTIN: I guess so.

BARBARA: Speaking of walking, your teacher called today. She said you've been going to therapy late.

DUSTIN: I've been busy.

BARBARA: Try to make it on time next week, all right?

DUSTIN: Fine.

BARBARA: Does Teddy ever help you walk?

DUSTIN: No. He used to watch me a lot, but now it's like I don't even have an impairment. He completely ignores it and asked me to climb out the window and splash in the puddles.
(*They both look out the window.*)

BARBARA: How does it feel to watch him play outside when you're in here?

DUSTIN: The same way it feels for him to sit there and watch me paint.

BARBARA: What do you mean?

DUSTIN: Do you feel bad 'cause you're not playing right now?
(*Barbara shakes her head no.*)

DUSTIN: Neither do I.

BARBARA: Things would just be a lot easier if you could walk.

DUSTIN: You mean I would get adopted into a real home faster.

BARBARA: That's not what I said.

DUSTIN: Well, look at Teddy. He can walk and he's still here with me.

BARBARA: Has Teddy talked to you about leaving?

DUSTIN: (*Defensively.*) No, why?

BARBARA: We've been working out an arrangement for a couple to adopt him.

DUSTIN: It'll probably fall through.

BARBARA: I don't think so. They're stopping by to see him again next week. It looks like this time it's really going to work out.

DUSTIN: Does he know that?

BARBARA: I told him.

DUSTIN: And he's still pretending he's blind.

BARBARA: Yeah, that's the problem. He has to be ready next week. He can't be running around refusing to take off a pair of dark glasses.

DUSTIN: Ya know, he asked me to describe my painting to him today.

BARBARA: Did you?

(*Teddy enters, having heard Dustin's last line, and bounces onto the bed.*)

DUSTIN: No. I mean, how do you describe a painting?

TEDDY: You did too describe it. It's all kinda blue. I think it's pretty.

DUSTIN: You can't see it.

TEDDY: I already know what it looks like.

BARBARA: You can't really know what it's like if you don't see it.

TEDDY: And you can't really know what it *feels* like if you do see it.

BARBARA: Honey, the whole idea of a painting is that they're to look at it. You can't get the effect of a painting by just hearing about it.

DUSTIN: See, I told you.

TEDDY: Nobody asked you. (*Teddy reaches under the bed for his orange juice and feels the braces.*)

DUSTIN: (*Forcefully.*) Your orange juice isn't under there, Teddy.

BARBARA: (*Turning to Teddy.*) You keep juice under your bed?

TEDDY: Let me guess, *you* don't, right?

DUSTIN: (*Forcefully.*) I put it back in the fridge.

TEDDY: Thanks.

BARBARA: Ted, the couple you met is going to drop by to visit with you again sometime next week, okay?

TEDDY: Me and Dustin don't need any visitors. We do just fine by ourselves.

BARBARA: They want to see you and show you your new home.

TEDDY: I can't see them. I'm blind.

DUSTIN: How did I know he was gonna say that?

BARBARA: Ted, you're not, and you have to stop playing this silly game.

TEDDY: How do you know I'm not?

DUSTIN: Teddy, stop.

TEDDY: I'm not doing anything wrong.

BARBARA: No one said you were, sweetie.

TEDDY: Then quit bugging me!

BARBARA: Pretending you can't see is not going to prevent you from being adopted.

TEDDY: I didn't say it was. Leave me alone.

DUSTIN: I told you it was hopeless.

BARBARA: Okay. Well, Dustin what do you say we show Teddy how to cooperate and get you to do some walking now?

DUSTIN: Why?

BARBARA: Just for a bit of extra practice.

DUSTIN: I left my braces at school.

BARBARA: They're not going to do you any good there. Get them home so you can practice.

DUSTIN: I wouldn't have time. I have to finish my art project.

BARBARA: Walk first, paint later.

TEDDY: Play first, walk later, and don't worry about painting.

BARBARA: Whatever, just get it straightened out, all right, Dustin?

TEDDY: And then he'll be well rounded just like you.

BARBARA: (*Playfully.*) All right, that's enough. I'll see you guys tomorrow.

DUSTIN: Okay.

TEDDY: (*Sarcastically.*) We'll all be looking forward to it.

BARBARA: Good. Then maybe I'll give you the cookies I have in my bag. (*Barbara swings her bag tauntingly over her shoulder, gives the boys a smile, and exits. There is silence, then Teddy reaches under his bed and pulls out the braces. Dustin stops painting to watch him. Teddy crosses to Dustin's bed and puts the braces back. Teddy lies down on Dustin's bed. Dustin continues painting. Teddy watches him intently.*)

DUSTIN: What do you want?

TEDDY: Nothing. I was just watching you paint.

DUSTIN: Well, don't.

TEDDY: (*He rolls over onto his stomach.*) Do you think you could teach me how to paint, Dustin?

DUSTIN: I told you it's too hard to teach. You would do better if you learned yourself.

TEDDY: But you could just teach me how to hold the brush, and then we could both paint.

DUSTIN: I've tried to teach you how to hold the brush. You won't listen to me.

TEDDY: I'll listen this time, I promise. Just put my hand on top of yours.

DUSTIN: No, Teddy. You're being stupid.

TEDDY: Please, Dustin. (*Teddy gets on his knees and walks over until he is standing next to Dustin.*)

DUSTIN: Well, what would you want to paint?

TEDDY: Something clear.

DUSTIN: You can't paint something clear. Not unless you leave the canvas blank.

TEDDY: Blank canvas could be white.

DUSTIN: Who's the painter here anyway? Look, just go back to your side of the room and let me paint on my own.

TEDDY: Dustin –

DUSTIN: I'm not gonna let you if you're going to be stupid and paint something like rain.

TEDDY: Dustin, what's your problem?

DUSTIN: Just shut up!

TEDDY: (*He pauses thoughtfully in silence for a while.*) Dustin, how come you hid your braces from Barbara?

DUSTIN: It doesn't matter.

TEDDY: Yes, it does.

DUSTIN: Because I didn't want to walk.

TEDDY: Why not?

DUSTIN: Could we just drop this?

TEDDY: No. I'm confused. Barbara said you wanted to walk.

DUSTIN: Well, I don't.

TEDDY: Why not?

(*Dustin doesn't answer.*)

TEDDY: You won't even try anymore.

DUSTIN: And you won't take off those damn glasses. We're even. What do you want to be blind for? Why the hell would you want to be blind?

TEDDY: If you tell me why you won't walk, I'll tell you why I wear these.

DUSTIN: I don't care why.

TEDDY: Well, I do.

DUSTIN: Teddy, there are more important things to me than walking, and ...

TEDDY: And what?

DUSTIN: And that's all.

TEDDY: It's because you can't do it perfect, right?

(*Dustin ignores him and returns to painting.*)

TEDDY: How come you never tell Barbara anything.

(*Dustin ignores him.*)

TEDDY: I could tell her if you want.

DUSTIN: Look! I don't want you to do anything but let me finish this. Go someplace that's not in the way.

TEDDY: (*Crosses over and lies down on the bed. Takes off his sunglasses, examines them for a while, then looks at Dustin.*) Dustin, you could wear these for a while if you let me paint with you.

DUSTIN: I don't want to wear your stupid dark glasses, Teddy. I'm busy. Just go away.

TEDDY: Okay. (*Teddy goes to exit.*)

DUSTIN: Teddy?

TEDDY: What?

DUSTIN: Never mind.

TEDDY: Dustin, are you okay? (*Moves toward Dustin and puts his hand on Dustin's shoulder.*)

DUSTIN: I'm fine.

(*Teddy turns to leave again and exits.*)

DUSTIN: Teddy – don't go.
(*Blackout.*)

SCENE THREE
*The lights come up on Teddy and Barbara sitting, eating cookies.
Dustin is painting.*

TEDDY: Dustin says you can't paint things if they're clear.
BARBARA: No. I guess not. Dustin's the artist here.
TEDDY: But I've seen paintings of glass before, or a window.
BARBARA: Have you?
TEDDY: Yeah. When I was really little, my mom took me to this art place. I think there was a painting with glass in it.
BARBARA: Do you remember much of that place?
TEDDY: Only that Mom would hold me up so I could touch the paintings, even though she wasn't supposed to. (*Pause.*) Barb, have you seen my Mom?
BARBARA: No, sweetie.
TEDDY: I don't remember, but I bet she was pretty. Dustin, you should've met my Mom. You would've liked her. She could even have helped you paint. Barbara, do you know where she is?
BARBARA: No, Ted. But you have some people who want to be your mom and dad.
TEDDY: Do they want to be Dustin's too?
BARBARA: They only want one child, and they like you.
TEDDY: Is it because Dustin can't walk?
(*Dustin turns to look at Teddy.*)
BARBARA: No.
TEDDY: If Dustin could walk, would they take him too?
BARBARA: I don't think so, Ted.
TEDDY: I want to stay with Dustin. We do fine by ourselves, right, Dustin?
DUSTIN: I guess.
BARBARA: Have you done any walking lately?
TEDDY: Yeah, I've done a lot.
BARBARA: (*Laughs.*) Not you. Dustin.
TEDDY: If you were trying to get me to walk instead of him, you wouldn't have to work anymore.
BARBARA: True, but we want Dustin to walk. It's a priority.
TEDDY: Whose priority?
DUSTIN: Teddy –
TEDDY: No. I want to know who wants him to walk.

BARBARA: Lots of people.

TEDDY: Does that mean Dustin too?

BARBARA: Well, Dustin agreed to it at the meeting in school. Right, Dustin?

DUSTIN: Yeah.

TEDDY: Then why isn't he walking?

DUSTIN: Teddy, cut it out.

TEDDY: I'm just trying to help. You said yourself …

DUSTIN: Teddy, shut up!

TEDDY: But you said …

DUSTIN: I can speak for myself.

TEDDY: Then why aren't you?

DUSTIN: If I wanted you to talk for me, I would have asked you. But I didn't ask. I don't need your help. Leave me alone and I'll do just fine.

BARBARA: Dustin –

DUSTIN: (*He wheels around to face her.*) And I don't need your help either. 'Cause you're *not* helping. You're always telling me I should walk. Why?

BARBARA: Because it's a sad thing to see a sixteen-year-old boy not be able to go outside and walk around because he won't try.

DUSTIN: It's sad for you, not me! Can't you see that?

BARBARA: But it's important for you to keep at it. You don't want to spend the rest of your life in a wheelchair, right?

DUSTIN: Maybe I do. How the hell would you know what I want? You never ask.

BARBARA: But it was your choice. You said …

DUSTIN: Yeah, of course I said I wanted to walk. They asked me when I was five. How was I supposed to know it meant wearing clumsy braces and dragging my feet along with my arms? Can't you see I don't want to do that?

BARBARA: Dustin, we had our first meeting, you said you'd start trying again. I'd hate to see you give all that up now.

DUSTIN: I haven't given anything up.

BARBARA: I know you feel awkward, but that's just because you haven't practiced enough.

DUSTIN: Yeah. And if I keep practicing, I'll be running marathons, just like the people on TV.

BARBARA: I didn't say that, but at least you'd be able to get around.

DUSTIN: I get around fine!

BARBARA: I'm just trying to help you.

DUSTIN: Why? You don't care about me. I'm just another job for you. I'm just another file that sits on your desk.

BARBARA: That's not true ...

DUSTIN: Then maybe you do this to make yourself feel good. A fat lady can make a kid walk. Wow, what a miracle worker!

BARBARA: Wait a minute now, that's not fair.

DUSTIN: And what you're doing is?

BARBARA: I'm doing this for you. It hurts me to see you confined to a wheelchair when you don't have to be.

DUSTIN: That's all you can see, isn't it? My legs? Well, if you were more observant, you might see that I don't mind that much. And if you do, well then, that's your problem. Just keep it to yourself.

TEDDY: Dustin –

DUSTIN: Shut up, Teddy.

BARBARA: It's not just me. Your teachers want to help too.

DUSTIN: If they really did, then they would quit trying to make me do something I don't want to do. Just give me a box of paints and show me how to move my wheelchair around better instead of trying to drag me out of it.

BARBARA: You can't just sit around and paint all the time.

DUSTIN: I want to paint. And if it will make you happy, I'll get onto the floor and do a few pushups every now and then.

BARBARA: Dustin –

DUSTIN: Barbara, just think of me instead of your job.

BARBARA: I am thinking about you. If you don't take the chance to walk now, I'm afraid you'll regret it later.

DUSTIN: And then I would blame you, and you would feel guilty, and you don't want that. See, you don't care about me, you care about yourself.

BARBARA: Dustin, maybe we could talk to your teachers about this.

DUSTIN: Maybe. But for right now I think I want to be alone.

BARBARA: All right. I think you should cool down. Come on, Teddy, let's go play.

TEDDY: In a minute.

(*Barbara exits.*)

TEDDY: Dustin –

DUSTIN: Go play, Teddy.

TEDDY: Dustin, don't be mad at me.

DUSTIN: Just leave me alone. You're the one who got me into this mess in the first place.

TEDDY: (*Frustrated, angry.*) You don't need to walk. You do it fine already.

DUSTIN: What?

TEDDY: It doesn't matter that you're in a wheelchair. You're always walking away. I can walk, but I'm still here.

DUSTIN: You're not talking about walking, you're talking about people turning away from each other. It's different, stupid.

TEDDY: You're the.stupid one. All you care about is painting, I'm here, too, you know.

DUSTIN: Yeah, well, I want to be alone right now.

TEDDY: (*Suddenly.*) Go away!

DUSTIN: What?

TEDDY: I hate you. That's all you ever tell me to do: "Go away, Teddy." "I don't want to play, Teddy." "I'm busy." Yeah, well, I don't care. I was just trying to be nice, that's all. But I don't care anymore. I wouldn't let you play if you wanted to.

(*Teddy throws a beanbag at Dustin. Dustin, moving to avoid it, knocks his painting off the easel.*)

DUSTIN: What did you do? What the hell did you do?

TEDDY: It's your fault. You didn't catch it.

DUSTIN: I don't believe you. What are you trying to do?

TEDDY: Dustin, stop it. I didn't mean it.

DUSTIN: It was wet. You messed it up.

TEDDY: You can fix it, right?

DUSTIN: Maybe. Don't worry about it.

TEDDY: I thought you'd catch it. Honest I did.

DUSTIN: Never mind.

TEDDY: Dustin, I didn't mean it. Don't be mad.

DUSTIN: I'm not.

TEDDY: I'm sorry.

DUSTIN: Teddy –

TEDDY: Dustin, I love you.

DUSTIN: Aw, come on, Teddy.

TEDDY: You're my brother. I can love you if I want.

DUSTIN: Don't.

TEDDY: Why?

DUSTIN: Just don't. It makes things hard on both of us.

TEDDY: So what. You're my brother.

DUSTIN: I am not your brother.

TEDDY: I can love you anyway.

(*Dustin looks at Teddy for a minute in silence.*)

TEDDY: Dustin? Why wouldn't you follow me out into the rain?

DUSTIN: It doesn't matter.

TEDDY: It does to me.

DUSTIN: I guess because people don't belong in rain. They just kind of stand out. It's like in painting. If you put a person, a real person, in a painting, they wouldn't seem to fit. They'd just look like they didn't belong in a perfect setting. You know what I mean?

TEDDY: No.

DUSTIN: Go play.

(Lights fade to black.)

SCENE FOUR

The stage is dimly lit. Dustin is lying in bed sleeping and Teddy is packing a suitcase that is lying open on his bed. He is talking to no one in particular as he is packing. The sound of rain hitting against the windowpane is noticeable, but soft. It will grow more noticeable as the scene progresses.

TEDDY: Ya know, sometimes I think it really wouldn't be so bad to be blind. You wouldn't have to worry about what everything looked like. You could make things look like you wanted them to. You could wear clothes that didn't match, and nobody would tell you you had no taste. They would think you dressed like that just 'cause you couldn't see. If we couldn't see, we'd start seeing the things inside people more.

(Teddy stops packing and wanders over to Dustin's easel. Picking up a paintbrush, he goes back to his bed, reaches under it, pulls out his bag of stuff, and adds the paintbrush to his collection. Teddy picks up the suitcase and walks to the door. Putting the suitcase down, he turns to look at Dustin.)

TEDDY: Dustin? *(Silence.)* You awake, Dustin? *(Silence.)* Dustin?

DUSTIN: *(Annoyed.)* What?

TEDDY: I want to talk to you.

DUSTIN: It's two o'clock in the morning. Go to sleep!

TEDDY: What's wrong?

DUSTIN: Just go to sleep.

TEDDY: Dustin? I'm leaving tomorrow. I want to talk to you.

DUSTIN: I'll talk to you in the morning. Now, go lie down.

TEDDY: Dustin —

DUSTIN: Teddy — leave me alone.

TEDDY: Dustin?

(When Dustin doesn't answer, Teddy reaches up and gently puts his hand on Dustin's face. Dustin bolts to a sitting position.)

DUSTIN: Quit it! You're not blind.

TEDDY: I'm cold. Just hold me a minute.

(The two boys look at each other for a minute, then Dustin turns over and lies down again, with his back to Teddy.)

TEDDY: Dustin … this is the last time … this is the last time … Can't you just … Forget it! This is the last time you'll see me. I'm the only thing you have, and I'm leaving.

DUSTIN: Good! Now, go to sleep.

(*Teddy turns away and goes back to his bed. He curls up and softly begins crying. Dustin is silent for a while. He then pulls himself into his wheelchair, talking softly to Teddy.*)

DUSTIN: I used to think that the morning light was yellow. That's the color streetlights are and the color the moon is and everything. Then one night I woke up and looked around. It was two o'clock, and it was blue. You know what I wanted to do, Teddy? I wanted to wake you up and show you that everything was blue, not yellow like I thought. But I didn't. It's different tonight. Everything should be blue in here, but it's not. Maybe I should paint the sky yellow, like you said, and red. Yeah, a red splash could mix in just fine. (*By this time the rain can be heard against the windowpane. Dustin has gotten into his wheelchair and now wheels over to Teddy's bed.*) Teddy? (*Pause.*) I need you. I'm scared.

TEDDY: (*Looks up and then goes to Dustin and sits in his lap.*) It's raining, Dustin. I can hear it.

DUSTIN: Yes, it's raining.

TEDDY: But you can't see it … no one can.

DUSTIN: It's too dark to see at night. You can hear it, and if you went outside, you could feel it.

TEDDY: I can feel it.

DUSTIN: Then let's paint it.

(*Teddy gets a canvas, palette, and brush and brings it to Dustin. Dustin puts Teddy's hand on his own, holding the brush. They begin making smooth strokes up and down, painting as they look out the window.*)

DUSTIN: When you paint rain, you have to move your hand gently. Yeah, like that. That's good.

TEDDY: As good as you?

DUSTIN: Better. You know how it feels, not just how it looks.

TEDDY: I'll show you how it feels.

DUSTIN: I was kidding when I said I wouldn't follow you out in the pouring rain. I would. We could go outside and play in the mud and climb trees. We could jump outside through the window too. It's only glass. You know how easy it is to break through glass. (*Lights out.*)

END OF PLAY

Who Is Chasing Whom!

A Play in One Act
By Lynne Alvarez

LYNNE ALVAREZ arrived in New York in 1978 planning to be a hotshot poet. On a whim, she accompanied a friend to a gathering of Hispanic writers at the Puerto Rican Travelling Theatre. At 31, she had never had a thought of writing a play, but was now hooked. Lynne wrote two plays under the auspices of Miriam Colon and the Puerto Rican Travelling Theatre: *Graciela*, which was presented at the Puerto Rican Travelling Theatre and *Guitarron*, which earned Lynne an NEA Fellowship and premiered in 1984 at *St. Clements Theatre* in New York.

Lynne was a member of New Dramatists for seven years where she wrote *Hidden Parts* (1981) which won the Kesselring Award in 1983. She also wrote *The Wonderful Tower of Humbert Lavoigent* (1983), which won two awards: The Le Compte De Nouey Award in 1984 and an FDG/CBS Award for Best Play and later, Best Production at Capital Repertory Company in Albany, New York in 1984/85. In 1984, the Actors Theatre of Louisville commissioned a one-act play which became the full-length play, *Thin Air; Tales from a Revolution*. *Thin Air* premiered at the San Diego Repertory Company in 1987 and won a Drama League Award and a Rockefeller Fellowship in 1988. Lynne won a second NEA Fellowship in 1989/90.

Lynne has also done commissioned translations and adaptations: *The Damsel and the Gorilla* or *The Red Madonna* by Fernando Arraval for INTAR in 1988; Tirso de Molina's *Don Juan of Seville* for Classic Stage Company (CSC) and an adaptation of Boccaccio's *Decameron* called *Tales From The Time of the Plague* for CSC as well. Lynne's adaptation of the children's story, *Rikki Tikki Tavi*, and a musical based on *The Pied Piper of Hamlin* called *RATS*, had their premier at the Repertory Theater of St. Louis in 1991 and 1992.

Most recently Lynne has been the recipient of a New York Foundation grant in 1994 and has created two plays for ACT's Young Conservatory including *The Reincarnation of Jaimie Brown* and *Eddie Mundo Edmundo*. She is the author of two books of poetry and her plays have been widely published and anthologized. Her most current play, *The Absence of Miracles and the Rise of the Middle Class* is a murder mystery about class war in New York City.

CHARACTERS

Who* is a dreamer for whom reality is never quite as it is for other people.

Whom* is a free spirit with a practical sense of the world.

*Both Who and Whom can be played in various ways which will slightly shift the emphasis of this theater piece. Both characters could be of the same sex, for instance; or they could be a couple; they could be different ethnically or in regards to age or size.

WHO IS CHASING WHOM!

SEQUENCE ONE

CHARACTER AND SET DESCRIPTION:
Who and Whom wear black leotards and tights. Who has an iridescent green fringe around each calf. Whom has iridescent orange fringe hanging from his sleeves. Both have on whiteface and wear gloves. At this point the set is a black curtain as backdrop. Bright spotlights should follow both characters. At some point a large sign, black with white letters will be lowered. It reads "*Who Is Chasing Whom.*"

ACTION I:

Who and Whom run around the curtain four or five times, going offstage and returning on the opposite side of the stage. They do not appear onstage at the same time. First we see Whom. Whom runs with long strides swinging his arms. Sometimes, center stage, he will leap and say, "Whee," enjoying himself.

Who, following him on stage just as Whom is going offstage, runs intensely with short steps, his arms pumping and his head down determinedly.

ACTION II:

Starting with the sixth time running across stage, Whom notices the audience. He grins and waves. Who keeps on running with great determination. Whom starts to play to the audience, perhaps he gives a special turn, or a somersault. He is so caught up that he lets Who get within 10 feet of him. This goes on during three more crossings of the stage.

Finally Whom is so enthralled with the audience, he stops and bows and smiles and moves his hands asking for applause. He bows again. Who appears and stops also and tiptoes within about six feet of Whom, trying to sneak up on him. Then he too becomes aware of the audience. He is sheepish and gives a shy bow.

Whom is still playing to the audience, perhaps has picked out one person who he is trying to please exorbitantly.

ACTION III:

> Who is torn between trying to catch Whom and being jealous of the audience's attention. Finally he cannot tolerate it and tries to copy Whom's bowing to the audience. Whom notices Who finally and they compete for lavishness of gesture in attracting the audience's attention.
>
> Then, Whom starts bowing faster and faster. Who tries to keep up with him and gets dizzy. He staggers around and around and then plops on the floor in a faint.
>
> Whom struts offstage smiling and waving to the audience.
> (Lights black out.)

END OF SEQUENCE ONE

SEQUENCE TWO

CHARACTER AND SET DESCRIPTION:

> This sequence is accompanied by music. (Snaredrum march.) Who is wearing black leotards but he is wearing a white doctor's coat over it. He carries a large telescope. Whom wears an orange cowboy hat and an orange vest over his leotards. He carries a giant magnifying glass. In this sequence the curtains are open and we see a large square black space. The walls or wall coverings are black. At one point a large sign descends which reads "Who Is Chasing Whom?" (In italics this time.)

ACTION I:

> This is closely choreographed in the sense that both characters will, when they make a definite move, be moving in unison. We find Who and Whom onstage. Each is using his particular instrument to examine the stage, curtains, orchestra pit, etc. Who, however, usually looks up, sometimes standing on tiptoe. Whom crouches low or lies on his stomach at times to examine things more closely. In this way there will be several times when Who is standing directly behind Whom looking up or over Whom's head while Whom is busily investigating something right in front of Who.
>
> They are never aware of each other although there are near misses.

ACTION II:

> At one point Whom leans on one hand on the stage. [He is sitting down at this time.] All of a sudden he notices his hand, not

recognizing it as his and begins to examine it with his magnifying glass.

Who also notices Whom's hand without knowing what it is. He also examines it with his telescope. He becomes excited and jumps exclaiming loudly, "Wow!"

They stare at the hand. Whom wiggles his fingers and they both laugh.

Then they become conscious of one another and gradually raise their instruments so that Who's telescope is staring into Whom's magnifying glass. The distortion startles them and Who staggers back and wipes his telescope. Whom wipes off his magnifying glass.

ACTION III:

As they are doing this, a huge sign with "Who Is Chasing Whom?" drifts down and lands with a bang left of center stage.

Whom does not notice. He is cleaning his glass. Who goes to the sign, reads it carefully. Then reads it again with his telescope and says, "oh-oh."

He quickly sits on the sign, trying to hide the words from Whom, but he can't quite cover it. Whom comes over and is curious. He starts to read it letter by letter with his magnifying glass. He comes to letters that Who is blocking and tries to move Who's legs. Who, then, lies on the sign and drapes one arm and one leg over the sign, hiding more letters. Whom wants terribly much to read the sign and moves an arm of Who's and then tries to move the leg. The arm falls over the letters again and then the leg. This goes on for a while with increasing frustration and violence on Whom's part and desperation on Who's part. Finally Whom throws Who off the sign entirely. Whom reads the sign quickly through his magnifying glass. He says, "oh-oh."

Who picks himself up, angrily. Whom starts running and the chase is on. Lights black out.

END OF SEQUENCE TWO

SEQUENCE THREE

CHARACTER AND SET DESCRIPTION:

Who wears black leotards and has long iridescent green plumes on his arms and head. Whom has on black leotards with iridescent orange plumes. This sequence also has music. It moves quickly. The curtains are still open as before. A large sign is hanging which says, *"Who Is Chasing ... "*

Action I:

> Who comes in swinging his arms and walking briskly. He moves
> his arms deliberately, he enjoys the plumes. He comes center stage
> and stands there waiting. He crosses his arms, then uncrosses them;
> he does this a few times. He looks at his wrist as if at a watch. He
> sees he does not have a watch there and checks the other wrist.
> Then he checks both forearms and both shoulders. Then he crosses
> his arms again and taps his foot nervously.
> All of a sudden he holds his crotch and looks guiltily from side to
> side. He has to go to the bathroom. He moves uncomfortable from
> foot to foot. He looks around to see if anyone is coming.

Action II:

> Who turns and goes toward the back of the stage with his back to
> the audience. He takes tiny shuffling steps keeping his knees
> together. He keeps checking, turning his head, to see if anyone is
> coming.
> He then sighs and makes motions as if he is urinating. He hums to
> himself while this is happening. It seems to go on and on. He gets
> impatient but can't stop.
> Whom comes onstage, leaping. He catches sight of Who and tenses,
> as if for a confrontation. He starts to sneak by but then sees that
> Who is urinating. This makes him laugh so hard he falls on the
> floor.

Action III:

> Whom picks himself up and goes over to Who. He taps him on the
> shoulder and startles him. Who is still urinating and is now in the
> conflict that he wants to hurry up so he can catch Whom, but he
> can't seem to stop.
> Whom sees this and laughs again until he falls on the floor. He gets
> up and teases Who by passing his plumes around Who's back and
> neck. This makes Who giggle, which makes things worse.
> Finally Whom slinks offstage like a vamp. Who watches him
> helplessly. Whom smiles wickedly and says, "Ta-Ta."
> (Lights black out.)

END OF SEQUENCE THREE

SEQUENCE FOUR

CHARACTER AND SET DESCRIPTION:

Whom and Whom are dressed as they were in Sequence One. There is no music in this sequence. Action takes place in front of the closed black curtain. A large sign, reading " ... *Whom*" is already hanging upstage right. There is a chair under it. Stage left is a large pile of objects that are pastel colored. They can be metal objects and plastic and rubber all in yellows, blues, and pinks. The pile is about eight feet tall and a foot wide. It is held in place by a clear plastic pole which can be withdrawn from the center.

ACTION I:

Whom walks out slowly, reading a letter. He sits on the chair. He is saying a steady stream of, "num, num, num, num, num, num, num," ... etc. as if reading the letter. At first he is very lively and then gradually the nums become sadder and sadder.

The nums fade away. Whom sags in the chair, overcome by sadness. The letter falls from his hands onto the floor. He doesn't care. His head droops.

ACTION II:

Who walks out. He sees Whom. Whom's shoulders are shaking as if he's crying. Who rushes to him to comfort him. He puts an arm around Whom's shoulders. Whom takes it off. Who tries to embrace him again. Whom pushes Who away. Who kneels by him. Whom gets up angrily and stalks across the stage. He pushes angrily against the stack of things which swing way over and then right themselves.

Whom exits. Who stares after him helplessly.

ACTION III:

Who gets up and dusts himself off. He sighs. He says, "Oh well," and shrugs exaggeratedly. He walks across the stage feigning nonchalance. Putting his hands into invisible pockets, kicking an invisible stone. He comes to the pile of things and with an air of great indifference, pushes them as Whom did.

Instead of swaying as they did before, the objects fly all over the place with a great clatter and splatter. Who ducks and covers his head, and runs offstage.

(The lights black out.)

END OF SEQUENCE FOUR

SEQUENCE FIVE

CHARACTER AND SET DESCRIPTION:
There is music with this sequence. Who and Whom are dressed in street clothes but with whiteface and gloves. The curtain is open. Hanging from the ceiling are hundreds of pastel-colored threads that reach to about a foot from the floor. We hear chimes. A large sign is on a stand. It says: *"Who Is Chasing Whom!"*

ACTION I:
Whom comes out. He sees the threads and is delighted. He runs through them first with his arms at his sides. He glides through them, letting them caress his face. He spreads his arms and zooms through them like an airplane. He takes off his shirt and rubs himself through them, sensuously. He says, "Mmmmmm-mmmmmmmmm," and "Aaahhhhhhhhhhh," as he does this.

ACTION II:
Who walks in and he sees Whom having so much fun. He rushes in yelling, "Whoopee!"
He runs through the threads. He hugs them. He grabs them in his hands and swings them. He grins broadly at Whom.
They both swoop through the threads. Whom is sensual but contained. Who is mad with joy, his movements are quicker and wilder. Sometimes both meet, they holds hands briefly. Then they meet more and more often. Finally Who is carried away and he embraces Whom passionately.

ACTION III:
Whom breaks from the embrace and continues dancing through the threads, self-absorbed.
Who is delighted with the embrace. He steals downstage. Carefully he takes a large red piece of cardboard from inside his shirt. He unfolds it carefully. It is a heart. He can hardly wait and nods happily to the audience. He turns to the stage thinking to see Whom. Whom is gone. Who calls out, "Yoo Hoo, Yoo Hoo."
He goes sweeping in a zigzag pattern through the threads, holding the heart aloft and runs offstage after Whom.

Curtain

END OF PLAY

The Dancers
By Horton Foote

HORTON FOOTE, Pulitzer Prize Winner, has had plays produced on Broadway, Off–Broadway, Off–Off–Broadway and many regional theatres. They include: THE CHASE, THE TRAVELING LADY, THE TRIP TO BOUNTIFUL, THE HABITATION OF DRAGONS, NIGHT SEASONS, IN A COFFIN IN EGYPT, TOMORROW, COURTSHIP, VALENTINE'S DAY, 1918, LILY DALE, THE WIDOW CLAIRE, COUSINS, THE DEATH OF PAPA, DIVIDING THE ESTATE, TALKING PICTURES, GETTING FRANKIE MARRIED–AND AFTERWARDS, and THE YOUNG MAN FROM ATLANTA. His films include: TO KILL A MOCKINGBIRD, BABY THE RAIN MUST FALL, TOMORROW, COURTSHIP, ON VALENTINE'S DAY, 1918, CONVICTS, TENDER MERCIES, THE TRIP TO BOUNTIFUL and OF MICE AND MEN.

ORIGINAL PRODUCTION

The Dancers was originally produced with the following cast:

Inez Stanley	Helen Wagner
Waitress	Mary Lou Taylor
Elizabeth Crews	Katherine Squire
Emily Crews	Joanne Woodward
Herman Stanley	William Erwin
Horace	James Broderick
Mary Catherine Davis	Janet De Gore
Verma Morrison	Gloria Jones
Mr. Tim Davis	Frank Overton
Mrs. Davis	Mary Haynsworth

CHARACTERS

A Waitress	Horace
Inez Stanley	Mary Catherine Davis
Elizabeth Crews	Velma Morrison
Emily Crews	Tom Davis
Herman Stanley	Mrs. Davis

PLACE

Harrison, Texas

TIME

Early summer, 1952

THE DANCERS

The stage is divided into four acting areas. Down Left is the living room of Inez and Herman Stanley. Down Right is part of a small-town drugstore. Upstage Right is the living room of Elizabeth Crews. Upstage Left is the yard and living room of Mary Catherine Davis. Since the action should flow continuously from one area to the other only the barest amount of furnishings should be used to suggest what each area represents. The lights are brought up on the drugstore, Down Right. A Waitress is there. Inez Stanley comes into the drugstore. She stands for a moment thinking. The Waitress goes over to her.

WAITRESS: Can I help you?

INEZ: Yes, you can if I can think of what I came in here for. Just gone completely out of my mind. I've been running around all day. You see, I'm expecting company tonight. My brother Horace. He's coming on a visit.

(*Elizabeth Crews and her daughter Emily come into the drugstore. Emily is about seventeen and very pretty. This afternoon, however, it is evident that she is unhappy.*)

INEZ: Hey ...

ELIZABETH: We've just been by your house.

INEZ: You have? Hello, Emily.

EMILY: Hello.

ELIZABETH: We made some divinity and took it over for Horace.

INEZ: Well, that's so sweet of you.

ELIZABETH: What time is he coming in?

INEZ: Six-thirty.

ELIZABETH: Are you meeting him?

INEZ: No—Herman. I've got to cook supper. Can I buy you all a drink?

ELIZABETH: No, we have to get Emily over to the beauty parlor.

INEZ: What are you wearing tonight, Emily?

ELIZABETH: She's wearing that sweet little net I got her the end of last summer. She's never worn it to a dance here.

INEZ: I don't think I've ever seen it. I'll bet it looks beautiful on her. I'm gonna make Horace bring you by the house so I can see you before the dance.

WAITRESS: Excuse me …

INEZ: Yes?

WAITRESS: Have you thought of what you wanted yet? I thought I could be getting it for you.

INEZ: That's sweet, honey … but I haven't thought of what I wanted yet. (*To Elizabeth and Emily.*) I feel so foolish, I came in here for something, and I can't remember what.

WAITRESS: Cosmetics?

INEZ: No … you go on. I'll think and call you.

WAITRESS: All right. (*She goes.*)

INEZ: Emily, I think it's so sweet of you to go to the dance with Horace. I know he's going to be thrilled when I tell him.

ELIZABETH: Well, you're thrilled too, aren't you, Emily?

EMILY: Yes, ma'm.

ELIZABETH: I told Emily she'd thank me someday for not permitting her to sit home and miss all the fun.

EMILY: Mama, it's five to four. My appointment is at four o'clock.

ELIZABETH: Well, you go on in the car.

EMILY: How are you gonna get home?

ELIZABETH: I'll get home. Don't worry about me.

EMILY: O.K. (*She starts out.*)

INEZ: 'Bye, Emily.

EMILY: 'Bye. (*She goes on out.*)

ELIZABETH: Does Horace have a car for tonight?

INEZ: Oh, yes. He's taking Herman's.

ELIZABETH: I just wondered. I wanted to offer ours if he didn't have one.

INEZ: That's very sweet—but we're giving him our car every night for the two weeks of his visit. Oh—I know what I'm after. Flowers. I have to order Emily's corsage for Horace. I came in here to use the telephone to call you to find out what color Emily's dress was going to be.

ELIZABETH: Blue.

INEZ: My favorite color. Walk me over to the florist.

ELIZABETH: All right.

(*They go out as the lights fade. The lights are brought up Downstage Left on the living room of Inez Stanley. Herman Stanley and his brother-in-law, Horace, come in. Herman is carrying Horace's suitcase. Herman is in his middle thirties. Horace is eighteen, thin, sensitive, but a likable boy.*)

HERMAN: Inez. Inez. We're here.

(*He puts the bag down in the living room. Inez comes running in from Right.*)

INEZ: You're early.

HERMAN: The bus was five minutes ahead of time.

INEZ: Is that so? Why, I never heard of that. (*She kisses her brother.*) Hello, honey.

HORACE: Hello, Sis.

INEZ: You look fine.

HORACE: Thank you.

INEZ: You haven't put on a bit of weight though.

HORACE: Haven't I?

INEZ: Not a bit. I'm just going to stuff food down you and put some weight on you while you're here. How's your appetite?

HORACE: Oh, it's real good. I eat all the time.

INEZ: Then why don't you put on some weight?

HORACE: I don't know. I guess I'm just the skinny type.

INEZ: How are the folks?

HORACE: Fine.

INEZ: Mother over her cold?

HORACE: Yes, she is.

INEZ: Dad's fine?

HORACE: Just fine.

INEZ: Oh, Herman, did you ask him?

HERMAN: Ask him what?

INEZ: Ask him what? About his tux.

HERMAN: No, I didn't …

INEZ: Honestly, Herman. Here we have him a date with the prettiest and most popular girl in Harrison and Herman says ask him what. You did bring it, didn't you, Bubber?

HORACE: Bring what?

INEZ: Your tux.

HORACE: Oh, sure.

INEZ: Well, guess who I've got you a date with. Aren't you curious?

HORACE: Uh. Huh.

INEZ: Well, guess …

(*A pause. He thinks.*)

HORACE: I don't know.

INEZ: Well, just try guessing …

HORACE: Well … uh … uh … (*He is a little embarrassed. He stands trying to think. No names come to him.*) I don't know.

INEZ: Emily Crews. Now isn't she a pretty girl?

HORACE: Yes. She is.

INEZ: And the most popular girl in this town. You know her mother is a very close friend of mine and she called me day before yesterday and she said, I hear Horace is coming to town and I said yes you were, and she said that the boy Emily is going with is in summer school and couldn't get away this weekend, and Emily said she wouldn't go to the dance at all but her mother said that she had insisted and wondered if you'd take her ...

HORACE: Her mother said. Does Emily want me to take her?

INEZ: That isn't the point, Bubber. The point is that her mother doesn't approve of the boy Emily is in love with and she likes you ...

HORACE: Who likes me?

INEZ: Emily's mother. And she thinks you would make a very nice couple.

HORACE: Oh. (*A pause.*) But what does Emily think?

INEZ: Emily doesn't know what to think, honey. I'm trying to explain that to you. She's in love.

HORACE: Where am I supposed to take her to?

INEZ: The dance.

HORACE: But, Inez, I don't dance well enough ... I don't like to go to dances ... yet ...

INEZ: Oh, Horace. Mother wrote me you were learning.

HORACE: Well ... I am learning. But I don't dance well enough yet.

INEZ: Horace, you just make me sick. The trouble with you is that you have no confidence in yourself. I bet you can dance.

HORACE: No, I can't ...

INEZ: Now let's see. (*Inez goes to the radio and turns it on. She comes back to him.*) Now come on. Show me what you've learned ...

HORACE: Aw, Sis ...

HERMAN: Inez. Why don't you let the boy alone?

INEZ: Now you keep out of this, Herman Stanley. He's my brother and he's a stick. He's missing all the fun in life and I'm not going to have him a stick. I've sat up nights thinking of social engagements to keep him busy every minute of these next two weeks—I've got three dances scheduled for him. So he can*not* not dance. Now come on, dance with me ...

(*He takes her by the arm awkwardly. He begins to lead her around the room.*)

INEZ: Now that's fine. That's just fine. Isn't that fine, Herman?

HERMAN: Uh. Huh.

INEZ: You see all you need is confidence. And I want you to promise me you'll talk plenty when you're with the girl, not just sit there in silence and only answer when you're asked a question ... Now promise me.

HORACE: I promise.

INEZ: Fine. Why, I think he dances real well. Don't you, Herman?

HERMAN: Yes, I do. Just fine, Inez.

INEZ: Just a lovely dancer, all he needs is confidence. He is very light on his feet. And he has a fine sense of rhythm—why, brother, you're a born dancer—

(*Horace is smiling over the compliments, half wanting to believe what they say, but then not so sure. He is dancing with her around the room as the lights fade. They are brought up on the area Upstage Right. Emily Crews is in her living room. She has on her dressing gown. She is crying. Elizabeth, her mother, comes in from Upstage Right.*)

ELIZABETH: Emily.

EMILY: Yes ma'm.

ELIZABETH: Do you know what time it is?

EMILY: Yes ma'm.

ELIZABETH: Then why in the world aren't you dressed?

EMILY: Because I don't feel good.

ELIZABETH: Emily ...

EMILY: I don't feel good ... (*She begins to cry.*) Oh, Mother. I don't want to go to the dance tonight. Please, ma'm, don't make me. I'll do anything in this world for you if you promise me ...

ELIZABETH: Emily. This is all settled. You are going to that dance. Do you understand me? You are going to that dance. That sweet, nice brother of Inez Stanley's will be here any minute ...

EMILY: Sweet, nice brother. He's a goon. That's what he is. A regular goon. A bore and a goon.

ELIZABETH: Emily ...

EMILY: That's all he is. Just sits and doesn't talk. Can't dance. I'm not going to any dance or any place else with him and that's final. (*She runs out Right.*)

ELIZABETH: Emily ... Emily ... You get ready this minute ... (*The doorbell rings. Yelling.*) Emily ... Emily ... Horace is here. I want you down those stairs in five minutes ... dressed.

(*She goes out Left and comes back in followed by Horace, all dressed up. He has a corsage box in his hand.*)

ELIZABETH: Hello, Horace.

HORACE: Good evening.

ELIZABETH: Sit down, won't you, Horace? Emily is a little late getting dressed. You know how girls are.

HORACE: Yes ma'm. (*He sits down. He seems a little awkward and shy.*)

ELIZABETH: Can I get you something to drink, Horace?

HORACE: No ma'm.

(*A pause. Elizabeth is obviously very nervous about whether Emily will behave or not.*)

ELIZABETH: Are you sure I can't get you a Coca-Cola or something?

HORACE: No. Thank you.

ELIZABETH: How's your family?

HORACE: Just fine, thank you.

ELIZABETH: I bet your sister was glad to see you.

HORACE: Yes, she was.

ELIZABETH: How's your family? Oh, I guess I asked you that, didn't I?

HORACE: Yes, you did.

> (*Elizabeth keeps glancing off Right, praying that Emily will put in an appearance.*)

ELIZABETH: I understand you've become quite an accomplished dancer...

HORACE: Oh ... well ... I ...

ELIZABETH: Inez tells me you do all the new steps.

HORACE: Well—I ...

ELIZABETH: Excuse me. Let me see what is keeping that girl.

> (*She goes running off Right. Horace gets up. He seems very nervous. He begins to practice his dancing. He seems more unsure of himself and awkward ... We can hear Elizabeth offstage knocking on Emily's door. At first Horace isn't conscious of the knocking or the ensuing conversation and goes on practicing his dancing. When he first becomes conscious of what's to follow he tries to pay no attention. Then gradually he moves over to the far Left side of the stage. The first thing we hear is Elizabeth's genteel tapping at Emily's door. Then she begins to call, softly at first, then louder and louder.*)

ELIZABETH: Emily. Emily. Emily Crews. Emily Carter Crews ... (*The pounding offstage is getting louder and louder.*) Emily. I can hear you in there. Now open that door.

EMILY: (*Screaming back.*) I won't. I told you I won't.

ELIZABETH: Emily Carter Crews. You open that door immediately.

EMILY: I won't.

ELIZABETH: I'm calling your father from downtown if you don't open that door right this very minute.

EMILY: I don't care. I won't come out.

ELIZABETH: Then I'll call him.

> (*She comes running in from Right. Horace quickly gets back to his chair and sits.*)

ELIZABETH: Excuse me, Horace.

> (*She crosses through the room and goes out Upstage Right. Horace seems very ill at ease. He looks at the box of flowers. He is very warm. He begins to fan himself. Elizabeth comes back in the room from Upstage Right. She is very nervous, but she tries to hide her nervousness in an overly social manner. Elizabeth has decided to tell a fib.*)

ELIZABETH: Horace, I am so sorry to have to ruin your evening, but my little girl isn't feeling well. She has a headache and a slight temperature and I've just called the doctor and he says he thinks it's very advisable that she stay in this evening. She's upstairs insisting she go, but I do feel under the circumstances I had just better keep her in. I hope you understand.

HORACE: Oh, yes ma'm. I do understand.

ELIZABETH: How long do you plan to visit us, Horace?

HORACE: Two weeks.

ELIZABETH: That's nice. (*They start walking offstage Left.*) Please call Emily tomorrow and ask her out again. She'll just be heartbroken if you don't.

HORACE: Yes ma'm. Good night.

ELIZABETH: Good night, Horace.

(*Horace goes out. Elizabeth calls out after him.*)

ELIZABETH: Can you see, Horace?

(*In the distance we hear Horace answer.*)

HORACE: Yes ma'm.

ELIZABETH: Now you be sure and call us tomorrow. You hear? (*She stands waiting for a moment. Then she walks back across stage to Upstage Right, screaming at the top of her voice.*) Emily Carter Crews. You have mortified me. You have mortified me to death. I have, for your information, called your father and he is interrupting his work and is coming home this very minute and he says to tell you that you are not to be allowed to leave this house again for two solid weeks. Is that perfectly clear?

(*She is screaming as she goes out Upstage Right. The lights are brought down. They are brought up immediately Downstage Right in the drugstore. It is half an hour later. Horace comes in. He seats himself at the counter. He still has the box of flowers. The drugstore is deserted. A Waitress is up near the front with her arms on the counter. She keeps glancing at a clock. Horace is examining a menu ... *)

HORACE: Can I have a chicken salad sandwich?

WAITRESS: We're all out of that.

HORACE: Oh. (*He goes back to reading the menu.*)

WAITRESS: If it's all the same to you, I'd rather not make a sandwich. I'm closing my doors in ten minutes.

HORACE: Oh. Well, what would you like to make?

WAITRESS: Any kind of ice cream or soft drinks. (*She looks up at the ice cream menu.*) Coffee is all gone.

HORACE: How about a chocolate ice cream soda?

WAITRESS: O.K. Coming up. (*She starts to mix the soda. She talks as she works.*) Going to the dance?

HORACE: No.

WAITRESS: The way you're all dressed up I thought for sure you were going.

HORACE: No. I was, but I changed my mind.

(*Mary Catherine Davis comes in the drugstore from Downstage Right. Somehow in her young head she has gotten the idea that she is a plain girl and in defiance for the pain of that fact she does everything she can to make herself look plainer.*)

WAITRESS: Hello, Mary Catherine. Been to the movies?

MARY CATHERINE: Yes, I have.

(*The Waitress puts the drink down in front of Horace. He begins to drink.*)

WAITRESS: What'll you have, Mary Catherine?

MARY CATHERINE: Vanilla ice cream.

WAITRESS: O.K. (*She gets the ice cream. She talks as she does so.*) There weren't many at the picture show tonight, I bet. I can always tell by whether we have a crowd in here or not after the first show. I guess everybody is at the dance.

MARY CATHERINE: I could have gone, but I didn't want to. I didn't want to miss the picture show. Emily Crews didn't go. Leo couldn't get home from summer school and she said she was refusing to go. Her mother made a date for her with some bore from out of town without consulting her and she was furious about it. I talked to her this afternoon. She said she didn't know yet how she would get out of it, but she would. She said she had some rights. Her mother doesn't approve of Leo and that's a shame because they are practically engaged.

WAITRESS: I think Emily is a very cute girl, don't you?

MARY CATHERINE: Oh, yes. I think she's darling.

(*Horace has finished his drink and is embarrassed by their talk. He is trying to get the Waitress' attention but doesn't quite know how. He finally calls to the Waitress.*)

HORACE: Miss ...

WAITRESS: Yes?

HORACE: How much do I owe you?

WAITRESS: Twenty cents.

HORACE: Thank you. (*He reaches in his pocket for the money.*)

WAITRESS: Emily has beautiful clothes, doesn't she?

MARY CATHERINE: Oh, yes. She does.

WAITRESS: Her folks are rich?

MARY CATHERINE: She has the prettiest things. But she's not a bit stuck up ...

(*Horace holds the money out to the waitress.*)

HORACE: Here you are.

WAITRESS: Thank you.

(*She takes the money and rings it up on the cash register. Horace goes on out. The waitress shakes her head as he goes.*)

WAITRESS: There's a goofy nut if I ever saw one. He's got flowers under his arm. He's wearing a tux and yet he's not going to the dance. Who is he?

MARY CATHERINE: I don't know. I never saw him before.

(*The Waitress walks to the edge of the area and looks out. She comes back shaking her head. She sits on the stool beside Mary Catherine.*)

WAITRESS: (*While laughing and shaking her head.*) I ought to call the sheriff and have him locked up. Do you know what he's doing?

MARY CATHERINE: No. What?

WAITRESS: Standing on the corner. Dancing back and forth. He's holding his arm up like he's got a girl and everything. Wouldn't it kill you?

(*Mary Catherine goes to the front and looks out.*)

WAITRESS: See him?

MARY CATHERINE: No. He's stopped.

WAITRESS: What's he doing?

MARY CATHERINE: Just standing there. Looking kind of lost. (*Mary Catherine comes back to the counter. She starts eating her ice cream again.*)

WAITRESS: Well—it takes all kinds.

MARY CATHERINE: I guess so.

(*She goes back to eating her ice cream. The lights are brought down. The lights are brought up on the area Downstage Left. The living room of the Stanley's. Inez is there reading a book. Herman comes in.*)

HERMAN: Hi, hon.

INEZ: Hello ...

HERMAN: What's the matter with you? You look down in the dumps.

INEZ: No. I'm just disgusted.

HERMAN: What are you disgusted about?

INEZ: Horace. I had everything planned so beautifully for him and then that silly Emily has to go and hurt his feelings.

HERMAN: Well, honey, that was pretty raw, the trick she pulled.

INEZ: I know. But he's a fool to let that get him down. He should have just gone to the dance by himself and proved her wrong ... Why, like I told him. Show her up. Rush a different girl every night. Be charming. Make yourself popular. But it's like trying to talk to a stone wall. He refused to go out anymore. He says he's going home tomorrow.

HERMAN: Where is he now?

INEZ: Gone to the movies.

HERMAN: Well, honey. I hate to say it, but in a way it serves you right. I've told you a thousand times if I've told you once. Leave the boy alone. He'll be all right. Only don't push him. You and your mother have pushed the boy and pushed him and pushed him.

INEZ: And I'm going to keep on pushing him. I let him off tonight because his feelings were hurt, but tomorrow I'm going to have a long talk with him.

HERMAN: Inez. Leave the boy alone.

INEZ: I won't leave him alone. He is my brother and I'm going to see that he learns to have a good time.

HERMAN: Inez ...

INEZ: Now you just let me handle this, Herman. He's starting to college next year and it's a most important time in his life. He had no fun in high school ...

HERMAN: Now he must have had some fun ...

INEZ: Not like other people. And he's not going through four years of college like a hermit with his nose stuck in some old book ... (*She jumps up.*) I'll never forgive Elizabeth for letting Emily behave this way. And I told her so. I said Elizabeth Crews. I am very upset ...

(*She is angrily walking up and down as the lights fade. They are brought up Downstage Right on the drugstore area. The Waitress is there alone. Mary Catherine comes in from Downstage Right.*)

WAITRESS: Did you go to the movies again tonight?

MARY CATHERINE: Uh-huh. Lila, do you remember when I was telling you about Emily's date and how she wouldn't go out with him because he was such a bore?

WAITRESS: Uh ...

MARY CATHERINE: Oh. I just feel awful. That was the boy sitting in here...

WAITRESS: Last night? ...

MARY CATHERINE: Yes. I went riding with Emily and some of the girls this afternoon and we passed by his sister's house and there sat the boy.

WAITRESS: Shh ... sh ...

(*She has seen Horace come into the area from Downstage Right. He comes to the counter. He seems very silent. He picks up a menu.*)

WAITRESS: Back again tonight?

HORACE: Uh-huh.

WAITRESS: What'll you have?

HORACE: A cup of coffee ...

WAITRESS: All out. We don't serve coffee after eight unless we happen to have some left over from suppertime ...

HORACE: Thanks. (*He gets up.*)

WAITRESS: Nothing else?

HORACE: No, thanks.

(*He goes over to the magazine rack. He picks up a magazine and starts looking through it. Emily Crews comes in from Downstage Right. She doesn't see Horace. She goes right over to Mary Catherine.*)

EMILY: Leora and I were riding around the square and we saw you sitting here ...

(*Mary Catherine points to Horace. Emily turns around and sees him. She looks a little embarrassed. He happens to glance up, and sees her.*)

HORACE: Hello, Emily.

EMILY: Hello, Horace ... Do you know Mary Catherine Davis?

HORACE: No. How do you do.

EMILY: I feel awfully bad about last night, Horace. My mother says that you know I wasn't really sick. I just wanted to tell you that it had nothing to do with you, Horace. It was a battle between me and my mother. Mary Catherine can tell you. I promised the boy I go with not to go out with any other boys ...

HORACE: Oh, that's all right. I understand.

EMILY: You see, we've gone steady for two years. All the other boys in town understand it and their feelings are not a bit hurt if I turn them down. Are they, Mary Catherine?

MARY CATHERINE: No.

EMILY: Mary Catherine is my best friend and she can tell you I'm not stuck up. And I would have gone anyway, except I was so mad at my mother ...

MARY CATHERINE: Emily is not stuck up a bit. Emily used to date all the boys before she began going with Leo steadily. She even had a date with Gus Meredith. All the other girls wouldn't go with him because they thought he was so fat and unattractive, but Emily said she wouldn't hurt his feelings for the world and she went with him. Didn't you, Emily?

EMILY: Uh-huh. How long are you going to be here, Horace?

HORACE: Well, I haven't decided, Emily.

EMILY: Well, I hope you're not still hurt with me.

HORACE: No, I'm not, Emily.

EMILY: Well, I'm glad for that. Mary Catherine, can you come with us?

MARY CATHERINE: No, I can't, Emily. Velma came in after the first show started and I promised to wait here for her and we'd walk home together.

EMILY: Come on. We can ride around and watch for her.

MARY CATHERINE: No. I don't dare. You know how sensitive Velma is. If she looked in here and saw I wasn't sitting at this counter she'd go right home and not speak to me again for two or three months.

EMILY: Velma's too sensitive. You shouldn't indulge her in it.

MARY CATHERINE: I'm willing to grant you that. But you all are going off to college next year and Velma and I are the only ones that are going to be left here and I can't afford to get her mad at me.

EMILY: O.K. I'll watch out for you and if we're still riding around when Velma gets out, we'll pick you up.

MARY CATHERINE: Fine ...

EMILY: 'Bye ...

MARY CATHERINE: 'Bye ...

EMILY: 'Bye, Horace.

HORACE: Good-bye, Emily.

(She goes out Downstage Right.)

MARY CATHERINE: She's a lovely girl. She was my closest friend until this year. Now we're still good friends, but we're not as close as we were. We had a long talk about it last week. I told her I understood. She and Eloise Dayton just naturally have a little more in common now. They're both going steady and they're both going to the same college. (*A pause.*) They're going to Sophie Newcomb. Are you going to college?

HORACE: Uh-huh.

MARY CATHERINE: You are? What college?

HORACE: The University ...

MARY CATHERINE: Oh, I know lots of people there. (*A pause.*) I had a long talk with Emily about my not getting to go. She said she thought it was wonderful that I wasn't showing any bitterness about it. (*A pause.*) I'm getting a job next week so I can save up enough money to go into Houston to business school. I'll probably work in Houston someday. If I don't get too lonely. Velma Morrison's oldest sister went into Houston and got herself a job but she almost died from loneliness. She's back here now working at the courthouse. Oh, well ... I don't think I'll get lonely. I think a change of scenery would be good for me.

(Velma Morrison comes in Downstage Right. She is about the same age as Mary Catherine. She is filled with excitement.)

VELMA: Mary Catherine, you're going to be furious with me. But Stanley Sewell came in right after you left and he said he'd never forgive me if I didn't go riding with him. I said I had to ask you first, as I had asked you to wait particularly for me and that I knew you were very sensitive.

MARY CATHERINE: I'm very sensitive. You're very sensitive ... I have never in my life stopped speaking to you over anything.

(A car horn is heard offstage.)

VELMA: Will you forgive me if I go?

MARY CATHERINE: Oh, sure.

(*Velma goes running out.*)

VELMA: Thank you. (*She disappears out the door.*)

MARY CATHERINE: I'm not nearly as close to Velma as I am to Emily. I think Emily's beautiful, don't you?

HORACE: Yes. She's very pretty.

MARY CATHERINE: Well, Lila's going to kill us if we don't stop holding her up. Which way do you go?

HORACE: Home.

MARY CATHERINE: I go that way too. We can walk together.

HORACE: O.K.

(*They go out of the area.*)

MARY CATHERINE: Good night, Lila.

WAITRESS: Good night.

(*They continue walking out downstage left as the lights fade. The lights are brought up on the living room of the Crew's house. Elizabeth Crews is there, crying. Emily comes in.*)

EMILY: Mother, what is it? Has something happened to Daddy?

ELIZABETH: No. He's in bed asleep.

EMILY: Then what is it?

ELIZABETH: Inez blessed me out and stopped speaking to me over last night. She says we've ruined the boy's whole vacation. You've broken his heart, given him all kinds of complexes and he's going home tomorrow ...

EMILY: But I saw him at the drugstore tonight and I had a long talk with him and he said he understood ...

ELIZABETH: But Inez doesn't understand. She says she'll never forgive either of us again. (*She starts to cry.*)

EMILY: Oh, Mother. I'm sorry ...

ELIZABETH: Emily, if you'll do me one favor ... I promise you I'll never ask another thing of you again as long as I live. And I will never nag you about going out with Leo again as long as I live ...

EMILY: What is the favor, Mother?

ELIZABETH: Let that boy take you to the dance day after tomorrow ...

EMILY: Now, Mother ...

ELIZABETH: Emily. I get down on my knees to you. Do me this one favor ... (*A pause.*) Emily ... Emily ... (*She is crying again.*)

EMILY: Now, Mother, please. Don't cry. I'll think about it. I'll call Leo and see what he says. But please don't cry like this ... Mother ... Mother ...

(*She is trying to console her as the lights fade. The lights are brought up on Upstage Left. It is Mary Catherine's yard and living room. Music can be heard in the distance. Horace and Mary Catherine come walking in Downstage Left and go up the Center of the stage until they reach the upstage area.*)

MARY CATHERINE: Well, this is where I live.

HORACE: In that house there?

MARY CATHERINE: Uh-huh. (*A pause.*)

HORACE: Where is that music coming from?

MARY CATHERINE: The Flats ...

HORACE: What's the Flats?

MARY CATHERINE: I don't know what it is. That's just what they call it. It's nothing but a bunch of barbecue restaurants and beer joints down there and they call it the Flats. There used to be a creek running down there that they called Willow Creek but it's all dry now. My father says when he was a boy, every time the river flooded, Willow Creek would fill up. The river doesn't overflow anymore since they took the raft out of it. I like to come out here at night and listen to the music. Do you like to dance? ...

HORACE: Well ... I ...

MARY CATHERINE: I love to dance.

HORACE: Well ... I don't dance too well.

MARY CATHERINE: There's nothing to it but confidence.

HORACE: That's what my sister says ...

MARY CATHERINE: I didn't learn for the longest kind of time for lack of confidence and then Emily gave me a long lecture about it and I got confidence and went ahead and learned. Would you like to come in for a while?

HORACE: Well ... if it's all right with you ...

MARY CATHERINE: I'd be glad to have you.

HORACE: Thank you.

(*They go into the area. Mary Catherine's father, Tom Davis, is seated there in his undershirt. He works in a garage.*)

MARY CATHERINE: Hello, Daddy.

TOM: Hello, baby.

MARY CATHERINE: Daddy, this is Horace.

TOM: Hello, son.

HORACE: Howdy do, sir. (*They shake hands.*)

MARY CATHERINE: Horace is Mrs. Inez Stanley's brother. He's here on a visit.

TOM: That's nice. Where's your home, son?

HORACE: Flatonia.

TOM: Oh, I see. Well are you young people going to visit for a while?

MARY CATHERINE: Yes sir.

TOM: Well, I'll leave you then. Good night.

MARY CATHERINE: Good night, Daddy.

HORACE: Good night, sir.

(*He goes out Upstage Left.*)

HORACE: What does your father do?

MARY CATHERINE: He works in a garage. He's a mechanic. What does your father do?

HORACE: He's a judge.

MARY CATHERINE: My father worries so because he can't afford to send me to college. My mother told him that was all foolishness. That I'd rather go to business school anyway.

HORACE: Had you rather go to business school?

MARY CATHERINE: I don't know. (*A pause.*) Not really. But I'd never tell him that. When I was in the seventh grade I thought I would die if I couldn't get there, but then when I was in the ninth, Mother talked to me one day and told me Daddy wasn't sleeping at nights for fear I'd be disappointed if he couldn't send me, so I told him the next night I decided I'd rather go to business school. He seemed relieved. (*A pause.*)

HORACE: Mary Catherine. I ... uh ... heard you say a while ago that you didn't dance because you lacked confidence and uh ... then I heard you say you talked it over with Emily and she told you what was wrong and you got the confidence and you went ahead ...

MARY CATHERINE: That's right ...

HORACE: Well ... It may sound silly and all to you ... seeing I'm about to start my first year at college ... but I'd like to ask you a question...

MARY CATHERINE: What is it, Horace?

HORACE: How do you get confidence?

MARY CATHERINE: Well, you just get it. Someone points it out to you that you lack it and then you get it ...

HORACE: Oh, is that how it's done?

MARY CATHERINE: That's how I did it.

HORACE: You see I lack confidence. And I ... sure would like to get it...

MARY CATHERINE: In what way do you lack confidence, Horace? ...

HORACE: Oh, in all kinds of ways. (*A pause.*) I'm not much of a mixer...

MARY CATHERINE: I think you're just mixing fine tonight.

HORACE: I know. That's what's giving me a little encouragement. You're the first girl I've ever really been able to talk to. I mean this way ...

MARY CATHERINE: Am I, Horace? ...

HORACE: Yes.

MARY CATHERINE: Well, I feel in some ways that's quite a compliment.

HORACE: Well, you should feel that way. (*A pause.*) Mary Catherine ...

MARY CATHERINE: Yes, Horace?

HORACE: I had about decided to go back home tomorrow or the next day, but I understand there's another dance at the end of the week...

MARY CATHERINE: Uh-huh. Day after tomorrow.

HORACE: Well ... I ... don't know if you have a date or not ... but if you don't have ... I feel if I could take you ... I would gain the confidence to go ... I mean ...

MARY CATHERINE: Well, Horace ... You see ...

HORACE: I know I'd gain the confidence. My sister is a swell dancer and she'll let me practice with her every living minute until it's time for the dance. Of course I don't know if I could learn to jitterbug by then or rumba or do anything fancy, you understand, but I know I could learn the fox-trot and I can waltz a little now ...

MARY CATHERINE: I'm sure you could.

HORACE: Well, will you go with me?

MARY CATHERINE: Yes, Horace. I'd love to ...

HORACE: Oh, thank you, Mary Catherine. I'll just practice night and day. I can't tell you how grateful Inez is going to be to you ... Mary Catherine, if we played the radio softly could we dance now?

MARY CATHERINE: Why certainly, Horace.

HORACE: You understand I'll make mistakes ...

MARY CATHERINE: I understand ... (*She turns the radio on very softly.*)

HORACE: All right.

MARY CATHERINE: Yes ...

(*He approaches her very cautiously and takes her in his arms. He begins awkwardly to dance. Mary Catherine is very pleased and happy.*)

MARY CATHERINE: Why, you're doing fine, Horace. Just fine.

HORACE: Thank you, Mary Catherine. Thank you.

(*They continue dancing. Horace is very pleased with himself although he is still dancing quite awkwardly. The lights fade. The lights are brought up on the area Downstage Left. It is early next morning. Inez is there reading. Horace comes in whistling. He seems brimming over with happiness.*)

INEZ: What are you so happy about?

HORACE: I'm just happy.

INEZ: Wait until you hear my news and you'll be happier.

HORACE: Is that so?

INEZ: Miss Emily has seen the light.

HORACE: What?

INEZ: She has succumbed.

HORACE: What do you mean?

INEZ: She has crawled on her knees.

HORACE: She's crawled on her knees? I don't get it ...

INEZ: She has eaten dirt.

HORACE: Sister, what's this all about?

INEZ: Last night around ten o'clock she called in the meekest kind of voice possible and said Inez, I've called up to apologize to you. I have apologized to Horace in the drugstore. Did she?

HORACE: Uh. Huh.

INEZ: And now I want to apologize to you and to tell you how sorry I am I behaved so badly ...

HORACE: Well. Isn't that nice of her, Inez?

INEZ: Wait a minute. You haven't heard the whole thing. And then Her Highness added tell Horace if he would like to invite me to the dance to call me and I'd be glad to accept. And furthermore, Elizabeth called this morning and said they were leaving for Houston to buy her the most expensive evening dress in sight. Just to impress you with.

HORACE: Oh ... (*He sits down on a chair.*)

INEZ: Brother. What is the matter with you? Now are you gonna start worrying about this dancin' business all over again? You are the biggest fool sometimes. We've got today and tomorrow to practice.

HORACE: Inez ...

INEZ: Yes?

HORACE: I already have a date with someone tomorrow ...

INEZ: You do?

HORACE: Yes. I met a girl last night at the drugstore and I asked her.

INEZ: What girl did you ask?

HORACE: Mary Catherine Davis ...

INEZ: Well, you've got to get right out of it. You've got to call her up and explain just what happened.

HORACE: But, Inez ...

INEZ: You've got to do it, Horace. They told me they are spending all kinds of money for that dress. I practically had to threaten Elizabeth with never speaking to her again to bring this all about. Why, she will never forgive me now if I turn around and tell her you can't go ... Horace. Don't look that way. I can't help it. For my sake, for your sister's sake, you've got to get out of this date with Mary Catherine Davis ... tell her ... tell her ... anything ...

HORACE: O.K. (*A pause. He starts out.*) What can I say?

INEZ: I don't know, Horace. (*A pause.*) Say ... well, just tell her the truth. That's the best thing. Tell her that Emily's mother is your sister's best friend and that Emily's mother has taken her into Houston to buy her a very expensive dress …

HORACE: What if Mary Catherine has bought a dress? …

INEZ: Well, she can't have bought an expensive dress …

HORACE: Why not?

INEZ: Because her people can't afford it. Honey, you'll be the envy of every young man in Harrison, bringing Emily Crews to the dance … Why, everybody will wonder just what it is you have …

HORACE: I'm not going to do it.

INEZ: Horace …

HORACE: I don't want to take Emily, I want to take Mary Catherine and that's just what I'm going to do.

INEZ: Horace …

HORACE: My mind is made up. Once and for all …

INEZ: Then what am I gonna do? (*She starts to cry.*) Who's gonna speak to Elizabeth? She'll bless me out putting her to all this trouble. Making her spend all this money and time … (*She is crying loudly now.*) Horace. You just can't do this to me. You just simply can't …

HORACE: I can't help it. I'm not taking Emily Crews—

INEZ: Horace …

HORACE: I am not taking Emily Crews.

(*He is firm. She is crying as the lights fade. The lights are brought up on Upstage Left area. Mary Catherine's father is seated there. He is in his undershirt. In the distance dance music can be heard. Mrs. Davis comes in from Left.*)

MRS. DAVIS: Don't you think you'd better put your shirt on, Tom? Mary Catherine's date will be here any minute.

TOM: What time is it?

MRS. DAVIS: Nine o'clock.

TOM: The dance has already started. I can hear the music from here.

MRS. DAVIS: I know. But you know young people, they'd die before they'd be the first to a dance. Put your shirt on, Tom.

TOM: O.K.

MRS. DAVIS: As soon as her date arrives we'll go.

TOM: O.K.

(*Mary Catherine comes in from Left. She has on an evening dress and she looks very pretty.*)

MRS. DAVIS: Why, Mary Catherine. You look lovely. Doesn't she look lovely, Tom?

TOM: Yes, she does.

MRS. DAVIS: Turn around, honey, and let me see you from the back. (*She does so.*) Just as pretty as you can be, Mary Catherine.

MARY CATHERINE: Thank you.

(*Horace comes in Downstage Left in his tux with a corsage box. He walks up the Center of the stage to the Upstage Left area.*)

MARY CATHERINE: That's Horace. (*She goes to the corner of the area.*) Hello, Horace.

HORACE: Hello, Mary Catherine.

MARY CATHERINE: You've met my mother and father.

HORACE: Yes, I have. I met your father the other night and your mother yesterday afternoon.

MRS. DAVIS: Hello, Horace.

TOM: Hello, son.

MRS. DAVIS: Well, we were just going. You all have a good time tonight.

HORACE: Thank you.

MRS. DAVIS: Come on, Tom.

TOM: All right. Good night and have a nice time.

MARY CATHERINE: Thank you, Daddy.

(*They go out Left. Horace hands her the corsage box. She takes it and opens it.*)

MARY CATHERINE: Oh, thank you, Horace. Thank you so much. (*She takes the flowers out.*) They're just lovely. Will you pin them on for me?

HORACE: I'll try. (*He takes the corsage and the pin. He begins to pin it on.*) Will about here be all right?

MARY CATHERINE: Just fine.

(*He pins the corsage on.*)

MARY CATHERINE: Emily told me about the mix-up between your sister and her mother. I appreciate your going ahead and taking me anyway. If you had wanted to get out of it I would have understood. Emily and I are very good friends ... and ...

HORACE: I didn't want to get out of it, Mary Catherine. I wanted to take you.

MARY CATHERINE: I'm glad you didn't want to get out of it. Emily offered to let me wear her new dress. But I had already bought one of my own.

HORACE: It's very pretty, Mary Catherine.

MARY CATHERINE: Thank you. (*A pause.*) Well, the dance has started. I can hear the music. Can't you?

HORACE: Yes.

MARY CATHERINE: Well, we'd better get going ...

HORACE: All right.

(*They start out.*)

HORACE: Mary Catherine. I hope you don't think this is silly, but could we practice just once more? ...

MARY CATHERINE: Certainly we could …

(*They start to dance. Horace has improved although he is no Fred Astaire. They are dancing around and suddenly Horace breaks away.*)

HORACE: Mary Catherine. I'm not good enough yet. I can't go. I'm sorry. Please, let's just stay here.

MARY CATHERINE: No, Horace. We have to go.

HORACE: Please, Mary Catherine …

MARY CATHERINE: I know just how you feel, Horace, but we have to go. (*A pause.*) I haven't told you the whole truth, Horace. This is my first dance too …

HORACE: It is?

MARY CATHERINE: Yes. I've been afraid to go. Afraid I wouldn't be popular. The last two dances I was asked to go and I said no.

HORACE: Then why did you accept when I asked you?

MARY CATHERINE: I don't know. I asked myself that afterwards. I guess because you gave me a kind of confidence. (*A pause. They dance again.*) You gave me confidence and I gave you confidence. What's the sense of getting confidence, Horace, if you're not going to use it?

(*A pause. They continue dancing.*)

HORACE: That's a pretty piece.

MARY CATHERINE: Yes, it is.

(*A pause. They dance again. Horace stops.*)

HORACE: I'm ready to go if you are, Mary Catherine.

MARY CATHERINE: I'm ready.

(*They start out.*)

MARY CATHERINE: Scared?

HORACE: A little.

MARY CATHERINE: So am I. But let's go.

HORACE: O.K.

(*They continue out the area down the Center of the stage and off Downstage Right as the music from the dance is heard.*)

END OF PLAY

The Pot Boiler

A Vaudeville Sketch
By Alice Gerstenberg

Adapted By Irvine N. Smith

CHARACTERS
    Thomas Pinikles Sud, a playwright
    Mrs. Ivory, a businesswoman
    Mr. Wouldby, a novice playwright
    Miss Ivory, the heroine
    Mr. Ruler, the hero
    Mrs. Pencil, the villainess
    Mr. Inkwell, the villain

SETTING
    A bare stage, dimly lit. There are two tables, one at Center and one at Down Right, and a number of chairs scattered around the stage. It is early afternoon.

THE POT BOILER

*Sud enters the theater through the audience and climbs up on stage.
He is gaudily and distinctively dressed. He carries a briefcase which
he puts on the Down Right table, and as he opens it and starts laying
out a variety of manuscripts, he calls off.*

SUD: Gus. Gus! Just some work lights, please. We're only rehearsing for
lines this afternoon. (*As lights come up on stage, Sud steps down toward
the front and calls to back of house.*) Oh, Joe—I'm expecting a young
man. It's all right; let him in.

WOULDBY: (*From back of auditorium.*) I'm here now, Mr. Sud.

SUD: Good, good. Come on up, Mr. Wouldby.

(*Sud goes back to his work at the table as Wouldby comes down to the
stage through the auditorium. Wouldby is very conservatively dressed, and
very mild and naive in his manner. He also carries a briefcase.*)

WOULDBY: (*Climbing up on stage.*) It's very good of you to let me in, Mr.
Sud. I've never watched a real playwright at work before.

SUD: (*Expansively.*) Well, I was fond of your father. I'm glad to help his son.
(*Pats Wouldby on the shoulder and goes to arrange chairs at the center
table.*)

WOULDBY: (*Following him.*) It must be wonderful to be the greatest
playwright of our day.

SUD: (*Pausing to reflect for a moment.*) Yes. Yes, it—it is.

WOULDBY: Everyone knows the famous Thomas Pinikles Sud.

SUD: (*Pausing again.*) Yes, the greatest figures in the theatrical world are
privileged to call themselves friends of mine.

WOULDBY: (*Following Sud who has gone back to work.*) Would—would—
would you read my script, sir?

SUD: (*Looks at script for a moment, amused condescension.*) Never roll a
script, young man. I can see very well that you don't even know the
first principles.

WOULDBY: But how can I learn them? No one will teach me.

SUD: Son, I shall do a great thing for you. I will let you stay and watch a
rehearsal of my latest play, *The Pot Boiler*.

WOULDBY: The ... uh, Pot Boiler?

SUD: Yes. In it I have used all the important dramatic principles.

WOULDBY: (*Fumbles in his briefcase for a pad of paper and pencil; puts on a
pair of glasses that look exactly like Sud's glasses.*) What are they?

SUD: Well, for example, Mrs. Pencil is the woman in the case.

WOULDBY: (*Puzzled.*) Pencil?

SUD: The villainess! Very symbolic, eh? I am known for the clever way in which I relate my characters to everyday objects.

WOULDBY: (*Doesn't understand at all.*) Oh.

SUD: Mr. Inkwell is the villain.

WOULDBY: (*Taking notes.*) Inkwell.

SUD: The heroine is—Miss Ivory.

WOULDBY: Ivory.

SUD: Mr. Ruler is the hero.

WOULDBY: Ruler.

SUD: And Mrs. Ivory is our clever businesswoman.

WOULDBY: (*Nodding.*) Mrs. Ivory.

SUD: I haven't finished writing the play yet, but we're going through it this afternoon as far as I have written—and then I shall see how to go on.

WOULDBY: You haven't finished—?

SUD: (*As actors enter.*) Ah, here are the actors now. Cast, cast—line up, please. (*He claps his hands.*) We have a guest. Hurry!

(*The actors line up reluctantly across the stage. Only Mrs. Pencil's personality reflects the role she plays. Miss Ivory is tough, gum-chewing, sexy. Mrs. Ivory is very young and girlish, giggly. Mr. Inkwell is shy, timid, retiring, easily embarrassed. Mr. Ruler is a bully, rough and unpleasant. Each accepts the order to "line up" characteristically.*)

SUD: Mr. Wouldby, this is my cast. Cast, this is Mr. Wouldby, an apprentice playwright.

(*The cast members respond to the introduction without enthusiasm.*)

SUD: Now, to work—to work! Let's clear the stage.

(*He gestures the cast Offstage and they disperse. Mrs. Pencil and Ruler go out Left; Miss Ivory, Mrs. Ivory and Inkwell exit Right.*)

SUD: Mr. Wouldby, you can sit over here with me.

(*As they move to the Down Right table.*)

SUD: Now, you must imagine that this room is the library in Mrs. Ivory's house. (*Claps his hands.*) Ready!

(*Mrs. Pencil enters from Left, acting out the pantomime which Sud describes to Wouldby.*)

SUD: The adventuress. She comes in. She has been out. She is worried. That nervous twitching of the lips and narrowing of the eyes are always full of suspense. She takes off her gloves, puts down her purse. That's good business! A door opens—she starts. By starting she shows you that she is guilty of something.

MISS IVORY: (*Entering from Right, sweetly.*) Oh, there you are, Mrs. Pencil.

MRS. PENCIL: Yes, I'm back.

MISS IVORY: Good. I thought I should have to drink my tea without you.

(*They sit at the table, Miss Ivory Up Center, Mrs. Pencil at the Left, and pantomime the pouring and drinking.*)

SUD: That tells the audience what time of day it is. Besides, drinking afternoon tea shows that Miss Ivory is in society.

WOULDBY: Very good, yes, indeed.

MRS. PENCIL: Isn't your mother going to join us?

SUD: That's only to show that the girl has a mother.

MISS IVORY: No, she is talking business with Mr. Inkwell.

MRS. PENCIL: (*Violent start.*) Inkwell!

MISS IVORY: Yes, do you know him?

MRS. PENCIL: (*Evasively.*) I—oh—no, no—

SUD: Do you catch it? Do you see how her nervousness suggests that there is a link between Mrs. Pencil and Inkwell? That's how I show my technique. The secret that every playwright keeps locked in his breast.

MISS IVORY: I am so sorry that mother has all this trouble with the bricklayers. They shouldn't have gone on strike just now, while you are visiting us.

SUD: That tells us that Mrs. Pencil is a guest in Miss Ivory's house.

MISS IVORY: When you were here last year, my father—

(*In unison, Miss Ivory and Mrs. Pencil put their right hands across their breasts, raise their heads, then turn heads to the left and lower them, dramatically.*)

SUD: The girl hesitates—they both look sorrowful. We had to cut down on the cast, so I killed off her father.

MRS. PENCIL: (*As they recover, speaking with an accent.*) Ah, my dear—we were such cloze friends—seence my arrival in zis countree—

SUD: You see I had to make her a foreigner. A villainess always talks with a foreign accent.

MRS. PENCIL: (*Normal speech.*) I haven't had much time to read particulars about the strike. Does your mother still refuse to arbitrate?

MISS IVORY: What right have the bricklayers to make rules for my mother? She would show her weakness if she gave in. I have faith that what she does is right!

SUD: The innocent heroine—so cool and pure and white!

(*Inkwell enters from the Right. As he and Mrs. Pencil see each other, they give a violent start of surprise and recognition, freezing in an exaggerated posture.*)

SUD: That's a dramatic scene! Doesn't that thrill your spine?

(*Inkwell and Mrs. Pencil break pose.*)

MISS IVORY: Mrs. Pencil, may I introduce Mr. Inkwell?

(*The two bow slightly.*)

MISS IVORY: Will you have a dish of tea, Mr. Inkwell?

SUD: Cup, cup of tea.

MISS IVORY: (*Reverting to character.*) Dish, *dish* of tea!

SUD: It's *cup*. I wrote *cup!*

MISS IVORY: Mr. Sud, when I was in England last year the Duke of Creighton himself offered me a *dish* of tea.

SUD: I don't give a damn about the Duke—I wrote *cup!*

MISS IVORY: Mr. Sud, I play only the smartest parts. It's *dish*—it's dish or I quit! Make up your mind.

SUD: (*Controlling himself.*) All right, all right. Say anything you like. (*Muttering to himself.*) I suggest bathtub!

MISS IVORY: (*Returning to her position triumphantly.*) Mr. Inkwell, will you have a dish of tea? And please tell me that you have ordered the strikers to come to mother's terms.

INKWELL: She is looking through her safe for more papers, so she asked me to wait in here.

SUD: That's an explanation of why he came in.

MISS IVORY: How many lumps?

SUD: Now that question of the number of lumps is very important—it gives a natural air to the scene.

WOULDBY: Yes, indeed!

MISS IVORY: I am going to the dining room to get some lemon for your tea.

INKWELL: Oh, please don't trouble—

MISS IVORY: No trouble at all. (*Exits Right.*)

SUD: When you want to get a character out, you've got to get 'em out!

INKWELL: (*Whirling on Mrs. Pencil.*) You here?

MRS. PENCIL: Shhh! I had to come. I couldn't live without you any longer.

INKWELL: But in this house?

MRS. PENCIL: I am her mother's friend.

INKWELL: You are indiscreet.

MRS. PENCIL: I was desperate for you. When I read about the strike I had to come!

SUD: Mrs. Pencil is the dreadful woman. A play can't exist without her.

WOULDBY: You mean she is his—

SUD: Oh, yes. The more fuss we make about her the better.

MRS. PENCIL: Oh, Clem, you aren't glad to see me! Oh, that I have lived for this!

(*Mrs. Pencil dashes about the stage, waving her hands and contorting her face. Sud watches her for a moment, then rises in astonishment and follows her.*)

SUD: Idiot! Can't you talk? Do you think I write my lines to be cut? How dare you cut my lines?

MRS. PENCIL: (*Dropping the action and taking her script off the table.*) I've done just what it says. (*Reads.*) "Mrs. Pencil shows extreme despair and passion."

SUD: (*Looks at quote.*) That's not the play! That's the motion picture version. (*Goes back to table, fumbling through various scripts.*)

WOULDBY: Have you the same script ready for the movies?

SUD: Certainly. I write in columns, alongside each other—play, motion-picture version, novel, serialization for newspapers and magazines ...

WOULDBY: All at once?

SUD: Certainly!

WOULDBY: What are all those little slips of paper?

SUD: Well, when I cut out a line someplace, I keep it—just in case I need it somewhere else.

WOULDBY: I see, I see. (*Writes in notebook.*) A great playwright must be economical with his ideas.

SUD: (*Handing slip to Mrs. Pencil.*) Exactly!

MRS. PENCIL: I see, Mr. Sud. Shall I go on?

SUD: (*Sitting down.*) Yes, Mrs. Pencil, go on.

MRS. PENCIL: Oh, Clem—I was so frightened when I read about the strikers. Even if you are their leader, they might turn and murder you.

INKWELL: Nonsense. I control the strikers. They come to me for orders. I'll stop this strike just as soon as old lady Ivory gives me my price.

MRS. PENCIL: But what do the bricklayers want?

INKWELL: (*Stepping up on chair and orating.*) They want shorter hours, better pay, better lighting ... better air ... (*Trails off.*)

SUD: After a moment. Well, go on, go on.

INKWELL: (*Apologetically.*) Well, pardon me, Mr. Sud—but you see you have me saying that the bricklayers want better light and better air. I mean, it doesn't sound right. You see, bricklayers work out of doors and the light and air there is ... well, it's in no way a criticism of your writing, sir ...

SUD: All right, leave out "lighting and air." that's simply some bad typing by my secretary. Go on, Inkwell.

(*Inkwell sits down at the right of the table and Mrs. Pencil sits down at the left.*)

INKWELL: See here, Kate, you keep out of this business. I won't be spied on by any woman.

MRS. PENCIL: (*In shocked whisper.*) Who is spying on you?

INKWELL: (*Whisper.*) You!

MRS. PENCIL: I?

SUD: Now we are coming to a big scene! There is nothing as effective as the repetition of the same words built to a climax. Begin again. Mrs. Pencil. "Who is spying on you?"

MRS. PENCIL: Who is spying on you?

INKWELL: You!

MRS. PENCIL: I?

INKWELL: You!

MRS. PENCIL: I?

INKWELL: You!

MRS. PENCIL: I?

SUD: (*Furious.*) Parrots! Nothing but parrots! Increase the stress—build the scene. Build! Build!

INKWELL: How can we build when you don't give us any lines?

SUD: What do you call yourselves actors for if you can't supply acting when the playwright uses dashes?! This is the biggest scene in the play. The very fact that I don't give you a lot of literary lines puts me in the class of the most forceful dramatists of the day. My plays are not wishy-washy lines. They are full of action—red blood, flesh and blood! Now you do your part—bing-bang stuff. Shake them in their chairs out there—make shivers run up and down their spines. Make them *feel* you. Now go to it, go to it! (*He conducts them as they speak.*)

INKWELL: You!

MRS. PENCIL: I?

INKWELL: You!

MRS. PENCIL: I?

INKWELL: You!

MRS. PENCIL: I?

SUD: Get it over, get it over! Mr. Wouldby, is it getting over?

WOULDBY: (*Looking at edge of stage.*) I don't see anything getting over.

SUD: He doesn't see it! You hear? He doesn't see it! Now begin again. And please, please, please—get it o-ver. O-ver! (*He conducts more violently.*)

MRS. PENCIL: Who is spying on you?

INKWELL: You!

MRS. PENCIL: I?

INKWELL: You!

MRS. PENCIL: I?

INKWELL: You!!

MRS. PENCIL: I??

INKWELL: You!!!

MRS. PENCIL: I???

INKWELL: (*Fiercely.*) *You!!!*

MRS. PENCIL: (*Violently.*) *I???*

INKWELL: (*Bellowing.*) Well, what do you call it, then—coming here after me like this??

MRS. PENCIL: (*Subsiding.*) What do you mean, like this?

SUD: (*Shrieks.*) Like what?

MRS. PENCIL: (*Doesn't understand.*) Like this?

SUD: Accent it—stress it—increase it! Like *what!*

MRS. PENCIL: Like this!

SUD: Like *what!*

MRS. PENCIL: (*Helplessly.*) Like this.

SUD: (*Running around the stage.*) The best scene in the play—ruined, ruined! I'm noted for my strong, laconic scenes and you make me suffer like this. Perfectly hopeless—nothing but animal sounds. Nothing but a machine! Oh, what's the use. Go on, go on! Now you see, Mr. Wouldby, how actors can make plays fail—

MRS. PENCIL: If you'd write us a decent play for once—

SUD: (*Whirls.*) No back-talk, madam. I haven't offered you a contract yet. If you can't play it any better, I'll let you go. Now, show us what you can do with the rest of the scene! (*To Wouldby.*) If she can't pound his chest right, the box-office will lose money on her.

WOULDBY: Must she pound him?

SUD: Certainly! Seeing a woman pounding a man's chest and hearing her scream is worth five dollars to anybody. Go on, Mrs. Pencil.

MRS. PENCIL: You are keeping something from me! You have deceived me! You dog, tell me. Tell me! (*She sets Inkwell up in front of her, quite lady-like, and pounds his chest with both fists.*) Who is she? Where is she? You are keeping something from me!

WOULDBY: Is she going to yank it out of his chest?

SUD: Pound! Pound! Get it over! (*He rushes between them, pushing Mrs. Pencil aside, and attacks Inkwell, pounding his chest with both hands.*) Tell me, you dog. Who is she? Where is she? You are keeping something from me! (*Whirls to Mrs. Pencil.*) I wrote "applause" here. You've got to get applause here—so pound!

INKWELL: Would you mind skipping the scene for today? I'll wear a chest protector tomorrow.

SUD: Just like an actor to have a personal prejudice against a part.

WOULDBY: But why must she pound him so hard?

SUD: Because he's the villain and the audience likes to see him get it.

WOULDBY: What has he done to make him the villain?

SUD: I didn't want an explanation here so I had to interrupt them—shhh, here comes Miss Ivory.

MISS IVORY: Here is the lemon for your tea, Mr. Inkwell.

SUD: Such interruptions reek with dramatic intensity!

MRS. PENCIL: (*Nervously.*) I—I think I'll take my—purse to my room! (*Exits Left.*)

SUD: Not a bad excuse, eh, the purse? I had to get her out!

WOULDBY: Oh, very natural—yes, indeed.

MISS IVORY: Well, Mr. Inkwell, I hope we may yet succeed in claiming you as a friend, instead of coddling you as an enemy.

INKWELL: If you treat all your enemies so well, what must you do for your friends.

MISS IVORY: We abuse those we love.

SUD: (*Proudly.*) Quite epigrammatic, eh?

INKWELL: Even abuse at such fair hands could only please.

SUD: Did you catch the subtlety of that remark?

MISS IVORY: (*Nervously.*) Wi—wi—will you have some more tea?

INKWELL: (*Suddenly.*) I don't want tea—I want you! I love you!

SUD: Wait a moment, wait a moment. That's far too abrupt! I've some better lines here somewhere. (*Searches through scripts.*) I cut some out of the beginning of the play. When the curtain went up, the maid was dusting the room and the Irish butler began making love to her. (*He finds a clipping and hands it to Inkwell.*) There, Inkwell, these should be better. Go on, please.

MISS IVORY: (*To Inkwell.*) Shall I go back?

INKWELL: Yes, please.

MISS IVORY: Wi—wi—will you have some more tea?

INKWELL: (*Romantically, in thick Irish brogue.*) I don't want tea—I want you! I love you! Oh, my darlin'—it is a terrible sensation, I 'ave for you, I 'ave. Put your little hand in moine, for the loikes of you I nivver...

(*All look dazed as Inkwell trails off and looks nervously at Sud.*)

INKWELL: I beg pardon, Mr. Sud, but this is a butler making love. I am playing the part of a gentleman—

SUD: (*Who has stamped Upstage in a rage.*) Haven't you any brains of your own? If a musician can transpose music at sight, can't you do the same with dialogue?

INKWELL: But a gentleman doesn't make love like a—

SUD: He *means* the same! Go on, go on, I can't stand these arguments. They'll give me a heart attack! Go on!

MISS IVORY: Oh, come on, Bob, say anything! Wi—wi—will you have some more tea?

INKWELL: (*Extemporizing nervously.*) I don't want tea! I want you! I love you! Oh, my darling—it is a wonderful feeling—this one—this feeling that I have for you—indeed, this one that I have—put your hand in mine—for a woman like you never before—uh, I have never before indeed—that is, such a woman—never before has such a woman as you—

SUD: Great Scott! Leave out the "which's" and "such's!" Get it clear for tomorrow's rehearsal.

INKWELL: I ought to have my name on the program as co-author.

SUD: You ought to have your name cut out of the program when you forget how to act!

INKWELL: Well, I'm worried about how the play is going to end.

SUD: I'm the playwright, leave that to me!

(Inkwell goes Upstage; there is a pause. Sud calls impatiently off Left.)

SUD: Mr. Ruler! Mr. Ruler!

RULER: What is it?

SUD: Pay some attention to your cue, please.

RULER: Beg pardon, sir—I didn't hear my cue.

SUD: Well, it's your business to listen for it.

RULER: They didn't give me my cue.

SUD: Well, what is your cue?

RULER: What is it?

SUD: I asked you what your cue was.

RULER: What is it?

SUD: Is your hearing perfectly clear?

RULER: Perfectly.

SUD: Then will you kindly tell me what your cue is!!

RULER: *What is it?*

SUD: I shall go mad! I'm dealing with lunatics! Mr. Ruler, once again I ask you—if you can *hear*— will you kindly read from your script and tell me what your cue is!

RULER: *(Yelling back.)* I've been trying to tell you that my cue is "What is it?"!!

SUD: Heart disease, heart disease. I shall die of it! That line was cut long ago! The trouble with you actors is that you can't forget.

WOULDBY: I always thought actors had to remember.

SUD: Any fool can remember!

RULER: *(Furious.)* See here, Mr. Sud—I don't take that kind of criticism. In fact, it's my first experience taking it from a playwright. In all the other companies I've been in, the director kept the playwright out. He wouldn't have him meddling about!

SUD: Mr. Ruler, I am backing this production. I haven't engaged you because you could act, but because you were born good looking— which is scarcely a compliment to your own efforts. Now if you please, we will proceed. I'll find a line here somewhere.

(As Ruler stamps Left angrily, Sud goes back to his pile of scripts and looks through them. He holds up a slip of paper.)

SUD: Ah, here's a precious line. Take it down, Mr. Ruler. "I was in the neighborhood looking for some real estate." Now, Mr. Ruler, you enter in time to interrupt Mr. Inkwell's declaration of love for Miss Ivory.

(Miss Ivory and Inkwell resume their positions. Ruler enters again.)

SUD: They spring apart—spring, Inkwell!

(Inkwell springs backwards.)

SUD: No, the house is not on fire—I didn't say jump.

INKWELL: "Spring" is the same as "jump."

SUD: This is no time to discuss synonyms. Go on, Miss Ivory.

MISS IVORY: Oh, hello, Jack. Where did you come from?

RULER: I was in the neighborhood looking for some real estate. Hello, Inkwell. How's the strike?

INKWELL: Well, if you could persuade Mrs. Ivory to—

RULER: No, Inkwell—I'm not converted to your view! I have my own theories!

SUD: Now we're coming to the kernel of the play's success. The new viewpoint! Use all the stock characters and situations you want, but add a new twist.

WOULDBY: What does Ruler think?

SUD: Listen.

RULER: I believe sternly in justice—the righteous expiation of sin. Only in that way can we progress to higher things.

SUD: Forms, not things!

RULER: Okay. Only in that way can we progress to higher forms, not things! The position I hold today is the result of my desire in a previous life. When the trumpet calls me into the next, there I shall reap the harvest of what I have sown here. Why should we help the bricklayers?

MISS IVORY: (*Who has been trying various postures without success.*) Mr. Sud.

SUD: Shhhhh.

RULER: If *they* chose in *their* past life to be born bricklayers here, have we the right—

MISS IVORY: Mr. Sud.

SUD: Shhhh.

RULER: I ask you—have we the right to tear down the building they designed when they were here before? Have we the right—

MISS IVORY: Mr. Sud!!

SUD: Well, what is it, Miss Ivory?

MISS IVORY: Excuse me, Mr. Sud, but all this time—while Ruler is talking—I don't know what to do with my hands. Couldn't you cut his lines?

RULER: I protest! Mr. Sud, I would resent having my part shortened just because the leading lady doesn't know what to do with her hands.

SUD: Well ...

RULER: Anyway, I think that in this speech of mine you have shown your real talent. To cut one word of it would do you a great injustice.

SUD: Thank you, quite so. Quite so! Miss Ivory, during this scene you might be—you might be—fanning yourself—to keep yourself the heroine, cool and pure and white.

MISS IVORY: Well, all right ...

WOULDBY: How well you understand human nature, Mr. Sud. The play is really more important than the actors, isn't it?

SUD: Of course. But actors are so superbly conceited—poor things.

RULER: Look here—

SUD: Quiet! Mrs. Ivory's entrance.

MRS. IVORY: (*Entering from Right.*) I couldn't find the papers in the safe. Ah, how do you do, Jack?

RULER: Good morning, Mrs. Ivory.

MRS. IVORY: Daughter dear—do you know anything about the papers in the safe?

SUD: Keep up the suspense, Inkwell.

INKWELL: I have no lines here.

SUD: A villain should sustain the suggestion of villainy whether he has lines or not. Look uneasy—tremble.

(*Inkwell does a highly exaggerated tremble, looking uneasy as he does so.*)

MRS. IVORY: But if I see him tremble, Mr. Sud, wouldn't I ask him if he had a chill?

SUD: It's not your business to be looking his way just then. Again, Inkwell.

(*Inkwell trembles. Sud yells at Mrs. Ivory.*)

SUD: Don't catch his eye!

MRS. IVORY: Will you tremble again, please?

(*Inkwell trembles again.*)

SUD: Count five for the tremble. Again please, "Daughter dear—do you know anything about the papers in the safe?"

MRS. IVORY: Daughter dear—do you know anything about the papers in the safe?

SUD: Everybody look away.

(*All do.*)

SUD: Tremble, Inkwell.

(*He does.*)

SUD: Now, everybody count five for the tremble.

(*All count five, moving their lips silently.*)

SUD: Now look at Inkwell.

(*All swing to look.*)

SUD: Again, please.

MRS. IVORY: Daughter dear—do you know anything about the papers in the safe?

SUD: (*Clapping his hands.*) One—two—three—four—five!

(*As all turn back:*)

MRS. IVORY: Those valuable papers!

SUD: That's it—go ahead!

MISS IVORY: I don't even know the combination, mother. Could they have been stolen?

WOULDBY: Did Inkwell really take them?

SUD: He's the villain, isn't he? I couldn't let Mr. Ruler do it.

MRS. IVORY: Oh, what shall I do? Where shall I look? Where, oh, where? (*As she crosses up behind the table, she knocks two revolvers onto the floor.*)

MISS IVORY: Oh! Revolvers!

RULER: Let me, Mrs. Ivory. (*Picks them up.*)

MISS IVORY: Where did they come from?

WOULDBY: Are they really going to use them?

SUD: Of course. I had to show the audience the revolvers were there, so Mrs. Ivory had to knock them off the table.

MRS. IVORY: (*Placing revolvers on table.*) I have to have these nearby when a strike is on. One never knows what to expect.

RULER: (*Touching pocket.*) Even I have one in my pocket.

INKWELL: (*Touching pocket.*) And I in mine.

MISS IVORY: Oh, dear, how dreadful! Suppose one of them should go off? Oh, do be careful!

INKWELL: (*Insinuatingly.*) Have you changed your mind, Mrs. Ivory? Have you decided to accept my proposition?

MISS IVORY: What is your proposition, Mr. Inkwell?

INKWELL: I believe your mother wishes to discuss it with you. Mr. Ruler, will you have a smoke with me in the conservatory? (*They exit.*)

SUD: (*Shouting after him excitedly.*) Conservatory!!

MISS IVORY: What does he want, Mother?

MRS. IVORY: (*Sinking down into chair.*) Oh, my daughter. How can I tell you? How can I? I am ruined—ruined! (*Sud conducts them.*)

MISS IVORY: *You—ruined?* Oh!

MRS. IVORY: Oh!

MISS IVORY: Oh!

SUD: (*To Wouldby.*) When you're hard up for conversation, use "oh's"!

MRS. IVORY: We have lived beyond our means. Oh, my child—I have only brought you misery.

MISS IVORY: Poor mother—don't take it that way. I love you. We will live differently—anything you say.

WOULDBY: How sweet and sacrificial.

SUD: Ah, she's pure Ivory—a chip off the old block.

MRS. IVORY: That is not all. Inkwell represents the bricklayers. He will continue the strike unless I can buy him off.

MISS IVORY: And you can't raise the money?

MRS. IVORY: He doesn't want money. He wants to marry you!

MISS IVORY: Oh!

MRS. IVORY: Oh.

MISS IVORY: Oh!!

MRS. IVORY: He will stop at nothing to get me into prison—any place to crush me. He has power. I have cause to fear him.

MISS IVORY: Oh, how terrible! How terrible! What am I to say? Oh, mother, and I can save you? And I hesitate? Yes, yes—I will, mother.

MRS. IVORY: Oh, my daughter. My child, my child.

MISS IVORY: Yes, mother, I will. Cost me what it may, I will. (*She reads the last line flatly.*)

SUD: Miss Ivory, show some feeling. Think how you feel when you read those lines.

MISS IVORY: I know how I feel when I read those lines. (*With great emotion.*) Yes, mother, I will. Cost me what it may, I will. Mr. Inkwell!

SUD: Abandonment, Miss Ivory—abandonment. Mr. Inkwelllll! Mr. Inkwellllll!!

MISS IVORY: Mr. Inkwelll! Mr. Inkwellllll!

MRS. IVORY: (*Following Miss Ivory.*) Wait—think—consider!

MISS IVORY: (*As Inkwell enters.*) Mr. Inkwell, I have decided. Yes—yes!

INKWELL: Ah, my dear!

MRS. IVORY: Oh!

RULER: (*Entering.*) My dear—what is it?

SUD: Now *there's* your line "What is it?" I tucked it in there!

MISS IVORY: I can't keep my promise to you, Mr. Ruler. Please don't ask me for an explanation.

RULER: (*Excitedly.*) What is it, Mrs. Ivory?

MRS. IVORY: Oh, I am broken-hearted, broken-hearted. She is going to marry Inkwell.

RULER: No, no! Not while I live.

MRS. IVORY: It must be! Come with me—I'll tell you, alone.

RULER: Not while I live! (*Mrs. Ivory leads Ruler off Right.*)

SUD: Mr. Ruler, Mr. Ruler! You leave far too easily. Wait! I remember a precious line from one of my last year's plays. It is perfectly fresh, none of the novelty worn off, and incontestably original. "I am coming back."

RULER: (*Coming back, concentrating.*) I am coming back. Yes, sir—I am coming back.

SUD: There is no "yes, sir" in it!

RULER: No, sir.

SUD: Do you wish to retire for a few minutes and commit it to memory?

RULER: No, sir, I think I have it. I am coming back. Cue, please, Mrs. Ivory.

MRS. IVORY: Come with me—I'll tell you, alone.

(*She tries to lead Ruler Offstage but he is very unwilling and she must turn and drag him with both hands as he says his lines.*)

RULER: Not while I live! I am coming back! I am coming back! *I am coming back!!!*

(*They exit.*)

INKWELL: Now that they have left us alone, my darling—let me tell you how I have waited for this moment.

MISS IVORY: No—let me pass—not now. I have said yes. Let it go at that—I cannot talk, not now! (*Exits Right.*)

MRS. PENCIL: (*Springs on from stage Left.*) Coward! Villain! I have been listening behind that door. All your vows to me were false!

INKWELL: (*Trying to choke her.*) Don't yell so!

MRS. PENCIL: I will yell!

SUD: Of course she will!! Shriek good, Mrs. Pencil.

MRS. PENCIL: (*Screaming.*) Ahhhhh! Ahhhhhh! Ahhhhh!

INKWELL: (*Trying to cover her mouth.*) Stop! Stop!

SUD: Struggle! Struggle! The audience loves it!

WOULDBY: But what did Inkwell do?

SUD: (*Watching fight, talking over his shoulder.*) Can't tell you—haven't decided yet! Explanation in last act! No time now! Reaching climax of play! (*To Inkwell and Mrs. Pencil.*) Keep it up! Keep it up!

MRS. PENCIL: Oh, the treachery—the perjury! You are not fit to live! I'll have my revenge! Revenge! (*She grabs revolver from the table.*) Bing! Bang! I hate you! I hate you! I hate you!
(*Inkwell falls.*)

MISS IVORY: (*Running on.*) Oh, who's hurt?

MRS. PENCIL: (*Aiming revolver.*) Don't come near him or I'll shoot you!

RULER: (*Running on.*) What's the matter?

MISS IVORY: Don't move or she'll shoot me.

RULER: (*Pulling out revolver.*) Harm her and I'll shoot *you!*

INKWELL: (*Lifting himself onto elbow, drawing revolver and aiming at Ruler.*) You thought you could be my rival—the girl said she would be mine! If you shoot the woman, she'll kill the girl. I'm going to save the girl. Shoot her and I'll kill *you!*

MRS. IVORY: (*Running on and seizing revolver from table.*) Stop, stop! Shoot him and I'll shoot to kill! I'll shoot to kill! I'll shoot to kill!

WOULDBY: My God, who shoots?

SUD: My God, I don't know. It's a deadlock! I don't know *who* should.

WOULDBY: (*Pulling out revolver and aiming at Sud.*) Oh, shoot the author!

ALL: Shoot the author! Shoot the author!
(*They all aim at Sud and shoot. As he staggers and falls the lights black out.*)

END OF PLAY

The Big Black Box
A Comedy In One Act
By Cleve Haubold

CHARACTERS
    Arnold
    The Box

DESCRIPTION OF CHARACTERS
    Arnold is a gullible Everyman of no particular age. He is rather
slight, physically, vocally and mentally. Arnold is neatly dressed in a
suit, wears a hat and carries an umbrella. His appearance and manner
suggest the comedian Stan Laurel.
    The Big Black Box is a smug and superior baritone.

SCENE
    A street. The only setting necessary is the box itself. Street signs,
hydrants and such may be added to suggest a street.

THE BIG BLACK BOX

At Rise: The big black Box is sitting there, chuckling and singing to itself.

BOX: Merrily we roll along, roll along, roll along,
Merrily we roll along, o'er the deep blue sea ...
(*It laughs and belches heartily. Arnold enters and crosses the Stage.*)

BOX: Nice day.

ARNOLD: Huh?

BOX: I just said it's a nice day.

ARNOLD: Is it?

BOX: I just said it. You don't have to agree if you don't want to.

ARNOLD: It's a nice day.

BOX: Thank you. Oh, don't run off.

ARNOLD: What?

BOX: I mean ... what's your hurry?

ARNOLD: I do not speak to strange boxes. So long. See you.

BOX: Merrily we roll along, roll along, roll along,
Merrily we roll along—

ARNOLD: You're singing.

BOX: You noticed!

ARNOLD: I don't miss much. Why are you singing?

BOX: I thought you didn't talk to strange boxes.

ARNOLD: I make that a very firm rule.

BOX: That's very wise of you.

ARNOLD: Why are you singing?

BOX: Oh ... no reason.

ARNOLD: I have never found a box to sing with no reason.

BOX: How perceptive you are, sir.

ARNOLD: So, why are you singing?

BOX: You'll find out.

ARNOLD: I'm not that interested.

BOX: Naturally. Of course not. Naturally. Merrily we roll along, roll along, roll along—

ARNOLD: Just sing your lid off. I don't care.

BOX: Naturally not. Merrily we roll along ... Ha, ha, hah.

ARNOLD: Now what are you laughing about? What?

BOX: Same thing I was singing about. But you wouldn't care. Ha, ha, hah.

ARNOLD: No, I wouldn't. I wouldn't, would not, wouldn't. Couldn't care less. Absolutely with effort could not care less. Good-bye.

BOX: Before you go ...

ARNOLD: Yes?

BOX: Have you got a light?

ARNOLD: Yes. Here.

BOX: Say, that's a nice lighter you've got there. Very nice indeed.

ARNOLD: Don't you want a light?

BOX: Don't be silly. Boxes don't smoke. I just wondered ... say, what is your name?

ARNOLD: Arnold. What's yours?

BOX: Boxes don't have names, Arnold.

ARNOLD: Oh.

BOX: I mean ... you've noticed that. Haven't you noticed that?

ARNOLD: I have. Now that you mention it.

BOX: Arnold. That's a good upstanding name. A name with something to it. Ar-nold!

ARNOLD: That's my name.

BOX: How lucky you are, Arnold, to have a name like that. How lucky you are. I wish I had a name like that.

ARNOLD: It's handy. People can call you by it.

BOX: Can they now?

ARNOLD: Oh, yes. Everyone does.

BOX: Fancy that. Everyone calls you by it?

ARNOLD: Everyone that knows it.

BOX: You are downright fortunate. Put down your umbrella and come here, Arnold.

ARNOLD: No.

BOX: Why not, Arnold? Just around in front so I can have a look at Arnold.

ARNOLD: What's inside?

BOX: I beg pardon?

ARNOLD: I said, "What's inside?"

BOX: I don't know you that well, Arnold. But if you look honest, well ... I might let you in on it.

ARNOLD: I look honest.

BOX: How do I know that?

ARNOLD: I have an honest name.

BOX: How do I know it's your name?

ARNOLD: I told you.

BOX: But if you look dishonest, that may not be your name. May not be your name at all. No I just don't know you at all, Arnold.

ARNOLD: Can you see me now?

BOX: A bit to the left. Now a bit closer.

ARNOLD: Closer?

BOX: Not much. Just a step.

ARNOLD: No.

BOX: Just half a step. What can that hurt?

ARNOLD: How do I know what's inside?

BOX: How're you ever going to find out?

ARNOLD: You don't look like much from here.

BOX: Appearances, Arnold. Only appearances. Arnold, you *don't* look dishonest.

ARNOLD: I'm not.

BOX: And I believe you. Now come a bit closer.

ARNOLD: How do I know you're trustworthy?

BOX: I'm trustworthy.

ARNOLD: How do I know?

BOX: Arnold, have I ever lied to you?

ARNOLD: You don't look unkind.

BOX: Down deep inside, I'm pure velvet.

ARNOLD: What color?

BOX: Oh, ho. Wouldn't you just like to know? Wouldn't you just!

ARNOLD: No. And I've got a bus to catch.

BOX: I'm fuchsia.

ARNOLD: Fuchsia? Really, pure fuchsia?

BOX: Pure, pure, oh pure. What else would it be?

ARNOLD: Pure fuchsia? I would like to see that?

BOX: I thought you would.

ARNOLD: Show me.

BOX: Come a little closer.

ARNOLD: Poke a little out the keyhole.

BOX: Oh, come now, Arnold. You couldn't expect me to do that!

ARNOLD: Are you sure it's pure fuchsia?

BOX: Who would know better than I?

ARNOLD: Well … here I am. Let's see it. Come on … please. I've always had a more than passing interest in fuchsia.

BOX: You're sincere?

ARNOLD: And trustworthy.

BOX: Admirable. Put a dollar through the keyhole.

ARNOLD: A dollar?

BOX: Then I'll open up. Just roll up a dollar and put it through the keyhole. You are sincere, aren't you?

ARNOLD: I'm sincere, but—

BOX: What are you worried about? It isn't as if you wouldn't know where your money is. And, of course, you'll get it right back. I just want to be sure you're sincere.

ARNOLD: I'll get it back?

BOX: What could happen to it, Arnold? I'm not a big spender.

ARNOLD: Well ... all right. Here.

BOX: ... And another.

ARNOLD: Another?

BOX: You either trust me or you don't.

ARNOLD: I'm not sure.

BOX: Arnold, do you place a price on your sincerity? Shame on you, Arnold. Go catch your bus.

ARNOLD: You've got my dollar.

BOX: I want your faith and confidence.

ARNOLD: Come on. Open up. You promised.

BOX: Did I? Put in another dollar, and I will.

ARNOLD: Are you sure?

BOX: Do I look deceitful?

ARNOLD: Well ... here.

BOX: You are a jewel, Arnold. A real jewel.

ARNOLD: So, open.

BOX: Oh, I will. I will. Come up real close, so you can get a good look.

ARNOLD: How much closer?

BOX: And ... you'll want your two dollars back, won't you? Real close. Right up to the front. Very very close. And lean over so you can see good.

ARNOLD: I knew you couldn't be trusted. There's my bus. I am going. Keep the two dollars. Dirty old box!

(*Arnold starts to go. The Box opens a crack.*)

BOX: If you're going to be that way about it ... here! You take your money. But don't you dare look at the fuchsia velvet!

ARNOLD: Keep the two dollars, I'll miss my bus.

BOX: For two dollars you could take a taxi.

(*Arnold comes toward the Box.*)

ARNOLD: You're not mad?

BOX: Mad? Why should I be mad? I'm hurt, I confess. A little hurt, but not mad. Take your two dollars and go. Put down your umbrella. Don't rumple the velvet. Just take your two dollars.

ARNOLD: You bet I will. I can't get my hand out. Your lid is closed on my hand.

BOX: How about that!

ARNOLD: I can't get my hand out. And I can't reach my two dollars.

BOX: Really now! That's odd.

ARNOLD: If you're as trustworthy and sincere as I am, you'll let go my hand.

BOX: Yes, I bet I would.

ARNOLD: I want my two dollars.

BOX: But, Arnold, it's down at the bottom. Just reach in a little farther, and you'll have it.

ARNOLD: No.

BOX: Oh, come on, Arnold! What are people going to say? "Look at Arnold. He's afraid to reach in and get his two dollars." Is that what you want them to say about you?

ARNOLD: Let go my hand. You can keep the two dollars.

BOX: No, no. I wouldn't hear of it that way. You've got to have your money back. Oh, while you're in, you might as well feel the velvet. That should show that I'm sincere.

ARNOLD: I want my hand.

BOX: Well, of course you do, Arnold. And you shall have it back just as soon as we can figure out how to do it. Why not reach your other hand down and lift the lid?

ARNOLD: No.

BOX: Arnold, sometimes your lack of trust distresses me. Let me think. I have it! Stick your hat in and wriggle it around. That should convince you. Go on. You're not going anywhere.

ARNOLD: It's my good hat.

BOX: I'll take that as a sign of your trust and confidence.

ARNOLD: There ... Something's got my hat!

BOX: Must be caught on the latch. Do you have a fountain pen?

ARNOLD: Yes.

BOX: Just the very thing. Just the right size and shape to poke the hat off the latch.

ARNOLD: You think so?

BOX: I am absolutely certain of it. Give it a try.

ARNOLD: Now something's got my fountain pen.

BOX: Arnold, you are a clumsy one! Is that a watch and chain you have on?

ARNOLD: It was my father's.

BOX: Then I'm sure it's a good one. Just slide the watch through the crack and let it swing around on the chain. It can't miss picking up everything.

ARNOLD: Something would get it.

BOX: What's this talk about "something"? There's nobody here but you and me. What would get it?

ARNOLD: I don't know.

BOX: See? A groundless fear.

ARNOLD: You would get it.

BOX: What would I want with a watch? I've got all the time in the world. But you're going to miss the next bus. Desperate situations demand desperate measures. I'm trying to help you. Try the watch.

ARNOLD: You're sure that something won't get it?

BOX: Positive.

ARNOLD: I've already lost my hat and fountain pen.

BOX: You haven't lost them, Arnold. You know precisely where they are.

ARNOLD: But you'll guarantee the watch and chain?

BOX: I guarantee them.

ARNOLD: There's no doubt in your mind?

BOX: Not a bit.

ARNOLD: Well … I'll try.

BOX: That's the boy.

ARNOLD: Something got my watch.

BOX: Son-of-a-gun!

ARNOLD: I am beginning to suspect something.

BOX: How 'bout that!

ARNOLD: I am beginning to suspect that you are deceitful. Deceitful and conniving. That is what I am beginning to suspect.

BOX: Oh, come off it, Arnold. Say, boy, if you lean down real close you can see the fuchsia velvet. Want to give that a try?

ARNOLD: No. I want you to let go.

BOX: Just a peek? You ought to get something for your money.

ARNOLD: You are greedy. Oh, how I hate a greedy box!

BOX: Don't kick.

ARNOLD: Let go. You want something else. What else you want?

BOX: Guess.

ARNOLD: Here is my neatly folded pocket handkerchief. You want my neatly folded pocket handkerchief? Is that what you want?

BOX: It's a start.

ARNOLD: Here's my whole entire wallet.

BOX: Keep on.

ARNOLD: How about a shoe?

BOX: Let's have it. And the other one, too.

ARNOLD: Now will you let go?

BOX: No.

ARNOLD: Take my coat and I'll tell you a secret about this coat. Sewn into the lining is a tinker-toy that I have carried for years as a talisman against evil. That's a real good thing to have on you.

BOX: That's the best yet.

ARNOLD: And you can have it.

BOX: Don't just flap your sleeves. Put it in.

ARNOLD: I can't get my coat off.

BOX: You can't?

ARNOLD: Can't get it off over my hand. You've got my hand. Let up for a minute and you've got the coat.

BOX: Now, Arnold, really! What do you think I am?

ARNOLD: I trusted you. Now you trust me.

BOX: Arnold, Arnold, Arnold. Shame.

ARNOLD: You don't think I'd run off, do you?

BOX: Well ...

ARNOLD: You don't sincerely think I'd run off and leave my two dollars, my good hat, my fountain pen, my father's watch and chain, my neatly folded pocket handkerchief, my whole entire wallet, my shoes, and my coat with my entire tinker-toy talisman against evil, do you?

BOX: I'll risk it. Put in all but the sleeve. Now, quick! The sleeve!

(*Arnold snatches his hand out of the box.*)

ARNOLD: Ha! You are a silly greedy box. Let them that be a lesson to you. Trick, trick, trick ... and I win! Now you don't have me, or my umbrella! Dirty, silly, greedy box!

BOX: Don't talk smart.

ARNOLD: He who laughs last, laughs best! Ho. Ho. Hee. Hee.

BOX: Oh, boy.

ARNOLD: I grant you that I shall have difficulty walking to the bus-stop without my shoes, and I shall miss my coat a great deal. But that really wasn't my good hat you got. And the fountain pen writes only with great difficulty. And it will leak, leak, leak on your fuchsia velvet. So there!

BOX: When's the next bus?

ARNOLD: It should be here in ... I shall miss my watch.

BOX: Want to peek at it?

ARNOLD: Definitely not. Don't you worry about me. I can get along without that watch. Of course, walking around without one's talisman is risky … But I'm out of reach now, and I intend to stay that way. Do you hear that? Do you hear that? I'm on my way. I am going. I am going to the bus-stop, and you'll never see me again. Good-bye!

BOX: Arnold …

(*The lid of the Box opens fully.*)

ARNOLD: It is fuchsia velvet!

BOX: All the way.

ARNOLD: No tricks now.

BOX: Arnold, you are too smart for me.

ARNOLD: You bet.

BOX: And look at all the goodies inside …

ARNOLD: I still don't trust you. Here. You want my umbrella? Take it.

BOX: What would I do with an umbrella?

ARNOLD: Then I can have it back?

BOX: Naturally.

ARNOLD: I've got it! You didn't get the umbrella! Here it is again. Can I have it back?

BOX: Take it. What do I care?

ARNOLD: I've got it now. I've got it back now. That really makes you mad, doesn't it! Just hopping mad!

BOX: Not particularly.

ARNOLD: Just to show you what I think of you … here it is. For keeps! (*He props the lid open with the umbrella.*) Boy, you're in a mess now. I hope it rains on your fuchsia velvet. What's the matter? Can't you talk with your lid open? Hey? Hello? What's the matter? Look, look, look. Here's my hand. Can't do anything about it, can you? Look. Here's the whole arm. Missed it that time, didn't you! Look here. I'm going to get my two dollars. Got 'em! See? One. Two. And my good hat. How about that! And my fountain pen. And my father's watch and chain. And my neatly folded pocket handkerchief. And my whole entire wallet. And my shoes. Both of 'em! Oh, boy! And my coat with the tinker-toy sewn into the lining as a talisman against …

(*The umbrella falls into the box. The lid slams shut, enclosing Arnold in the box. He begins to shout and struggle, but the sounds die out shortly.*)

BOX: Merrily we roll along, roll along, roll along,
Merrily we roll along, o'er the deep blue sea …
(*It belches with soul-satisfying resonance. And just sits there. Curtain.*)

END OF PLAY

The Matsuyama Mirror

A Play in One Act
by Velina Hasu Houston

Adapted from an ancient Japanese fairy tale

For Kiyoshi

VELINA HASU HOUSTON The award-wining author of over a dozen plays, Houston's plays have been produced at the Old Globe Theatre, Manhattan Theatre Club, Negro Ensemble Company, Syracuse Stage, Smithsonian Institution, the Kennedy Center, A Contemporary Theatre, Whole Theatre, The Asia Society, Japan Society, Odyssey Theatre Ensemble, Theatre of Yugen, East West Players, in Japan and other U.S. theaters. Her critically acclaimed signature play *Tea,* which was selected as on of the top ten plays written by women worldwide in 1986 by the Susan Smith Blackburn Prize of London, has a long production history in regional theaters and radio. Other plays include *Kokoro, American Dreams, Asa Ga Kimashita, Necessities, The Matsuyama Mirror, As Sometimes in a Dead Man's Face, O-manju, The Revenant, Princess Ka'iulani: Half of Forever,* and more. Her many recent commissions include projects with the Asia Society, Honolulu Theatre for Youth, University of Hawaii's Kennedy Theatre and Cornerstone Theater Company. For film and television, Houston has written works-for-hire for Sidney Poiter's Verdon-Cedric Productions, Columbia Pictures, several indie producers, PBS' "Wonder Works," Lancit Media/PBS-KCET's "The Puzzle Place," and the American Film Institute. Lauded by Poitier with the Remy-Martin New Vision Award in film, Houston's work has been recognized by the Kennedy Center's New Visions/New Voices program. Selected as a woman of merit by the National Japanese American Historical Society and included in *Transpacific's* Top 100 Asian Americans, Houston is a two-time Rockefeller fellow, a Sidney. F. Brody fellow, a James Zumberge fellow, California Arts Council fellow, Los Angelos Endowment for the Arts fellow as well as the recipient of many other awards including national first prizes in the Lorraine Hansberry Playwriting Award and the David Library Playwriting Award for American Freedom. She is author/editor of *The Politics of Life: Four Plays by Asian American Women* (Temple University Press) and the upcoming *A Storm Is Blowing From Paradise: Plays from the Asian Diaspora* (Temple). She heads the playwriting program at USC's School of Theatre and serves periodically as a visiting associate professor of screenwriting at UCLA's School of Theater, Film and Television. A Phi Beta Kappa, she holds an M.F.A. from UCLA and is a Ph.D candidate in Critical Studies in Cinema at USC's School of Cinema-Television. Her work is the subject of several Japanese and U.S. television and radio documentaries. She is the mother of Shotokan green belt Kiyoshi Houston, age nine. Representatives: Mary Harden of Bret Adams, Ltd. (theater), Merrily Kane of The Artists Agency (film, television); Michael C. Donaldson, Esq., Berton & Donaldson.

ORIGINAL PRODUCTION

The Matsuyama Mirror was originally produced in spring, 1995, as a co-production of Honolulu Theatre for Youth and Kuma Kahua Theatre, Honolulu, Hawaii. It was directed by Pamela Sterling with the following cast:

Aiko	Denise Tajiri
Okaasan	Nyla Fujii
Tooriko	Reay Kaplan
Otoosan	James McCarthy
Yukiko Obasan	Nan Asuncion
Kokeshi Dolls	Danielle Gentzler, Kanoa Jones, Melissa La Rosa, and Laura Soong.

CHARACTERS

Aiko, a Japanese girl, 12
Okaasan, her mother, also The Grand Mistress of Matsuyama
Otoosan, her father
Tooriko, her sister, 16
Yukiko Obasan, her aunt
The Kokeshi Dolls
Kuro-Ko

TIME AND PLACE

Matsuyama, Japan. The late 1600s.

With thanks to Brian Nelson, June Angela, Pamela Sterling, Andrew Berger at Lincoln Center Institute, the Kennedy Center's New Vision/New Voices Program, Honolulu Theatre for Youth and Kuma Kahua.

The Matsuyama Mirror

PROLOGUE

Koto music. A Kuro-Ko, a traditional Japanese theater stage assistant, dances about the stage setting props and assumes the waki position at the side of the stage.

SCENE ONE

Aiko and Tooriko's bedroom. Feminine and girlish. Aiko, her long black hair in pigtails, sits on a colorful futon, folding origami paper. Okaasan enters with a tray of tea, musubi and fruit. Aiko bows her head towards her mother. Their love for one another is apparent. Okaasan peels the fruit and they share the refreshment.

AIKO: Will it be today, Okaasan? You said it would be yesterday.

OKAASAN: The horses tire easily in the snow. Otoosan did not expect snow.

AIKO: The horses may tire, but not Father.

OKAASAN: Maybe not, but he never does well with the unexpected.

AIKO: I hope he brings me a pretty kokeshi doll.

OKAASAN: The kokeshi are for decoration. I make you soft dolls for play.

AIKO: But I like the kokeshi; they are so colorful and beautiful.

OKAASAN: Everything you do seems to fly in the face of tradition. Anyway, perhaps the time for dolls is over.

AIKO: *(Surprised.)* Why?

OKAASAN: Father thinks you are too old for dolls.

AIKO: Oneesan is too old for dolls, but not I. I want to keep my dolls forever. They are my playmates.

OKAASAN: Your sister is your playmate.

AIKO: Oneesan is too old. She has forgotten how to play.

OKAASAN: I hope you never forget how to play.

AIKO: Forget? I shall never stop playing.

OKAASAN: One day, all women must stop. But, in your heart, you must remember.

AIKO: Okaasan, why must all things be the same for all females? What if one of us is different?

OKAASAN: And just who is this different one? Could it be Aiko the great child empress, protector of our rice fields and persimmon orchard?

AIKO: Yes! Aiko the adventuress! My dolls are my court! We will frolic, drink tea, and never live in anyone's shadow!

OKAASAN: And what about a husband, honorable adventuress?

AIKO: No-no-never-never-no! That would interfere with tea and sweets!

OKAASAN: (*Laughs.*) Oh, Aiko-chan, then the world would be turned around and upside down!

AIKO: Then maybe I belong in a topsy turvy world!

OKAASAN: (*A sigh as she playfully touches Aiko's braids.*) Dear Aiko-chan, it is hard to imagine you all grown up, married, with children of your own.

AIKO: I only grew one inch in the last three years, so I shall be a girl forever.

OKAASAN: When you become a lady, Otoosan will take away your dolls and bring a handsome suitor who will take you for his bride.

AIKO: When does it start, this questionable condition of being a lady?

OKAASAN: It starts in the body.

AIKO: Yes?

OKAASAN: (*Hesitant.*) Here. (*Points to her abdomen.*)

AIKO: What starts?

OKAASAN: Well … your body will … prepare itself for children. You may feel frightened or sad. You will … bleed and—

AIKO: Bleed? Is someone going to cut me?

OKAASAN: It is a … cleansing.

AIKO: But I am not dirty!

OKAASAN: A *purification*. And then you are a woman and you must prepare yourself for all that means.

AIKO: And when does this stop, this war in my body?

OKAASAN: When the sun goes down on the last battle.

AIKO: I shall pray not to grow even another fraction of an inch!

OKAASAN: Even Issunboshi, the little one-inch man, wanted to grow.

AIKO: I will trade places with him. Put me in a chestnut shell with a pearl for my pillow and a petal for my blanket.

OKAASAN: Oh, Aiko-chan, you live in fairy tales.

AIKO: Not today …

OKAASAN: Dear child. Do not think of it as war; think of it as power.

AIKO: What victory is there in bleeding to death?

OKAASAN: This is bleeding *to life*. It gives you the power to have children; it is a sign of your fertility.

AIKO: Does Otoosan think I am bleeding? Is that why he does not wish for me to have any more dolls?

OKAASAN: He knows the time is coming when his last little girl changes forever. (*A beat.*) Shall I tell you a secret?

AIKO: Oh yes!

OKAASAN: These dolls of yours were once my dolls.

AIKO: But why did your father never take them away?

OKAASAN: They sat on the table looking beautiful. At night, I slipped them into my kimono and played with them in bed. When he caught me, I said I wanted to save them for the daughters I would someday have. After you and Tooriko came, however, I lost interest in dolls.

AIKO: How is that possible?

OKAASAN: (*A smile.*) It is a mystery.

AIKO: I never will.

OKAASAN: Time will tell. Your choices may change.

AIKO: And if they do not?

OKAASAN: Then I guess we will have to change the world, find a place for an adventuress to fit!

AIKO: But what would Father say?

OKAASAN: He would curse the day that *my* father taught me to read and write!

AIKO: And then you taught me!

OKAASAN: I will always teach you, for I grew you inside of me like a flower. Come to me with every fear you have, no matter how small, ne, Aiko-chan?

AIKO: Can you make the war stop?

OKAASAN: (*A gentle laugh.*) You expect incredible magic, little one. Think of it as the discovery of something very precious inside of you.

AIKO: You mean like a buried treasure?

OKAASAN: If you like.

AIKO: War, blood, buried treasure. It sounds like something for boys!

OKAASAN: It is exclusively for girls. Your older sister is bleeding.

AIKO: (*A shriek.*) Oneesan? Honto? (*Looks around.*) Where?

OKAASAN: … privately …

AIKO: But she never cries out in pain.

OKAASAN: Maybe it is something that she welcomes.

AIKO: If she were nicer, she would not bleed.

OKAASAN: Your sister bleeds once a month.

AIKO: Once a month? But that is so often!

OKAASAN: It keeps a woman honest.

AIKO: Then men must bleed, too, so there will always be truth.

OKAASAN: Men do bleed.

AIKO: Once a month?

OKAASAN: Perhaps not often enough. (*A beat.*) But always in love and war.

AIKO: So I want neither love nor war. (*A beat.*) Okaasan, will Tooriko make babies now?

OKAASAN: Give her time, my child. She has only been married one season.

AIKO: Does she know how to make a baby?

OKAASAN: What do you mean?

AIKO: Does she know the recipe?

OKAASAN: (*Looks away to hide her amusement.*) Oh, I am certain she has learned it by now.

(*Enter Tooriko with a basket of sewing. Her seriousness and formality are stark contrasts to Aiko's exuberance.*)

TOORIKO: Good evening, Okaasan. (*To Aiko.*) Aiko, I heard you all the way down the corridor talking as loud as a boy. Let me tell you something, little sister, you have no choice. Life is love and war and that is all. Here. (*Hands her a sewing basket.*) Make yourself useful. Sew. (*Pinches Aiko.*) And never you mind about whether or not I shall have children! My husband is so busy cutting lumber in the mountains that I may as well not worry about it either.

(*Aiko ignores the offering of sewing and Tooriko gives her a reproachful glance.*)

TOORIKO: Sew and improve your domestic skills!

AIKO: Ane, I do not wish to sew this evening! Otoosan will be home any moment and he is bringing me a new doll.

TOORIKO: Your embroidery work is less than perfect. When the childhood fat wears off your fingers, perhaps they will be more dexterous.

AIKO: My fingers are not fat! Yours are too skinny, like chopsticks. Chopstick-Fingers-Oneesan!

TOORIKO: (*Thrusts basket at Aiko again.*) Here is your sewing for today. Take it. Mother. Make her take it. (*Sighs deeply.*) I thought I was rid of this little ladybug when I married, but I am stuck here more often than I like waiting for my husband—and waiting on this spoiled child.

AIKO: Dear, sweet sister.

(*Okaasan takes it and hands it to Aiko who accepts it graciously, which irritates Tooriko.*)

OKAASAN: Aiko-chan, let us embroider flowers.

TOORIKO: Embroider lilies. Be precise. Make it a present for Aunt Yukiko.

AIKO: I do not wish to sew for our grumpy old aunt.

OKAASAN: Aiko-chan! Do not speak that way of Obasan!

AIKO: She always unbraids my pigtails!

TOORIKO: Because they make you look like a little girl.

AIKO: I *am* a little girl!

TOORIKO: You must start behaving your age.

AIKO: I will not act old like you.

TOORIKO: I am not old!

AIKO: You are cursed with bleeding, so you are old!

TOORIKO: (*Surprised.*) How do you know about that? Did you watch me changing my clothing, you nuisance?

AIKO: I just know, that is all.

TOORIKO: Be still and sew.

OKAASAN: *I* told Aiko-chan about the menses.

TOORIKO: She is too young to understand.

AIKO: Is that so? But you just said that I am a lady!

TOORIKO: I take it back. You are a … (*Tries to think of a word.*) … you are a little azuki bean.

AIKO: (*Laughs.*) If I am a little bean, then you are a big bean!

OKAASAN: Aiko-chan, enough.

AIKO: Marriage has made sister a weed. Perhaps that is what I shall embroider. Any suggestions, dear sister?

TOORIKO: Yes. Embroider your lips together.

OKAASAN: Girls, please.

TOORIKO: This … this condition of women is not for your amusement — or mine. Or anyone else's.

AIKO: I am sorry.

TOORIKO: Very well.

AIKO: Tell me, Oneesan, does it hurt when you bleed?

TOORIKO: Ladies do not discuss such things.

AIKO: Do tell!

TOORIKO: (*Wanting to terrify her.*) If you must know, it hurts like ten horses trampling on your stomach, like the high winds of a typhoon twisting, grinding through your gut.

AIKO: Oh my goodness!

TOORIKO: It is the beginning of life; you will see. It starts and secrets unfold.

AIKO: Secrets? What secrets?

TOORIKO: Woman secrets!

AIKO: Like what!

OKAASAN: Do not tease little Aiko so, Tooriko-san.

TOORIKO: Like playing games with your husband.

AIKO: Grown-up men play games with women?

TOORIKO: Oh yes.

OKAASAN: Tooriko!

AIKO: How odd. What kinds of games?

OKAASAN: That is enough.

TOORIKO: But you, with all your spice, will never know the power of it. You will sit here and merely bleed and whine and your suitors will run away in the snow looking for more domestically suitable mates.

OKAASAN: Tooriko, are you talking about the acquisition of a pet or wife.

AIKO: Can Father stop the pain of trampling horses?

TOORIKO: (*Laughs.*) Otoosan? He can do nothing in this matter but look the other way when the condition begins.

OKAASAN: In fact, your father will suddenly become speechless.

AIKO: Father? But why? He is a strong man.

OKAASAN: Because his little girl becomes a woman. Is it not true, Tooriko, that your father never knows what to say to you anymore?

TOORIKO: He found such a nice husband for me.

OKAASAN: But does he speak?

TOORIKO: Only when necessary.

OKAASAN: But, then again, when my condition began, my father talked incessantly about anything *but* my condition. I was always still his flower. Tooriko-chan. You also must be a flower.

TOORIKO: Be rebellious while you can, Aiko-chan. One day your petals will be heavy.

AIKO: Then I shall shed them and bloom anew, looking up at the sun.

OKAASAN: The worlds of love and marriage demand much of us, Aiko-chan.

AIKO: Are you happy, Okaasan?

OKAASAN: Without question.

AIKO: So you will not tell me to bend to the ground blind to the sun, will you?

OKAASAN: Never, but neither should you make time stand still.

AIKO: Even though your father is dead, are you not still a flower, Okaasan?

OKAASAN: Sometimes in the morning when I wake up from dreams, I feel like my father's daughter. Then I look around me and realize that I am now my husband's wife and my children's mother.

AIKO: Now I *know* I do not wish to grow up. What a somber business!

OKAASAN: Not at all. Without this "business," I would not have you or Tooriko.

AIKO: But there is no time to play! Tooriko-san, I will have to keep you from being a willow tree, weeping for eternity.

TOORIKO: I will not weep! I will stand erect like a pine. I will see over the mountains.

AIKO: Pining pine tree! Pining, pining pine tree!

TOORIKO: Oh the joys of having a little monkey sister!

AIKO: Thank you, big monkey sister!

OKAASAN: (*Breaking them up.*) Girls, girls, please. Maybe you are not deserving of presents from your father's travels.

AIKO: Gentle mother. How you tease us! If there were not dolls in Father's satchel, I would look at you and say you, after all, are the best gift.

TOORIKO: Enough, enough.

OKAASAN: Oh, let her be a child, Tooriko-san. Enjoy her.

TOORIKO: Of course. Tell me when you start to bleed, sister, and I might tell you about the power.

AIKO: Power?

OKAASAN: Tooriko!

TOORIKO: Oh yes. You will gain a power greater than the greatest magic.

AIKO: You lie! You just want to trick me, put me at ease so the trampling of horses will be that much more shocking.

OKAASAN: My little warriors. I hope your father brings you shields and swords so that your battles can be fought to a proper and deserving finish.

TOORIKO: What will Father bring us? Did he give you any idea, Okaasan?

AIKO: I hope he brings me a tall kokeshi doll with painted red lips and beautiful blackened teeth!

TOORIKO: I would like a lacquer comb with polished abalone shell.

(*Okaasan has wandered to a window and stares outward into the night.*)

AIKO: What would you like, Okaasan?

OKAASAN: (*Distracted.*) What?

AIKO: What would you like Father to bring for you?

OKAASAN: (*Concerned.*) Just him. (*Looks out of the window again.*) There is so much snow.

AIKO: He will find his way safely. I will pray for him and he shall come.

OKAASAN: He should be within the limits of town by midnight. Perhaps I should go looking for him.

TOORIKO: It is too cold for women to go outside.

AIKO: Sometimes rules have to be broken.

OKAASAN: As a child, I went into the snow when my mother said to stay by the fire. And I stayed by the fire when my mother bade me to get some fresh air.

TOORIKO: I stayed by the fire when you told me.

OKAASAN: Yes.

AIKO: I did not!

OKAASAN: That is so. (*Becomes distracted by the snow again.*) Has the snow stopped yet?

TOORIKO: (*Looks out of window.*) No. It is falling, falling as if it will fall forever.

(*Lights crossfade to Scene Two … *)

SCENE TWO

A low light fades in on the bedroom. Aiko sleeps restlessly. Tooriko sits up anxiously. There is a large candle. Aiko stirs and Tooriko tries to hide her anxiety.

TOORIKO: Go back to sleep.

AIKO: Oneesan?

TOORIKO: What now?

AIKO: … Tell me about the power.

TOORIKO: No. There is no power, only the suffering.

AIKO: I knew you were fibbing today!

TOORIKO: All right, you want to know about the power? Fine, I will tell you since you will probably never get a chance to use it on someone.

(*Aiko leans forward with anticipation.*)

TOORIKO: If you even hint at the fact that you are having your monthly bleeding, your husband will bring you sweets and have the maid cook your favorite foods.

AIKO: Truly?

TOORIKO: If you want time alone to dream, you hint again and he suddenly must leave the room. If you say that the bleeding is very heavy, he will not even want to sup with you or share the bed with you.

AIKO: Truly? Then I could play all night.

TOORIKO: Yes. I have never known such peace.

(*Tooriko looks out of the window, nervously picks up her sewing, and starts to work on a piece of embroidery.*)

AIKO: Why must you sew at twilight?

TOORIKO: Because there is too much snow.

AIKO: Let it snow now that Father is home. Did he bring gifts? Did you see him before you fell asleep?

(*Tooriko glances at her and then looks away quickly.*)

TOORIKO: Here. Sew to keep your mind off our troubles.

AIKO: What troubles?

TOORIKO: Nothing. There are no troubles.

AIKO: Father still has not returned home?

TOORIKO: You told Okaasan that rules sometimes have to be broken! She took the horse and rode into town to check on Father's traveling party.

AIKO: What? How long ago?

TOORIKO: Several hours.

AIKO: I shall go find her!

(*Aiko tries to leave and Tooriko stops her.*)

TOORIKO: A lady waits.

AIKO: I ride just as well as Father. Let me go!

TOORIKO: Not a man in Ehime prefecture will have you as a wife if you keep acting like this.

AIKO: Good riddance. I will wait for a man who will allow me to think.

TOORIKO: Then you will be waiting for a long, long time.

AIKO: Go to sleep, sister.

TOORIKO: No, Aiko, you cannot go.

(*They struggle as sounds of horses are heard from offstage. Aiko tries to run out, but is stopped by Otoosan who enters covered with snow. He conceals grimness with a smile for his children. He carries a satchel filled to capacity.*)

OTOOSAN: Good daughters. Hello.

TOORIKO: (*Bows low.*) Welcome home, Otoosan.

AIKO: Welcome, Father.

OTOOSAN: Where are you going in such a hurry, Aiko?

TOORIKO: She was going out in the snow to find you!

AIKO: Where is mother?

OTOOSAN: It is so cold.

AIKO: Otoosan, where is she? With the horses?

TOORIKO: Quiet, Aiko!

(*He sits fighting emotion as Tooriko helps him off with his coat. He and Tooriko sit around the candle. Incredulous, Aiko puts on her father's coat and prepares to leave.*)

OTOOSAN: Take off my coat and sit, Aiko.

AIKO: Tell me where she is, when she will be here.

OTOOSAN: Sit.

(*Otoosan takes the coat off of her and forces her to sit by the candle.*)

OTOOSAN: Children, your mother has ... left us.

AIKO: What? Where has she gone?

OTOOSAN: ... there has been ... an accident.

(*The breath is knocked out of Aiko. She sits motionlessly. Tooriko is quiet with shock for a moment and then she weeps uncontrollably.*)

AIKO: (*With an eerie calmness.*) You must tell me what has happened to my mother.

OTOOSAN: ... we will not see her again.

AIKO: What have you done to her?

TOORIKO: Aiko! Please. What has happened, Otoosan?

OTOOSAN: It is not for women to hear such things.

AIKO: I will hear everything if you say I shall never see my mother again. Tell me.

OTOOSAN: The snow. An accident with the horses. Her head struck a rock. When they found her, she was already—

TOORIKO: Say no more.

AIKO: Speak!

OTOOSAN: Too late, too late.

AIKO: Is that all you have to say?

TOORIKO: *Silence,* Aiko!

OTOOSAN: It is not for men to weep and curse fate.

AIKO: What then? To sit there like a piece of stone?

TOORIKO: Aiko!

OTOOSAN: Yes.

AIKO: How can you? What are you?

OTOOSAN: The bearer of our pain so that you can go on. (*Looks downward.*)

AIKO: (*Dazed.*) Was there a lot of blood?

OTOOSAN: (*Surprised by the question.*) Yes.

AIKO: (*Quietly.*) Women have lots of blood.

OTOOSAN: Yes.

AIKO: Were there horses trampling and high winds blowing?

OTOOSAN: (*Surprised again.*) Yes, Aiko.

TOORIKO: After she struck her head, perhaps there was no pain, just quiet ...

OTOOSAN: ... very quiet ...

> (*The three sit quietly as Tooriko tries to suppress tears. Otoosan tries to suppress them as well. Aiko is surprised by this show of emotion; Tooriko is disturbed by it.*)

TOORIKO: Oh, this family. Pull yourself together, Father.

OTOOSAN: Your mother drifts in the wind tonight, seeking her next existence. We must keep the sky clear; we must not weep.

AIKO: Bring her back. (*To the ether.*) Come back, Okaasan. Come back!

OTOOSAN: Enough, gentle Aiko-chan. ... we must go on as usual ...

AIKO: How?

TOORIKO: Shall we sit around like fools and weep?

AIKO: You never loved her like I did.

TOORIKO: I am older and I have loved her longer. (*A beat.*) It is not our way to weep.

AIKO: Is it not equally as foolish to pretend that nothing has happened?

> (*Otoosan calms himself and reaches for the satchel. He takes out two packages.*)

OTOOSAN: Here. Your gifts. Come. Let us be as curious and happy as we always are when I return from my journeys.

AIKO: I want no gift, only the return of my mother.

OTOOSAN: What do you think I brought you, Aiko-chan?

AIKO: Who will I ask for help when I am learning new embroidery?

TOORIKO: I will help you.

AIKO: You do not help. You order.

OTOOSAN: We will all help each other.

AIKO: Tooriko-san will only help herself and her husband.

TOORIKO: What is wrong with that? If you ever grow up, you will bring a husband to live here with you and Otoosan. You will know secrets that will make you selfish sometimes, too.

OTOOSAN: Yes, Aiko. I will find you a strong, patient man.

TOORIKO: In this case, perhaps a saint is required.

OTOOSAN: And Tooriko will always be near. Her husband plans to build their new house just on the other side of the village.

AIKO: It might as well be on the other side of the universe.

TOORIKO: Otoosan, she is topsy-turvy. I walk a straight and level path.

OTOOSAN: When I am gone, you two sisters will be all that is left of our family. Can you not be civil to one another? Come, Aiko-chan. Come sit by me.

AIKO: Who will cook tonight, Otoosan?

TOORIKO: I will cook.

AIKO: You? The taste will kill us all!

OTOOSAN: I have sent word to your aunt and she will come tomorrow to help us.

AIKO: Aunt Yukiko!

OTOOSAN: This is a time to find strength in family. Yukiko Obasan is good and kind.

AIKO: And as rough as a tree trunk.

TOORIKO: But as sturdy and lasting.

OTOOSAN: Are you not curious about your present, Aiko? Perhaps it will give you a little light in this darkness?

AIKO: (*She is.*) Not really. Not now.

OTOOSAN: Please, Aiko.

AIKO: Never mind.

OTOOSAN: Then if I have brought a new doll, must I find another little girl to give it to?

AIKO: Otoosan? What is death like? Could the gods have made a mistake? Can they be persuaded to give her back?

OTOOSAN: Open your present, dear child.

AIKO: She said she would be here.

TOORIKO: Stop it, Aiko-chan.

AIKO: How can I behold these gifts at such a time?

TOORIKO: Because we need to. If I stare at the tatami all night and cry, then I will not make it to morning.

OTOOSAN: Here, Tooriko-san.

(*He hands her a gift. She opens it. It is a scarf.*)

TOORIKO: Thank you, Otoosan. I shall save it.

OTOOSAN: Do not save it. Wear it. Make yourself look beautiful. Today. Now. And for you, Aiko-chan.

(*He takes out a silver, sparkling box. Immediately, the Kuro-ko tinkles wind chimes and Aiko looks around, startled as if she hears something. Aiko holds the box and slowly opens it, scattering dust. She takes out a large silver and gold lacquered mirror with angel hair hanging in shreds from it. It leaves her in a state of awe. Tooriko is afraid of it.*)

AIKO: What is it, Father?

OTOOSAN: It is called a "mirror."

AIKO: " ... mirror ... "

TOORIKO: I have never heard of such a thing. Does it belong in the house?

OTOOSAN: It is magic. Look in the glass.

(*Aiko does and is startled.*)

AIKO: There is a girl in the glass!

OTOOSAN: (*Laughs.*) And who does she look like?

(*Aiko dares look again. She gasps. Tooriko is curious, but is controlled by her fear.*)

AIKO: It is Mother, when she was a young girl!

(*Tooriko screams in fright and Otoosan silences her with a gentle look.*)

OTOOSAN: It is you, Aiko-chan.

AIKO: (*Looks again.*) She looks like Okaasan.

OTOOSAN: (*Sadly.*) Yes. A young lady.

AIKO: Her eyes are so black. Okaasan has become a child in this mirror. How can that be so? What have you done? Have you put mother in the mirror? Can I get her out?

TOORIKO: No! No! We will all be cursed.

OTOOSAN: Whenever you miss your mother, you must look in this mirror and you will find her looking back at you.

AIKO: … magic … mother …

(*A warm, loving woman's laughter is heard only by Aiko who jumps in surprise and fear.*)

TOORIKO: (*Staring at her.*) You are possessed.

AIKO: That is not me in the mirror! It is a spirit.

OTOOSAN: It is you and you are the best memory of your mother. No one else in Matsuyama has such a mirror. You will be the talk of the town.

TOORIKO: And not just because of this mirror.

(*Aiko brandishes the mirror towards her sister who jumps in fright.*)

TOORIKO: Keep that thing away from me!

(*Otoosan laughs, but Tooriko begins to cry again.*)

AIKO: Come, look in the mirror, sister! It truly is Mother!

TOORIKO: No!

AIKO: See something above and beyond your straight and level path. Just this once.

TOORIKO: No! Please!

AIKO: Very well then. I shall keep the secrets of the mirror.

TOORIKO: Have them!

AIKO: The mirror will lead me to Okaasan.

TOORIKO: I will have nothing to do with such black magic.

OTOOSAN: It is healing magic.

TOORIKO: I will have tea instead.

OTOOSAN: I brought your mother a porcelain doll.

(*He offers it to Tooriko, but she motions for him to offer it to Aiko. He hands it to Aiko. Her pleasure gives Tooriko pleasure.*)

OTOOSAN: For you, Aiko-chan.

(*Aiko takes it.*)

AIKO: Thank you, Otoosan.

TOORIKO: Thank you.

OTOOSAN: I wish that I could have brought back more … I wish …

(*He picks up his things and leaves. Tooriko tries to blow out the candle and Aiko stops her.*)

AIKO: Leave it be.

TOORIKO: But it is almost burned away. There is no use for it.

AIKO: Let it burn and, when it is gone, I want its scent to linger in my hair and kimono.

TOORIKO: (*Urging her.*) You must stop dreaming, little sister. Learn to be practical. As you can see, our parents are not immortal.

AIKO: But they are. Mother lives.

TOORIKO: Aiko-chan, childhood is a butterfly feeding on the dew of youth. And the dew disappears quickly. You *must* grow up.

AIKO: No. I must wait for Mother.

TOORIKO: Oh, how can you behave so when she has died this night?

AIKO: She is only hiding.

TOORIKO: And you have been struck by the moon. Do you not see that the gods have punished her for riding out into the snow like a soldier?

AIKO: She *is* a soldier, a soldier of the soul, like me! I shall ride, too, and I will return in one piece with Mother at my side.

TOORIKO: Dear Aiko.

AIKO: She is somewhere and I shall find her.

TOORIKO: (*Sighs.*) Maybe in another life.

AIKO: No! In this one!

(*Tooriko leaves. Aiko stares into the mirror as the Kuro-ko tinkles the wind chimes. Lights crossfade to Scene Three ... *)

SCENE THREE

Lights fade in on the bedroom. Yukiko Obasan cleans the room with an obsessive efficiency. When she begins to dust, she sees Aiko's collection of kokeshi dolls and sighs in disgust. Aiko tiptoes into the room and Yukiko whirls around with a sixth sense.

YUKIKO OBASAN: Why are you sneaking in here?

AIKO: I did not wish to disturb you, Obasan.

YUKIKO OBASAN: Come here. Now.

AIKO: No, thank you.

YUKIKO OBASAN: How my sister let you run around in those pigtails at your age is beyond me.

(*Yukiko Obasan tries to unbraid Aiko's pigtails as Aiko fidgets.*)

YUKIKO OBASAN: Stop wiggling like a snake.

(*Aiko leaps from her aunt's arms.*)

AIKO: Are you so familiar with snakes?

YUKIKO OBASAN: It is time to be rid of your dolls as well.

AIKO: You cannot take away my toys!

YUKIKO OBASAN: Now that I am running this household for your father, it is time you acted your age.

AIKO: You sleep in my mother's bed!

YUKIKO OBASAN: (*Embarrassed.*) Where else am I to sleep? In the stables with the horses?

AIKO: I am certain that could be arranged.

YUKIKO OBASAN: A mother dies, her sister comes to help. Good because we share the same blood.

AIKO: Blood?

YUKIKO OBASAN: As custom has it, I must help.

AIKO: By marrying your sister's husband?

YUKIKO OBASAN: Look at you, so unlady-like. Come here and sit down so that I may loosen your hair from this most inappropriate style.

AIKO: This is my hair, wild and free. I shall never do what you say. You came here with food to make my father stop being sad. Now you sleep in my mother's bed. She will come back and you will be chased out in the middle of the night!

YUKIKO OBASAN: And will you stay here all alone when your father must travel to market? How will a child fend for herself?

AIKO: I am an adventuress.

YUKIKO OBASAN: Is that so? What if goblins and ogres come?

AIKO: I will think them to death! (*A beat.*) Besides, I will not be alone. I will be here with my mother and my mirror.

YUKIKO OBASAN: Your what? "Mirror"?

AIKO: Never you mind. It is a special gift from my father that is none of *your* business.

YUKIKO OBASAN: Aiko-chan ... I am your ... new mother.

AIKO: No, thank you.

YUKIKO OBASAN: I will cook for you and help you with your sewing. And, like my sister, I can read and write. I will help you with those lessons as well.

AIKO: (*Fidgeting.*) No, thank you.

YUKIKO OBASAN: Be still.

AIKO: No!

(*Aiko tries to leave the room and her aunt stops her.*)

YUKIKO OBASAN: I said sit! I will teach you civility if it is the last thing I do.

(*Aiko fights, tears falling, and Yukiko Obasan forces her to sit while she undoes Aiko's ponytail. Aiko cries.*)

AIKO: You smell like onions.

YUKIKO OBASAN: Thank you, dear child.

AIKO: Or like soggy squid that has sat in the sun for days.

YUKIKO OBASAN: Bless you, sweet princess.

AIKO: And I also detect a strong odor of fermented soy beans.

YUKIKO OBASAN: Healthy foods for the body.

AIKO: Why do you cook so much food for my father.

YUKIKO OBASAN: For all of you, to help you forget.

AIKO: I forget nothing.

YUKIKO OBASAN: May I prepare something special for you? Is there something that you would like?

AIKO: Yes. Mongolian bamboo shoots.

YUKIKO OBASAN: I would have to go to Mongolia for that.

AIKO: (*That's her point; with malevolent delight.*) Yes.

(*Yukiko Obasan finishes unbraiding her ponytail.*)

YUKIKO OBASAN: There. Now see how beautiful you look. The young men of Matsuyama will stand in line to have the hand of a lady like you.

(*Yukiko Obasan opens Aiko's mouth and examines her teeth.*)

YUKIKO OBASAN: And you have perfect teeth as well.

AIKO: That is what father says when he buys a new horse.

(*Yukiko Obasan tries to manage the strain as she puts the kokeshi dolls into a furoshiki and ties it up.*)

YUKIKO OBASAN: Now I want you to show me that you are willing to cooperate. Take these dolls to the attic.

(*Aiko opens the furoshiki and studies her dolls with love.*)

YUKIKO OBASAN: They are just things. Little girl things.

(*Aiko slips her mirror out of her kimono sleeve, stares into it as wind chimes tinkle. Startled, Yukiko Obasan looks around.*)

YUKIKO OBASAN: Did you just hear something?

(*Aiko puts the mirror away.*)

AIKO: Okaasan says I may keep my dolls.

YUKIKO OBASAN: What is that you are hiding in your sleeve?

AIKO: Just a thing.

YUKIKO OBASAN: Let me see it.

AIKO: I think not.

YUKIKO OBASAN: Your mother is gone now. (*Gently.*) She can speak no more.

AIKO: You cannot silence a true mother.

(*At her wit's end, Yukiko Obasan returns the dolls to the furoshiki.*)

YUKIKO OBASAN: If you do not put these away, I will use them in the cooking fire tonight.

AIKO: I hate you! You are a thief!

(*Aiko takes the package and leaves angrily. Yukiko feels tormented and inept. Lights crossfade from downstage right. An open road. Aiko wears a scarf around her head and a jacket. She carries two furoshiki. She sits looking from right to left. Tooriko appears also dressed warmly. She is surprised to find her sister.*)

TOORIKO: What are you doing on the outer roadway?

AIKO: I am going to town.

TOORIKO: By yourself? Come back to the house this instant.

AIKO: I am a young lady, am I not? I may travel the world alone.

TOORIKO: Silly Aiko-chan. You will get sick in this chill.

AIKO: Mother leaves and now you leave. I am left to live with our aunt and father. Yukiko Obasan is pretending to be our mother.

TOORIKO: She is only trying to help. You are too young to be without a mother.

AIKO: I am terribly old.

TOORIKO: Do you require a cane?

AIKO: Do not tell Father that I am on the roadway.

TOORIKO: What have you there in your furoshiki?

AIKO: My dolls.

TOORIKO: You run away with your dolls and no food to eat?

AIKO: I am not running away!

TOORIKO: Even so, the road to town is a long one. Dolls will not keep you warm.

AIKO: Yukiko Obasan was going to burn them in the fire.

TOORIKO: You are exaggerating. Come back to the house with me. I will protect your dolls.

AIKO: Why?

TOORIKO: Because I must. Come, little bean of mine.

AIKO: Maybe she will even burn me in the fire if she thinks I am no longer of any good use.

TOORIKO: (*Softening.*) Little sister. I understand. Perhaps we should hide the dolls in a special place.

AIKO: She would find them. She has explored every nook and cranny of our home in just a few days. She wants to do the same with us: clean us out, dust us off, and try to make us hers.

TOORIKO: Come. Together we will find a place for your dolls.

AIKO: You would break a rule for me?

TOORIKO: Today I will.

AIKO: Why today?

TOORIKO: Because my husband will come for me in the morning and I will return to my home.

AIKO: I see.

TOORIKO: Come, little sister. Let us carry out our family task.

AIKO: She will never let me keep them.

TOORIKO: We shall tell her that we must save them for your daughters.

AIKO: *My* daughters!

TOORIKO: One day you will have daughters.

AIKO: No, I will have sons, so they need never worry about being good ladies.

TOORIKO: But sons must worry about being men.

AIKO: Human beings are not designed very well.

TOORIKO: But we are. When you become a lady, you will wonder why it took so long.

AIKO: Who wants horses and typhoons?

TOORIKO: You will see. Come.

AIKO: You go on back to the house. I will come shortly. I want to see if it will snow.

TOORIKO: It has not snowed since our mother passed.

AIKO: Since she *went away.* (*A beat.*) The snow will come again.

TOORIKO: Very well. I cannot stand the cold.

AIKO: It is warm. Bury your feet in the snow and it feels like a blanket.

TOORIKO: (*A smile.*) Dreamer child.

(*Tooriko exits, patting Aiko on the head. Aiko cries. She unwraps her dolls and kisses them. She takes out her mirror and stares at it.*)

AIKO: Mother? Where are you? Can you hear me? Your flower grows and there is fear.

(*She smiles at the reflection as wind chimes tinkle and the woman's laughter is heard. Aiko looks around as if trying to find the voice. She puts everything away and runs about in a hurry.*)

AIKO: Mother? Okaasan? Is that you?

(*Aiko stumbles and falls. The Kuro-ko goes to her side and holds her. Lights black out.*)

SCENE FOUR

Immediate lights up. There is a scrim that represents Aiko's lacquered mirror. Images of Aiko appear on the scrim. Aiko is on the ground and being held by the Kuro-ko. She looks up and stares at the scrim "mirror." She tries to run towards it but cannot, as if there is an invisible force in her way. Wind chimes tinkle and the laughter is heard again.

AIKO: Okaasan? I know it is you! I knew you would not abandon your promises. Okaasan!

(*Aiko tries to approach the scrim again, but this time is yanked back by the invisible force. She begins to dance as if being pulled by this force. Kuro-ko and Tooriko, wearing a mask, join Aiko in her dance. Classic shakuhachi music fades in. She falls beside the mirror and is surrounded by red chiffon scarves (these can be pulled from the handle of the mirror). The stream of scarves is endless and overwhelms her. The invisible force pulls her in frenzy as she begins to dance again. The scarves are a part of a red chiffon kimono which she puts on during the dance. The scarves trail on the floor and are long enough to billow. The dance comes to a pitch and Aiko collapses on the floor. The music ceases. Aiko whimpers and moans. She is so exhausted that she cannot lift her head. Then the wind chimes begin to tinkle again. Exit Tooriko. The Kuro-ko pushes Aiko towards the scrim and resumes the waki position. The scrim is backlit and the images of Aiko disappear. Behind the scrim appear three figures. They run in giggling and shuffling, like children at play. They are representations of kokeshi dolls. They wear masks and headgear that reflect the wooden texture and painted markings of the dolls. Their simple kimono are in the same style as their masks. They have butterfly wings on their backs. They are innocent and curious. Their tone is staccato, rhythmic. They speak in high register, with upward inflection. They stare at Aiko's figure through the scrim.)*

KOKESHI: What is it?

FIRST KOKESHI: It is a doll.

SECOND AND THIRD KOKESHI: What a beautiful doll. Let us invite it to play with us.

(Through a split in the scrim, the kokeshi hesitantly approach Aiko. They touch and sniff her. One pulls a long chain of lilies out of her kimono sleeve and tickles Aiko's nose with it. One pokes at her.)

SECOND KOKESHI: Hello, little doll!

AIKO: (*Weakly.*) Have you seen my mother?

(The kokeshi jump and gasp.)

THIRD KOKESHI: Why it is not a doll at all!

FIRST KOKESHI: It certainly is not one of us. (*Touches Aiko's forehead.*)

THIRD KOKESHI: (*Uses a special power to make this discovery.*) It … is a little girl.

SECOND KOKESHI: How lovely! We need a little girl to play with!

FIRST KOKESHI: I do not remember girls.

THIRD KOKESHI: Remember soft and sweet, pink hearts, ticklish feet.

SECOND KOKESHI: Remember from the fairy tales, the little girls with far to go.

FIRST KOKESHI: Oh yes! I remember!

(The second and third kokeshi want to take Aiko into their world.)

FIRST KOKESHI: But wait. I think she is hurt.

KOKESHI: We will have to take her home with us. We will have to make her our own.

THIRD KOKESHI: What is your name, little girl?

(The kokeshi surround Aiko with the chain of lilies. They hold her like a baby, and fan and caress her.)

THIRD KOKESHI: (*As if in a trance with her special powers.*) She is Aiko. She wants to be here with us.

SECOND KOKESHI: But she asked for "mother." Who is "mother?"

THIRD KOKESHI: We will ask the Grand Mistress of Matsuyama.

SECOND KOKESHI: Oh no. We must play first.

FIRST KOKESHI: She cannot play. She is hurt.

(*They all sniff her again.*)

THIRD KOKESHI: But we can make her well.

FIRST KOKESHI: But she is not a kokeshi doll. Maybe she is not meant to enter the mirror.

SECOND KOKESHI: You always want to make the rules for our play. I say we should take her home.

THIRD KOKESHI: I have never had a girl toy before.

(*Aiko sneezes and the kokeshi run for the scrim. They stand just inside and stare at her. She struggles to raise her head and sees them.*)

AIKO: Please help me.

KOKESHI: Are you going to blow up?

AIKO: I simply sneezed.

KOKESHI: Sneezed! (*They giggle.*) You are a good girl toy.

AIKO: I need to find my mother.

KOKESHI: Mother? What is "mother?"

AIKO: (*Startled.*) Wait a minute. I know you.

KOKESHI: Oh no, never-never-no.

AIKO: Yes! You are my dolls!

KOKESHI: (*Laughter.*) We do not belong to you! We belong to spring!

AIKO: (*Confused.*) Do you not remember? I saved you from my wicked aunt Yukiko just yesterday.

FIRST KOKESHI: What is "yesterday?"

AIKO: The day before today.

SECOND KOKESHI: What is "today?"

AIKO: It is time.

THIRD KOKESHI: What is time?

AIKO: Minutes and hours that tell you when to eat, sleep, when to stop playing—

FIRST KOKESHI: Stop playing?!

KOKESHI: What?!

FIRST KOKESHI: How absurd!

SECOND KOKESHI: Utterly boring!

THIRD KOKESHI: There is no time here.

KOKESHI: Let us play! You are one of us now!

(*The kokeshi giggle like human wind chimes. Aiko begins crawling to the scrim. Finally, she reaches it. The kokeshi look at one another and finally decide to drag her in. The minute she enters their world, Aiko is renewed. The kokeshi are delighted. They remove her red kimono and cast it outside the scrim. The Japanese children's song, "Haru Ga Kita," fades in (an instrumental version). They begin playing with great delight, using the lily chain as a toy. They dance and skip. Outside the scrim, Otoosan enters and sees the red kimono. It startles him. He picks up the mirror and looks around in panic.*)

OTOOSAN: Aiko-chan? Aiko!

(*He touches the red kimono and raises his fingers to his nose to smell them. He licks his fingers to taste. His panic heightens.*)

OTOOSAN: Aiko!

(*He runs out. Aiko suddenly looks in his direction. She goes to the edge of the scrim and the kokeshi pull her back.*)

KOKESHI: Where are you going? Do not leave us.

AIKO: It is time for dinner. I must put you away.

KOKESHI: We need never be put away again. We play forever.

AIKO: But surely you must stop to eat and sleep?

KOKESHI: Oh no. We are never hungry.

AIKO: But you must have reading and writing lessons with your tutor.

KOKESHI: Oh no. Never-never-no.

AIKO: What about your sewing? Are your stitches perfect?

KOKESHI: Perfect life. No curse. Never nervous.

AIKO: But sometimes you have to follow rules, do you not?

KOKESHI: We know everything that a doll must know to be happy. Do you know everything that a little girl must know to be happy?

AIKO: (*Sadly.*) No.

KOKESHI: Then you need a teacher.

FIRST KOKESHI: Perhaps the Grand Mistress?

SECOND KOKESHI: Oh, but we are having so much fun at play. Can it not wait?

AIKO: I want to find my mother. I have something very important to tell her.

SECOND KOKESHI: What could be more important than playing?

AIKO: Something is happening to me that only my mother can explain.

THIRD KOKESHI: Remember, she is from a different world. Things happen to little girls.

FIRST & SECOND KOKESHI: Oh dear!

FIRST KOKESHI: Are you dying? In fairy tales, human beings die.

SECOND KOKESHI Are you lost in the woods?

THIRD KOKESHI: Did you tell a lie?

KOKESHI: Lying is bad.

AIKO: I have run away from home.

KOKESHI: (*Gasp.*) Why?

AIKO: Because my aunt has stolen my father.

KOKESHI: Ummm. Stealing is very bad.

AIKO: She loves him and—

KOKESHI: Oh! Love is very, very good!

AIKO: But the worst of it is I have been cursed.

(*Kokeshi gasp in unison.*)

FIRST KOKESHI: Is it catching?

AIKO: No. You are dolls. You are safe from this condition.

SECOND KOKESHI: Condition?

AIKO: Of course, some say it is power.

FIRST KOKESHI: Like magic?!

AIKO: I am not certain, but something tells me that I do not want it in my life.

SECOND KOKESHI: Why not?

AIKO: Because it will make me bleed.

THIRD KOKESHI: Ah. I know what it is.

FIRST & SECOND KOKESHI: What is it? What is it?

THIRD KOKESHI: It is the most interesting things about little girls.

SECOND KOKESHI: Uh-oh! What have you done?

AIKO: I have done nothing wrong!

THIRD KOKESHI: It is not something that you *do*. It just happens.

FIRST KOKESHI: What is it? Does she have an illness?

THIRD KOKESHI: Little girls ... grow up.

AIKO: I am afraid that is what is happening to me.

KOKESHI: We are sorry. So sorry.

(*Aiko points outside of the scrim to the red kimono.*)

AIKO: I have been bleeding inside.

SECOND KOKESHI: What is bleeding?

AIKO: When your insides start to come out.

THIRD KOKESHI: And your body changes.

FIRST & SECOND KOKESHI: Oh my.

FIRST KOKESHI: It sounds like death.

AIKO: It is meant to be a sign of life.

THIRD KOKESHI: That is the power!

SECOND KOKESHI: But you are not bleeding now.

AIKO: (*Startled.*) That is true! The bleeding has stopped.

FIRST KOKESHI: So you must stay. You are safe here.

SECOND KOKESHI: No horses!

THIRD KOKESHI: No typhoons!

FIRST KOKESHI: Nothing will stop you from playing.

THIRD KOKESHI: We will take you to see the Grand Mistress.

AIKO: I will agree to your desires if you promise to help me find my mother. Is she here? Has she been here? I heard her laughter.

(*The kokeshi giggle and pull Aiko in different directions as "Haru Ga Kita" fades up again. Upstage, from behind the scrim, a figure in a long, exaggerated kimono decorated with lilies appears. It is the spirit of Okaasan. A shroud of lilies is over her head. She walks slowly, formally. The kokeshi and Aiko do not notice her. Finally, she encircles the play group and they stop. The kokeshi fall to their knees in bows. Aiko is in awe and then recognition sets in.*)

AIKO: Okaasan?

KOKESHI: Honorable Respectable Sincere Loving Sensitive Creative Kind Beautiful Grand Mistress of Matsuyama!

AIKO: No, this is my mother.

KOKESHI: Shhhh!

AIKO: And you are my dolls.

KOKESHI: Quiet!

AIKO: I fell in the snow and I looked in the mirror and ... (*To Grand Mistress.*) Are you my mother?

OKAASAN: I am all mothers.

AIKO: Will you be mine today?

OKAASAN: Are you a flower?

AIKO: Yes.

OKAASAN: Then I know I can help you because I am also a flower.

KOKESHI: Tulips! Daisies! Chrysanthemums! Lilies!

AIKO: Mother, I—

OKAASAN: Yes.

AIKO: I am bleeding.

OKAASAN: Ah ...

KOKESHI: Poor little girl.

OKAASAN: Oh no. We must offer congratulations.

AIKO: Congratulations?

OKAASAN: Yes. You are becoming powerful.

KOKESHI: Ohhhh!

OKAASAN: Can you not feel it?

AIKO: (*Confused.*) No.

OKAASAN: Aiko-chan, it is dinner time and you are here playing. Forever playing. Is that what you desire?

AIKO: Father has married Yukiko Obasan and she sleeps in your bed and snoops all over the house.

OKAASAN: Father needs a wife and you need a mother.

(*Aiko wants to reach out to the Grand Mistress, but cannot touch her, as if there is an invisible wall between them. They reach their finger tips towards one another.*)

AIKO: I intended to go home for dinner, but my dolls want to play and play.

KOKESHI: Jump and roll and skip and leap!

OKAASAN: Then, at some point, you must make a decision.

AIKO: I came looking for you, Okaasan, because of the curse.

OKAASAN: Is it a curse?

AIKO: Yes! Horses and typhoons!

OKAASAN: But it endows us as well, with richness, fruitfulness, boys and girls.

KOKESHI: Make us one little, two little, three little girls!

AIKO: I cannot forget horses and typhoons.

OKAASAN: Are you bleeding now?

KOKESHI: Nooooo.

OKAASAN: In a world like this, there is no blood or death. Just light.

KOKESHI: Sunbeams, moonbeams, starry bright!

AIKO: You said it was unlikely that I could avoid bleeding.

OKAASAN: Little dolls cannot bleed. Stay here and roll in the clouds all your life long, Aiko. You need never look into a human face again.

AIKO: But I am not a doll!

OKAASAN: Are you certain?

KOKESHI: She smells like a girl!

AIKO: These are the dolls. My silly kokeshi.

OKAASAN: Then, dear one, shall you return home for dinner and sit at the table as an adult with your father and aunt ... your new mother?

AIKO: New mother? I only have *one* mother.

OKAASAN: Never turn away from love, my child. (*A beat.*) Shall you go home now?

KOKESHI: Oh no! Do not go!

OKAASAN: Or do you choose to be a doll and play forever?

KOKESHI: Oh yes! Come, Aiko the adventuress!

AIKO: But I do not like your sister.

OKAASAN: She is not the only thing you must accept. There is Otoosan. He is different now, trying to find his way in a world that excludes me. Tooriko-san also struggles with the unevenness of a new life.

AIKO: You mean she is not happy?

OKAASAN: She is *learning*. That means some days are pink and others grey. (*A beat.*) Then there are all the rules.

KOKESHI: Despicable!

OKAASAN: But, without order, life is like an unkept house.

AIKO: But Yukiko Obasan wants to take away my dolls.

OKAASAN: She knows that your body is speaking new languages. She wants to help you learn them.

AIKO: She wants me to wear my hair "like a lady!"
(*The kokeshi begin to giggle and tug at Aiko.*)

AIKO: Tell them to stop playing, Okaasan.

OKAASAN: But that is what they are created to do. What of you, my young lady? What is it that you are meant to be and do?

KOKESHI: Come play with us, little girl.

AIKO: Stop it, you silly dolls.

KOKESHI: Silly is good! Silly, willy, shrilly, frilly!

OKAASAN: Say the word and I shall close the doors to that other world.
(*Aiko looks toward the opening of the scrim. Outside the scrim, the Kuro-*)

ko scatters crimson petals around the stage and dances with the red chiffon scarved kimono as if beckoning her.)

AIKO: But if I go back, will you come with me, Okaasan?

OKAASAN: I cannot.

AIKO: Will you always be in the mirror?

OKAASAN: I will grow young with you.

AIKO: But every time I look into it, you will be there?

OKAASAN: All your life you will look in the mirror and be reminded of your mother.

AIKO: (*Sadly.*) But it will not really be you, will it?

OKAASAN: That is a difficult question. (*A beat.*) It will be you. And it will be your mother in you. It will be what she was and what you both can be in another time.

AIKO: Dolls are so lucky.

OKAASAN: Are they? They shall never breathe, never make a memory that allows them to live forever.

AIKO: A flower.

OKAASAN: Yes. A flower.

(*Aiko steps towards the scrim and the kokeshi frown sadly.)*

KOKESHI: Oh no.

FIRST KOKESHI: Do not leave us.

SECOND KOKESHI: Do not go away to that place!

THIRD KOKESHI: They will change you, rearrange you!

AIKO: It is time for dinner.

KOKESHI: (*A friendly warning.*) But the bleeding will return!

AIKO: Yes. Like a river.

THIRD KOKESHI: Horses!

FIRST & SECOND KOKESHI: Typhoon!

AIKO: Silly kokeshi. Sweet things. Today I must go to my aunt who knows a language that I must learn.

FIRST KOKESHI: But it will hurt so much to grow up.

AIKO: Perhaps.

SECOND KOKESHI: Do not let her burn us up in the fire!

AIKO: I shall protect you with my dying breath.

THIRD KOKESHI: Do not forget about us!

AIKO: Do not forget about me when I am no longer a little girl. (*Bowing to her mother.*) Sayoonara, Okaasan.

OKAASAN: Endure, persevere, ne, Aiko-san.

KOKESHI: Carry on!

AIKO: You really should rest, dear dolls.

KOKESHI: Oh no! We cannot sleep! Too much fun to reap! We will think of you and try not to be blue!

AIKO: Goodbye!

KOKESHI: Let us play, let us play, let us play!

(*Aiko steps through the scrim and immediately, back lights fade on the scrim. Shakuhachi music fades in. Aiko grows weak and loses her balance. The Kuro-ko aids her. She falls and crawls toward the red kimono and crimson petals. Music ceases. With determination Aiko pulls herself to standing, politely refusing the help of the Kuro-ko who bows to her honorably. As Aiko exits, the Kuro-ko assumes the waki position. Lights crossfade to Scene Five ...)*

SCENE FIVE

Lights up downstage center. Otoosan and Yukiko Obasan kneel at a low table eating a meal. Yukiko Obasan eats ravenously. She is visibly with child. She is exhausted and her attitude is considerably more humble. Aiko enters.

AIKO: Otoosan?

(*Otoosan drops his food in shock. Yukiko Obasan faints.*)

OTOOSAN: Anta. Aiko!

AIKO: Hello, Father.

OTOOSAN: Aiko ...

AIKO: Is she all right?

OTOOSAN: (*Not looking in Yukiko's direction.*) Yes, yes. (*Then looks at her and immediately holds her in his arms and fans her.*) No, I mean— (*Stops and looks at Aiko with incredulity.*) I ... I thought you were dead.

AIKO: I am very alive. Did you look for me all night?

OTOOSAN: All night? Aiko-chan, you have been gone for two winters!

AIKO: (*Surprised.*) Two winters? (*She stares at Obasan's stomach.*) I see.

OTOOSAN: That night, I saw blood in the snow. I had given you up for dead, but we could not find your body. Your aunt looked for you tirelessly. Where have you been?

(*Yukiko moans.*)

OTOOSAN: Anta. Wake up, wake up.

(*Aiko stares at her aunt.*)

AIKO: She felt it important to find me? But she is with child now, a new child, a little girl for you, for this house.

OTOOSAN: She cried for you, Aiko-chan.

AIKO: For me?

OTOOSAN: Yes. She felt that she had failed you.

(*Aiko stares at her father's hand which clasps her aunt's hand tightly. Aiko unwraps her furoshiki to reveal the red petals and materials. Otoosan is shocked.*)

AIKO: I have been bleeding.

OTOOSAN: Has someone hurt you?

AIKO: Whoever makes girls into women. But I have come home to learn.
(*Otoosan does not comprehend at first. Yukiko Obasan sputters awake and stares wide-eyed at Aiko. She kowtows to Aiko.*)

YUKIKO OBASAN: You are a ghost returned from the dead! What can I offer you, most honorable spirit?
(*Aiko touches her aunt's hand with affection, but Yukiko jumps.*)

AIKO: I am sorry, dear aunt.

YUKIKO OBASAN: Honorable Spirit, may I feed you fruit and tea?

AIKO: It is Aiko, just Aiko. Touch me, aunt.

YUKIKO OBASAN: No, no.

OTOOSAN: It is all right. She has returned. She was lost.

YUKIKO OBASAN: Aiko? Is it truly you?

AIKO: Yes, Obasan.

YUKIKO OBASAN: I was afraid you died out in the cold, all because of what I wanted to do with your dolls. What has happened to you? Have you been hurt?

AIKO: I have become a woman, Obasan.

YUKIKO OBASAN: My dear child, dear young woman.
(*Aiko sits beside her aunt.*)

AIKO: Will it always hurt?

YUKIKO OBASAN: Maybe, maybe not. But you must think of it as a clean pain.

AIKO: Clean?

YUKIKO OBASAN: It is never dirty. It is never unkind. It is a river of life.
(*Pats her stomach.*) It flowed in me and now a child will be born. It will be a girl. I can hear her sing at night when the moon glows.

AIKO: Here. Then you must have these. (*Gives her the furoshiki.*) You may take my dolls now.

YUKIKO OBASAN: No. Please keep them.

AIKO: Are you sure?

YUKIKO OBASAN: They are a part of you, and of your mother.

AIKO: If you truly do not mind, I would like to keep them. Maybe you will allow your new child to be my little sister and I will hand these down to her.

YUKIKO OBASAN: How kind of you.

AIKO: As for you father, you must no longer be silent.

OTOOSAN: Aiko!

AIKO: You must tell us your secrets.

OTOOSAN: It is not the custom.

AIKO: But I need to hear you, Otoosan.

YUKIKO OBASAN: He will be with me when the child is born.

AIKO: Is that true?

OTOOSAN: (*Embarrassed.*) I have asked for permission.

AIKO: My little sister ... she will need to have beautiful dolls to play with.

And when she becomes a young woman, I will hold her in my arms
and sing songs to her.

YUKIKO OBASAN: We will polish the dolls and keep them in view, for
memories must live, be touched, tasted. Is that not so, Otoosan?

OTOOSAN: I—well— (*He's left speechless as he stares at the red petals.*)

AIKO: Speak, Otoosan.

OTOOSAN: I ... I see your mother in your face.

(*Aiko takes out the mirror and stares into it. She hears the wind chimes
and laughter. It makes her smile. It is almost as if Otoosan and Obasan
hear it as well. They look around the room and then try to deny with their
expression that anything is out of sorts.*)

AIKO: This mirror can reflect the whole world. And, after all, that is what
we see when we look at other people, at flowers, at the mountains.
Reflections of the light.

(*While speaking, Aiko moves downstage center. Scrim lights up; we see the
Grand Mistress and kokeshi at play. Tooriko enters carrying a baby in
bunting. Aiko looks around in wonder.*)

AIKO: Ah ... think of all the new little girls ... !

(*As lights fade out, the kokeshi sing "Haru Ga Kita":*)

KOKESHI: Haru Ga Kita, Haru Ga Kita
Doko Ni Kita, Yama Ni Kita
Sato Ni Kita, No Ni Mo Kita
Hana Ga Saku, Hana Ga Saku
Doko Ni Saku, Yama Ni Saku
Sato Ni Saku, No Ni Mo Saku.

END OF PLAY

La Dispute

by Marivaux

Translated by Timberlake Wertenbaker

ORIGINAL PRODUCTION

La Dispute was performed on BBC Radio 3 in 1987. It was directed by David Johnston, with music by Gordon Langford. The cast was as follows:

Hermiane...Maggie McCarthy
The Prince ....Ronald Herdman
Mesrou...Alton Kumalo
Carise...Valerie Murray
Eglé..Maureen O'Brien
Azor ....Gary Cady
Adine ....Jane Leonard
Mesrin..James Macpherson

CHARACTERS

HERMIANE

THE PRINCE

MESROU

CARISE

EGLÉ

AZOR

ADINE

MESRIN

MESLIS

DINA

COURTIERS

SETTING

The action takes place in the country.

LA DISPUTE

SCENE ONE
The Prince, Hermiane, Carise, Mesrou.

HERMIANE: Where are you taking me, your Highness? This country looks wild and isolated and I see no signs of the entertainment you promised me.

THE PRINCE: (*Laughing.*) Everything will be ready.

HERMIANE: I don't understand. What is that strange building over there? What is the meaning of those extraordinarily high walls around it? Where are we going?

THE PRINCE: We are going to watch an unusual spectacle, Hermiane. Remember the question we discussed last night: you maintained against the whole of my court that it was not your sex but ours which had first been unfaithful in love.

HERMIANE: Yes, your Highness, and I still maintain it. The first unfaithfulness could only have been committed by someone who was bold enough to blush at nothing. Now, ever since the beginning of this corrupt world, women have been – and still are – naturally timid and reserved. How then could they be the first to fall into a pattern of vicious behavior that requires such daring, such libertine feelings and such insolence? No, your Highness, it doesn't make sense.

THE PRINCE: Indeed, Hermiane, it doesn't make sense to me either and you needn't argue with me on that subject. I share your feelings against everyone else, as you know.

HERMIANE: Yes, but I'm afraid that is only out of gallantry, your Highness.

THE PRINCE: Gallantry? I haven't noticed it, Hermiane. It is true that I love you and perhaps that fact helped to convince me you were right, but this has happened in such a subtle way I've not been aware of it. I have no respect for the hearts of men: deal with them as you will. I'm certain man's heart is indeed more unfaithful than a woman's. Mine alone must be excepted from this rule and that is only because it is you who are the object of my love. If it were anyone else it would no longer be so.

HERMIANE: Your words betray irony, your Highness.

THE PRINCE: Then I shall be punished soon enough. You will soon have the means to silence me if you find I don't agree with you.

HERMIANE: What do you mean?

THE PRINCE: We must look to Nature for our answers. Surely only Nature can decide once and for all who was the first to be unfaithful and I'm certain her decision will prove us right.

HERMIANE: Please explain yourself.

THE PRINCE: There is only one way to know whether the two of us are right in believing that it was a man who was responsible for the first unfaithfulness: and that is to be there at the beginning of the world.

HERMIANE: Quite. But we weren't.

THE PRINCE: No, but we will be. We will soon watch men and women exactly as they were at the beginning. Ah, here we are. Carise, Mesrou, is everything ready?

CARISE/MESROU: Yes, your Highness.

THE PRINCE: Hermiane, the world and its first loves are about to appear before us exactly as they were, or at least as they must have been. The events may not be precisely the same, but the characters will be. You are about to see hearts in the same state they were at the beginning of the world and souls as fresh as in those first days, or even more fresh. Carise, Mesrou, you may go now. Warn us when you are about to begin.

CARISE/MESROU: Yes, your Highness.

THE PRINCE: Come this way, Hermiane.

SCENE TWO
Hermiane, The Prince.

HERMIANE: You've excited my curiosity, your Highness.

THE PRINCE: I'll explain. Some eighteen or nineteen years ago the dispute we had yesterday took place at my father's court. It lasted a long time and became heated. My father disagreed with our view, Hermiane, but he was a man of science and decided to make a foolproof experiment. He found four newborn babies and had them taken to this forest. Two of them were of your sex and two of mine. He gave each one of them extensive grounds and built separate houses for them in which they still live. In that way, none ever met any of the others and they know only Mesrou and his sister Carise who brought them up and still care for them. My father chose black people as their guardians so that they'd be even more surprised when they met each other. Today, for the first time, these young people will be given the freedom to leave their enclosures and meet one another. They speak our language and we can listen to their conversation, which will be the same as it was in the beginning of the world. The first loves are about to begin, Hermiane. Let us watch what happens.

(*Sound of trumpets.*)

There's the fanfare. Our young people are about to appear. This gallery runs along the whole building; we'll watch them unseen and listen.

SCENE THREE
Carise, Eglé.

CARISE: Don't be afraid, Eglé. Follow me.

EGLÉ: Oh, Carise, where are we going?

CARISE: Look: here are grounds you've never seen before. You can walk through them without danger.

EGLÉ: What do I see, Carise? So many new worlds!

CARISE: No it's always the same world. You didn't know how big it was.

EGLÉ: Look at all these countries, these dwellings. I feel very small in such a wide space. I like it, but it frightens me as well. (*She looks and stops by a stream.*) Oh, look, Carise. What's this water rolling on the ground. I've never seen such a thing happen in my world.

CARISE: That's called a stream.

EGLÉ: (*Looking.*) Carise, come here, quickly. Look. There's something living in the stream. It looks like a person. It seems to be as surprised by me as I am by it.

CARISE: (*Laughing.*) It's yourself you're seeing. All streams do that.

EGLÉ: That's me? There? That's my face?

CARISE: Yes.

EGLÉ: But do you know that it's very beautiful. Yes, it is a most enchanting object. If only I'd known that before!

CARISE: It's true that you are beautiful, Eglé.

EGLÉ: Beautiful? I'm absolutely ravishing. What a delightful discovery. Look, the stream repeats all of my expressions and there's not one I don't like. You and Mesrou must have been very happy to look at me all these years. I could spend my whole life looking at myself. Oh, I'm going to love myself very much from now on.

CARISE: I have to attend to something in your house, Eglé, do you mind staying alone?

EGLÉ: No, no, I won't be bored as long as the stream stays with me.

SCENE FOUR

Eglé is alone for a moment, then Azor appears, facing her.

EGLÉ: I'm so beautiful I'll never tire of looking at myself. (*She sees Azor. Frightened.*) Oh. What's this? Another person just like me. No, no, don't come any closer. (*To herself.*) The person laughs. The person seems to be admiring me. (*To Azor.*) Wait, please. Don't move. (*To herself.*) And yet, the person looks at me with such a gentle expression. (*To Azor.*) Can you speak?

AZOR: Yes. It was the pleasure of seeing you that had made me speechless.

EGLÉ: The person hears me and answers me in a very pleasant manner.

AZOR: You enchant me.

EGLÉ: Good.

AZOR: You delight me.

EGLÉ: I like you too.

AZOR: Why then do you forbid me to come any closer?

EGLÉ: I'm no longer forbidding you with as much conviction as before.

AZOR: Then I'll come closer.

EGLÉ: Yes, I would enjoy that. No, wait. I'm so agitated.

AZOR: I obey you because I'm yours.

EGLÉ: The person obeys me! Well then, come a little closer. You can't really be mine if you stay so far away. Ah, yes. It's you. (*To herself.*) The person's very well put together. Do you know, you're almost as beautiful as I am.

AZOR: Being so close to you is making me die of happiness. I want to give myself to you. I don't know what I feel, I don't know how to say it.

EGLÉ: That's how I feel.

AZOR: I'm happy. I'm fainting.

EGLÉ: I'm sighing.

AZOR: It doesn't matter how close I am to you, I still can't see enough of you.

EGLÉ: That's what I think too. But I don't know how we can see more of each other. It's impossible for us to be any closer.

AZOR: My heart wants your hands.

EGLÉ: Here: take my hands. My heart gives them to you. Are you any happier now?

AZOR: Yes, but not more at peace.

EGLÉ: Nor am I, we're alike in all things.

AZOR: Oh, no, there's such a difference between us. The whole of me can't even compare with your eyes. They're so soft.

EGLÉ: But yours are lively.

AZOR: You're so pretty, so delicate.

EGLÉ: Yes, but I assure you it wouldn't suit you to be as pretty as I am. I wouldn't want you to be any different from the way you are. It's another kind of perfection. I don't deny mine, but you must keep yours.

AZOR: I won't change then.

EGLÉ: Ah, tell me, where were you before I knew you?

AZOR: In a world of my own. But I won't ever go back there since you don't live there and I want to have your hands with me forever. I can no longer manage without them, nor can my mouth deprive itself of kissing them.

EGLÉ: And my hands can no longer be deprived of the kisses of your mouth. Shh. I hear a noise. These must be the people from my world. Hide behind this tree or they'll be frightened. I'll call you.

AZOR: But I can't see you from behind that tree.

EGLÉ: All you need do is look into that water. My face is there, you'll see it.

SCENE FIVE
Mesrou, Carise, Eglé.

EGLÉ: He's only just gone and I'm already suffering. Ah, Carise.

CARISE: You seem troubled Eglé, what's the matter?

MESROU: Her eyes are softer than usual today.

EGLÉ: Carise, Mesrou, I have very important news: you believe there are only three of us in this world, but you're wrong: there are four of us. I've acquired an object that was holding my hand a few moments ago.

CARISE: Holding your hand? Why didn't you call for help?

EGLÉ: Help against what, Carise? Against the pleasure it gave me? I was very pleased to have my hand held. It was being held with my consent. This person kissed my hand all the time and I want to call the person back so it can kiss my hand again and give me and itself all that pleasure.

MESROU: I know who it is. I believe I saw him hiding behind the tree. This object is called a man, Eglé, and his name is Azor. We already know him.

EGLÉ: Azor? That's Azor? What a lovely name. Dear Azor, dear man. He'll come back soon.

CARISE: I'm not surprised he loves you and that you love him. You were made for each other.

EGLÉ: Quite. We guessed as much ourselves. (*She calls.*) Azor, my Azor, come here quickly, come here, dear Man.

SCENE SIX
Carise, Eglé, Mesrou, Azor.

AZOR: Carise, Mesrou, you're here. These are friends of mine.

EGLÉ: (*Cheerfully.*) They've just told me. They've also declared you were made on purpose for me and I'm made on purpose for you. That's why we love each other so much. I'm your Eglé, and you're my Azor.

MESROU: One is the man, the other the woman.

EGLÉ: Here's my hand, Azor. It'll make up for your having had to hide. (*To Carise and Mesrou.*) That's what he was doing with my hand before. You see there wasn't any need to call for help, was there?

CARISE: Children, I've told you already that your destiny is to be enchanted by one another.

EGLÉ: (*Holding Azor's hand.*) That's obvious.

CARISE: But if you want to love each other forever, you'll have to observe one rule.

EGLÉ: Yes, I know. To be always in each other's company.

CARISE: No: the opposite. You must occasionally deprive yourselves of the happiness of seeing each other.

EGLÉ: How now?

AZOR: What?

CARISE: Yes. If you don't observe this rule you'll soon see this happiness diminish and you'll become indifferent to one another.

EGLÉ: (*Laughing.*) Indifferent! My Azor indifferent? Hahaha. What an amusing thought. Hahah.

AZOR: (*Laughing.*) How little Carise knows.

MESROU: Don't laugh at Carise, she's giving you excellent advice. It's only by doing what she suggests, that is by separating occasionally, that Carise and I have continued to love each other.

EGLÉ: Yes, that might work for you. You're both so black you must have run away in terror the first time you saw each other. Hahaha.

AZOR: The best the two of you could hope for was to learn to tolerate each other.

EGLÉ: And if you saw each other all the time you'd be repelled because you have nothing beautiful to show each other. I know that I love you, but I never miss you when I don't see you. I don't need your presence at all. Now why is that? It's because you don't please me. But Azor and I are enchanted with each other. He's so handsome and I'm so lovely, so appealing, we're transported every time we look at each other.

AZOR: Let me have your hand again, Eglé. You see how much I suffer when I can't hold her hand. And when I'm holding it I want to die if I can't kiss it, and when I've kissed it I still want to die. And that's only her hand.

EGLÉ: The man is right and I feel everything he's described in the same way. That's what's happened to us and when you talk about our happiness you do it without understanding anything about it. Even we who feel this happiness don't understand it. It's – infinite.

MESROU: We're only asking you to separate for two or three hours a day.

EGLÉ: No. We can't manage a minute.

MESROU: What a pity.

EGLÉ: You're beginning to irritate me, Mesrou. What will happen if Azor and I see too much of each other? Will we become ugly? Will we stop being enchanting?

CARISE: No, but you'll stop feeling that you are.

EGLÉ: How can we possibly stop feeling something that we are?

AZOR: Eglé will always be my Eglé.

EGLÉ: And Azor always my Azor.

MESROU: Yes, we understand that, but you don't know what might happen. Suppose I were to become as handsome as Azor or that Carise were suddenly as beautiful as Eglé.

EGLÉ: Why should we care about that?

CARISE: If you'd had a surfeit of seeing each other, you might be tempted to leave one another and to love us.

EGLÉ: Why should we be tempted? Does one leave what one loves? What sort of thinking is that? Azor and I love each other, that's all there is to it. You may become as beautiful as you wish, what does it matter to us? That will be your concern. We already have ours.

AZOR: Carise and Mesrou will never understand. They would have to be in our place to know what has happened.

MESROU: As you wish.

AZOR: My love is my life, Mesrou.

EGLÉ: Have you heard that, Carise. His life. How can he leave me? He has to live, and so do I.

AZOR: Yes, my life. Ah, how is it possible to be so beautiful, to have such beautiful eyes, such a beautiful mouth, to have everything so beautiful?

EGLÉ: I love it when he admires me.

MESROU: He does adore you.

AZOR: Yes, Mesrou, you've said that very well. I adore. Mesrou finally understands me. Eglé, I adore you.

EGLÉ: (*Gasping.*) Adore me, Azor, but let me breathe a little. Ah, that's better.

CARISE: I'm delighted to see so much tenderness between you, but you will not preserve it unless you listen to us. You must make an effort to be wise. Eglé, give this portrait to Azor. It will make your absence easier for him to bear.

EGLÉ: What's this? Ah, it's me. Yes, I recognize myself. It's a much better image of me than the one in the stream. All of my beauty is there; yes, it's very much me. How wonderful it is to find oneself everywhere. Look Azor, look at my attractions.

AZOR: It's Eglé, it's my beloved woman. But it's not as beautiful as the real Eglé.

MESROU: At least it represents her.

AZOR: Yes, it does. Let me kiss the portrait then. (*He kisses it.*) It only makes me want the real Eglé more.

EGLÉ: Yes and there's another problem. When he kisses the portrait, it's my copy who has everything. I have nothing.

AZOR: Give me your hand and I'll make amends.

EGLÉ: I want a portrait of Azor to play with.

MESROU: You can have his portrait or your own. Which one would you prefer?

EGLÉ: I'll have both, please.

MESROU: You have to choose one: I want to keep the other.

EGLÉ: I suppose I don't really need Azor's portrait because I already have his image in my mind. I'll take my own portrait then and that way I can have both images together.

CARISE: Here is another kind of portrait. It's called a mirror and if you push this button here, it will open. We must leave now. We'll come back in a little while. In the meantime, please remember what we said about short separations.

SCENE SEVEN
Azor, Eglé.

EGLÉ: I can't open the box, Azor, why don't you try? Carise said to push this button.

AZOR: (*Opening it and looking.*) There. But I only see myself in there. Yes, it's the same face I saw in the stream.

EGLÉ: Let me see. No, Azor, you're wrong. Look. It's me again. It's your Eglé exactly as she is. Come and see for yourself.

AZOR: You're right. It is you. No, wait. Look, now there are two of us in there. Half you and half me. I'd prefer it to be just you, I can't see as much of you when I'm in there as well.

EGLÉ: I like seeing a little of you in there. You don't spoil anything, I assure you. Come a little closer. Stay still.

AZOR: Our faces look as if they're about to touch in there. Now they are touching. What happiness for my face.

EGLÉ: I can feel your face and I like it.

AZOR: What if our mouths were to come a little closer?
(*They kiss.*)

EGLÉ: Look, you've disturbed us in there and I can only see myself now. This mirror is an admirable invention.

AZOR: So is the portrait, I want to kiss it again. (*He kisses it.*)

EGLÉ: Azor, do you think Carise and Mesrou are good people?

AZOR: Yes, I do and they wish us the very best. I wanted to talk to you about the advice they gave us.

EGLÉ: About those separations? I was thinking about that as well.

AZOR: Yes, my Eglé. Their predictions have frightened me. I'm not worried as far as I'm concerned, but I don't want you to become bored with me. I'd be desperate if that ever happened.

EGLÉ: Yes, but you must also take care of yourself. You must never tire of adoring me. I know I'm beautiful but now your fears have frightened me.

AZOR: No, no. *You* needn't be afraid. Eglé ... what are you thinking about now?

EGLÉ: I've taken everything into consideration and come to a decision. Let's cause ourselves some pain and agree to separate for two hours. Your heart and its adoration of me mean even more to me than your presence. Although I also like your presence very much.

AZOR: What? Separate? Us?

EGLÉ: Ah, Azor, we must separate immediately. If we wait even a moment, I'll no longer want to part from you.

AZOR: Alas, I don't have the strength to separate.

EGLÉ: And I'm rapidly losing mine.
(*Azor starts crying.*)

EGLÉ: Are you crying, my poor Azor? Stay then. As long as there's no danger.

AZOR: But you said there was a danger.

EGLÉ: Then go.

AZOR: Yes, I'll go. Good-bye, Eglé. Good-bye.

SCENE EIGHT
Eglé, alone.

EGLÉ: Alas, he's gone. I'm all alone. I can no longer hear his voice. (*She sighs.*) Azor. Azor. I ought never to have sent my man away. (*She looks at herself in the mirror.*) Look at that face. Carise and Mesrou don't know what they are talking about: separations aren't necessary to make someone love that face forever. If only I'd looked at myself more carefully I would have known better than to send Azor away.

Azor … Oh well, I'll go and sit by the stream again. At least it's another mirror.

SCENE NINE
Eglé, Adine.

ADINE: What's this?

EGLÉ: Oh. This seems to be yet another person.

ADINE: A new object. I'll get closer and have a look.

EGLÉ: The person's studying me with care, but it doesn't seem to feel admiration for me. This is not another Azor. (*She looks at herself in the mirror.*) Nor is it an Eglé, no, definitely not. And yet, it seems to be making comparisons.

ADINE: I don't know what to think of that face. It lacks something; it's rather insipid.

EGLÉ: There's something about this person I don't like.

ADINE: Does it have a language? Let's see. Hm, hm. Are you a person?

EGLÉ: Yes, I am very much a person.

ADINE: Well? (*Pause.*) Have you nothing to say to me?

EGLÉ: No. People are usually eager to speak to me.

ADINE: But aren't you delighted by me?

EGLÉ: By you? I am the one who delights others.

ADINE: What? You're not overjoyed to see me?

EGLÉ: Neither overjoyed nor particularly displeased. Why should I care whether I see you or not?

ADINE: This is very strange. I show myself to you, you look at me. And yet you feel nothing. You must be looking somewhere else by mistake. Gaze upon me with a little more care. Now. How do you find me?

EGLÉ: You, you, you. Who cares about you? I've already told you that I'm the one who is gazed upon. I'm the one who's spoken to and told about the impression I've made. That's how it is. How can you ask me to look at you when I myself am here?

ADINE: Surely it's the one who is the more beautiful who waits for others to notice her and gaze upon her in astonishment.

EGLÉ: Then what are you waiting for? Be astonished.

ADINE: Didn't you hear me? I said it was the more beautiful one who waits for the admiration of others.

EGLÉ: And I've told you the more beautiful one is waiting.

ADINE: If I am not that one, then where is she? There are three people in this world and they are all lost in admiration of me.

EGLÉ: I know nothing about these people of yours, but there are three who are enchanted with me and who treat me as I deserve to be treated.

ADINE: I know that I am beautiful, so beautiful I delight myself every time I look at myself. You see how things are.

EGLÉ: What is this tale you're telling me? I who am speaking to you can never look at myself without becoming totally enraptured.

ADINE: Enraptured? I admit you're quite passable, even rather pleasant. You see that I'm not like you and that I'm making an effort to be fair.

EGLÉ: (*Aside.*) I'd like to beat her with her fairness.

ADINE: You're not seriously thinking of entering into a dispute with me over who is the more beautiful, are you? Why, one need only look.

EGLÉ: But it's by looking that I find you rather ugly.

ADINE: That's because you can't help finding me beautiful and you're jealous.

EGLÉ: The only thing that prevents me from finding you beautiful is your face.

ADINE: My face? Oh, you can't vex me that way. I've seen my face. Go and ask the waters of the stream about my face. Ask Mesrin who adores me.

EGLÉ: The waters of the stream are making fun of you and they've already told me that there is nothing more beautiful than my own face. I know nothing about this Mesrin of yours but he will need only catch a glimpse of my face to stop looking at you. Furthermore I have an Azor who's worth much more than your Mesrin, an Azor I love and who is almost as enchanting as I am. And he says I am his life. You're nobody's life. *And* I have a mirror which confirms everything the stream and Azor have already told me. Can anything beat that?

ADINE: (*Laughing.*) A mirror? You have a mirror as well? What can a mirror do for you except make you look at yourself. Hahaha.

EGLÉ: Hahaha. I knew I wouldn't like her.

ADINE: Here. Take a look at this mirror which tells the truth. Learn to know yourself better and to keep quiet.

EGLÉ: Why don't you take this one and look at yourself in there. It will teach you how mediocre you are and to adopt a tone of modesty when speaking to me.

ADINE: Go away. I have no use for you if you will persist in your refusal to admire me. I'm turning my back on you. There.

EGLÉ: As for me, I don't even know you're here.

ADINE: What a madwoman.

EGLÉ: She's deluded. What world can such a person have come from? There's Carise, I'll ask her.

SCENE TEN
Carise, Adine, Eglé.

CARISE: What are you two doing so far apart? Why aren't you talking to each other?

ADINE: That's a new person I've come across. She's been thrown into despair by my beauty.

EGLÉ: Have you ever seen a duller object than that one over there, Carise? She's a silly person who aspires to astonish me. She keeps asking me what I feel when I look at her. She seems to expect me to be happy when I see her. She actually said to me: "Gaze upon me, how do you find me?" She even has the arrogance to think herself as beautiful as I am.

ADINE: I didn't say that. I said I was more beautiful than you. That's obvious as soon as you look into the mirror.

CARISE: Gently, gently. Don't be angry with each other. You must enjoy being together and add to it the pleasure of knowing yourselves to be both adored. Eglé is adored by Azor whom she cherishes and Adine by Mesrin whom she loves in return. Come, come, be friends.

EGLÉ: I will as soon as she rids herself of her delusions of beauty.

ADINE: I know how to bring her to her senses. I'll take her Azor away from her, not that I care anything for him, but I'll do anything for a little peace.

EGLÉ: Where's that idiot friend of hers, Mesrin? If I come across him, she can beware. Good-bye, I must leave. I can't stand her presence any more.

ADINE: Hahaha, It's my merits which cause her aversion.

EGLÉ: Hahaha. What an unpleasant face.

SCENE ELEVEN
Adine, Carise.

CARISE: Don't pay attention, Adine, let her go.

ADINE: I feel sorry for her, that's all.

CARISE: It's time for your music lesson.

ADINE: I'm coming, but I see Mesrin and I want to have a word with him.

CARISE: But you only left him a moment ago.

ADINE: I'll only be a moment.

SCENE TWELVE

Mesrin, Carise, Adine.

ADINE: (*Calls.*) Mesrin!

MESRIN: (*Running to her.*) Adine. Ah, it's you. It's my Adine. She's come back to me. I've been so impatient. Oh, I'm so happy.

ADINE: No, no, restrain your happiness, Mesrin, I haven't come back. I only happened to be here.

MESRIN: Then you must happen to stay with me, Adine.

CARISE: Be quick, Adine, or we won't have time for your lesson.

ADINE: Yes, yes. Mesrin, I am beautiful, am I not?

MESRIN: Beautiful! Oh, so beautiful!

ADINE: You see, Carise, he doesn't hesitate. He describes what he sees.

MESRIN: You are divine, you are beauty incarnate.

ADINE: Yes, that's what I think too. And yet it seems that Carise, you and I are all mistaken: I'm not beautiful, I'm ugly.

MESRIN: Ugly? My Adine ugly?

ADINE: Yes, your own Adine. When I left you, Mesrin, I came upon a person from another world. And this person wasn't astonished by my presence as you are, she wasn't enraptured; no, this person demanded of me that I be delighted by her. And when I refused, she accused me of being ugly.

MESRIN: What an outrage!

ADINE: And she said you would leave me the moment you set eyes on her.

CARISE: That's because she was vexed with you, Adine.

MESRIN: Are you absolutely certain this was a real person?

ADINE: She said she was and she looked like a person – more or less.

CARISE: She is a person.

ADINE: She may come this way and when you see her I want you to scorn her. I want you to be horrified by her.

MESRIN: She must be revolting.

ADINE: She's called…wait, what is she called…

CARISE: Eglé.

ADINE: Ah yes, she's an Eglé. You'll know her by an angry, scowling face, which isn't as dark as Carise's but isn't as white as mine. It's just a color, a nondescript color.

MESRIN: Which isn't attractive.

ADINE: Oh, no, not at all. Indeed it can hardly be called a color at all. And her eyes. How can I describe her eyes? They are eyes that look, that's all. Her mouth is neither very large nor very small, it's a mouth to speak with. Her figure's upright and it would be similar to ours if only it were more pleasant to look at. She has hands that move about, and long, thin fingers. And her voice is rough and cross. You'll recognize her as soon as you see her.

MESRIN: Look, I see a person over there, coming this way. Leave it to me: I'll send her back to her world thoroughly humbled.

ADINE: Yes. Humiliate her. Mortify her.

MESRIN: Don't worry. And now please let me have your hand.

ADINE: Take it, Mesrin, it's here for you.

CARISE: You've said all you wanted to say, Adine, let's go.

ADINE: Only when he's finished kissing my hand.

CARISE: Leave her alone, Mesrin, I'm in a hurry.

ADINE: Good-bye, my love, I'll come back soon. Don't forget to avenge me.

MESRIN: How can I fail when I am so angry with this person? Good-bye, my enchantress.

SCENE THIRTEEN
Mesrin, Azor.

MESRIN: A color that's neither black nor white. An upright figure. A mouth that speaks. Where shall I find her? (*Seeing Azor.*) Is that her over there? Is that Eglé? No, I don't think it can be. That person isn't deformed.

AZOR: Hello. You seem to be very similar to me.

MESRIN: That's what I was thinking.

AZOR: Are you a man then?

MESRIN: So I've been told.

AZOR: That's what I've been told as well.

MESRIN: You say you've been told: do you know some other people?

AZOR: Yes, I know all the people in this world. Two are black and one is white.

MESRIN: It's the same for me. Where are you from?

AZOR: The world.

MESRIN: Do you mean my world?

AZOR: I don't know. There seem to be so many worlds suddenly.

MESRIN: It doesn't matter anyway. I like your face. Put your hand in mine, we must love each other.

AZOR: You make me feel merry, and I like to look at you, although you're not exactly lovely.

MESRIN: Nor are you. What I like about you is that you're a man.

AZOR: That's it. That's my feeling for you. You're a good companion, I'm a good companion and I don't care about your looks.

MESRIN: Looking at you brings me good cheer. When do you take your meals?

AZOR: Every day.

MESRIN: So do I. Let's take our meals together, for our amusement and to keep us merry. We'll laugh, we'll jump about, isn't that right? I'm in such good spirits I'm already jumping. (*He jumps.*)

AZOR: I'm jumping as well. There will be the two of us, there might even be three of us: I'll tell my pale beauty about this. Now, she does have looks I care about. Wait until you see her: she's worth more than the two of us put together.

MESRIN: I can believe that, my friend, because you and I are absolutely nothing next to someone I know, and who'll soon join us. She's a delight, and she has these soft white hands and she allows me to kiss them.

AZOR: Hands, eh? Well my pale beauty also has hands which are heavenly and she allows me to caress them as much as I want to. I'm expecting them right now.

MESRIN: Good, because I've just left the hands that belong to me and that reminds me I must leave you to attend to a little affair. Stay here until I come back with my dear Adine and let's jump some more to celebrate this happy meeting. Hahaha. Jump.

AZOR: Hahahaha. I'm jumping.

SCENE FOURTEEN
Azor, Mesrin, Eglé.

MESRIN: Look, look over there. There's a beautiful object which is listening to us.

EGLÉ: There's something standing next to Azor which looks most pleasing.

AZOR: That's my pale beauty, my Eglé.

MESRIN: (*To himself.*) Eglé? Adine calls that a scowling face?

AZOR: Ah, Eglé, I'm so happy.

EGLÉ: Is this a new friend who has suddenly appeared to us?

AZOR: Yes, he's a companion of mine. He's called a man and he comes from a world not far from here.

MESRIN: But this world is the best world.

EGLÉ: Why? Is there more to see here than in your world?

MESRIN: Oh yes, much more.

EGLÉ: Why then, you must stay here.

AZOR: That's just what we were saying. He's good and full of cheer and I love him. Not in the way I love you, my lovely Eglé, because I adore my Eglé, whereas I'm not too bothered about him. But I love to be in his company and to speak to him about you, about your mouth, about your eyes, about your hands. Ah, your hands, I've been languishing for your hands. Let me kiss them.

MESRIN: You kiss that hand, Azor and I'll kiss the other one.

EGLÉ: Ah.

AZOR: No. Wait. I want the other hand as well. This isn't your pale beauty, it's mine and both of these hands belong to me. There's nothing for you here.

EGLÉ: He wasn't doing any harm, Azor. By the way, it's time for you to go now. Remember how necessary separations are to our love. Yours hasn't lasted long enough.

AZOR: But I haven't seen you for hours!

EGLÉ: You're wrong. I know it hasn't been long enough. I'm determined to keep to what we've resolved.

AZOR: You'll be here all by yourself.

EGLÉ: I'll manage.

MESRIN: Don't upset her, friend.

AZOR: Are you angry with me, Eglé?

EGLÉ: Why are you being so stubborn? Weren't you told how dangerous it was for us to see too much of each other?

AZOR: It may not be true.

EGLÉ: I'm certain it wasn't a lie.

AZOR: I'll leave then, for your sake, but I'll be back soon. Come, my friend, you said you had some business to attend to. Come with me and help me pass the time.

MESRIN: Yes ... but ...

EGLÉ: What is it, friend?

MESRIN: I've been walking for such a long time.

EGLÉ: Then your friend must stay here and rest, Azor.

MESRIN: Yes, and I'll keep the beautiful woman company. That way she won't feel bored.

AZOR: She said she wanted to be alone, friend. If she needs to be entertained, I can do it much better than you. Let's go.

EGLÉ: (*Angry, aside.*) Go then.

SCENE FIFTEEN
Carise, Eglé.

CARISE: You seem very thoughtful, Eglé.

EGLÉ: Yes. I'm thoughtful about the fact that I'm in a bad mood.

CARISE: Are you feeling sad?

EGLÉ: No, Carise, it's not sadness, it's a kind of confusion.

CARISE: About what?

EGLÉ: You said before one never knew what might happen to love.

CARISE: Yes.

EGLÉ: Well, I don't know what's happening to me.

CARISE: What's wrong with you?

EGLÉ: It seems to me I'm angry with myself, I'm angry with Azor, I'm angry with everybody.

CARISE: Why are you angry with yourself?

EGLÉ: Because although I have the intention of loving Azor forever, I'm beginning to fear I might fail.

CARISE: Is that possible?

EGLÉ: Yes. I'm very cross with Azor and I suspect his behavior is at fault.

CARISE: I think it may be that you want to find fault with him.

EGLÉ: If you keep answering me in that manner, I'll soon be angry with you as well.

CARISE: You are indeed in a bad mood. What has Azor done to you?

EGLÉ: Azor and I agreed to separate. He left but then he came back almost as soon as he'd gone. He wants to be with me all the time and what you predicted has begun to happen already.

CARISE: What? Could you suddenly love him less?

EGLÉ: Yes. It's not my fault if the pleasure one takes in seeing someone vanishes when one sees them too often.

CARISE: But you said that was impossible.

EGLÉ: Don't quibble with me. What did I know? I said that because I was so ignorant at the time.

CARISE: Eglé, I can't believe that it is Azor's desire to be with you all the time that's making you dislike him. You haven't known him long enough for that.

EGLÉ: Oh, I've known him long enough. We've already had three conversations together. Apparently, the length of these meetings has proved nefarious.

CARISE: You're not saying in what way you feel he has wronged you.

EGLÉ: He's wronged me in many ways. To begin with, he behaved with me in a most irritating manner. My hands are my own, I believe, I may do with them what I please, and he won't allow them to be kissed.

CARISE: And who wanted to kiss your hands?

EGLÉ: A friend Azor found recently and who's called a man.

CARISE: And you found this friend attractive?

EGLÉ: Yes, delightful. He has a more gentle manner than Azor and he was kind enough to offer to keep me company. Then Azor had the caprice of forbidding him the pleasure of my hand and me the pleasure of his company. He argued with his friend and then took him away. He never even asked what I wanted. Ha! Am I no longer my own mistress? Doesn't Azor trust me? Is he afraid someone else might love me?

CARISE: He may be afraid of your finding his friend too attractive.

EGLÉ: Then it's up to Azor to make himself a little more attractive to me. As for the rest, I like being loved by people and if Azor had a hundred friends instead of one, I'd want them all to love me. Azor wants my beauty to be there for him alone, but I think it should be there to be enjoyed by everybody.

CARISE: I believe your distaste for Azor isn't caused by that but by your present preference for Azor's friend.

EGLÉ: Do you think so? You could be right.

CARISE: Aren't you ashamed of your unfaithfulness?

EGLÉ: Yes, a little, but I'm still very ignorant about these matters.

CARISE: It's not ignorance, Eglé. You promised to love Azor and to remain faithful.

EGLÉ: Yes, but I promised that when he was the only one around. I didn't know about the existence of his friend then.

CARISE: You must admit those are not good reasons for being unfaithful and you denied them when Mesrou and I spoke to you before.

EGLÉ: You're right; they're not very good. I have one now that's irrefutable: It's simply that Azor's friend is better than Azor.

CARISE: You're wrong about that as well. It's not that he's better but that he's newer.

EGLÉ: Yes, but to be newer is a considerable advantage. It's an attractive quality and one that Azor completely lacks.

CARISE: Add to this that this newcomer is about to love you.

EGLÉ: Just so: I hope he is about to love me. That's another attraction.

CARISE: Whereas Azor is no longer about to love you.

EGLÉ: No, because he loves me already.

CARISE: You can't be very pleased with such peculiar reasons for your change of heart.

EGLÉ: I'm not pleased with anything. On the one hand, this change makes me sad, on the other, it makes me happy. I have no more control over the one than over the other. They are both equally important to me. Now, to which do I owe the most? Should I give myself pain or should I give myself pleasure? I challenge you to answer me.

CARISE: Consult your own heart: it'll condemn your unfaithfulness.

EGLÉ: You haven't been listening, Carise. My heart condemns it, but my heart also approves it. My heart says yes, my heart says no. It's of two minds. I suppose I might as well choose the most convenient.

CARISE: I'll tell you what to do. Avoid Azor's friend. That's the best way to resolve your struggle. Let's go quickly.

EGLÉ: I believe it's too late to go. The struggle is coming this way: Azor's friend is walking towards us.

CARISE: It doesn't matter. Make an effort, Eglé and don't look at him.

SCENE SIXTEEN
Mesrou, Mesrin, Eglé, Carise.

MESROU: (*Trying to hold Mesrin back.*) Help me, Carise, he's running away from me. Don't let him come near: he wants to be unfaithful.

CARISE: Don't come any closer.

MESRIN: Why not?

CARISE: Because I forbid it. Mesrou and I must have some authority over you, we are your masters.

MESRIN: (*In revolt.*) Masters? You? I don't understand the notion of a master.

CARISE: Very well. If I can't order you not to come near, let me at least beg it out of you. And Eglé will add her prayers to mine.

EGLÉ: Me? Not at all. I don't wish to add any prayers of mine.

CARISE: Let's go, Eglé. You don't even know if he loves you.

EGLÉ: I need only ask him. What do you want with me, handsome friend?

MESRIN: I want to see you, gaze upon your beauty, admire you and call you my dear soul.

EGLÉ: You see, Carise, he's even talking about his soul. And do you love me?

MESRIN: Desperately.

EGLÉ: Didn't I tell you so, Carise?

MESRIN: Do you love me as well?

EGLÉ: I would prefer not to love you because there is Azor who loves me and is relying on me.

MESROU: Mesrin, follow Eglé's example and don't be unfaithful.

EGLÉ: Mesrin! So your name is Mesrin.

MESRIN: Yes.

EGLÉ: You're Adine's friend.

MESRIN: I was her friend but I don't even want her portrait any more.

EGLÉ: Give it to me. (*To herself.*) Adine's portrait and her friend. He has that merit as well. Carise, here are too many excellent qualities together and I can no longer resist them. Come here Mesrin, and let me love you.

MESRIN: What an enchanting hand, give it to me.

EGLÉ: I've gained an incomparable friend.

MESROU: Why do you want to leave Adine, Mesrin? What complaints do you have against her?

MESRIN: I'm not leaving Adine because I want to, but because Eglé's beautiful face commands it.

EGLÉ: He has eyes to see, that's all.

MESRIN: I know I am being unfaithful but there is nothing I can do about it.

EGLÉ: I've forced him to it, we've forced each other.

CARISE: Adine and Azor will be thrown into despair.

MESRIN: I'm sorry.

EGLÉ: What can we do?

CARISE: I could put an end to their unhappiness by making them love each other. Will you agree to that?

MESRIN: Yes, do it.

EGLÉ: No, wait. I want Azor to miss me, I feel my beauty deserves such a tribute. And it won't hurt Adine to suffer a little. It will teach her to know herself better.

SCENE SEVENTEEN
Mesrou, Eglé, Carise, Azor, Mesrin.

MESROU: I see Azor.

MESRIN: I now feel embarrassed before my friend. He'll be very surprised.

CARISE: It appears from the look on his face that he's already guessed the harm you've done him.

EGLÉ: Yes, he does look sad and he has a right to feel so.

AZOR: (*Approaches, shamefacedly.*) Eglé...

EGLÉ: Azor, are you upset?

AZOR: Yes.

EGLÉ: Very upset?

AZOR: Very.

EGLÉ: Yes, I see that you are. But how do you know that I love Mesrin?

AZOR: What?

MESRIN: Yes, my friend.

AZOR: Eglé loves you and no longer cares for me?

EGLÉ: Yes.

AZOR: (*Gaily.*) Nothing could be better. Please go on loving each other. I no longer care for you either, Eglé. I'll be back in a moment, wait for me here.

EGLÉ: Stop. What do you mean, you no longer love me? What does that mean?

AZOR: I'll explain later.

SCENE EIGHTEEN
Mesrou, Carise, Eglé, Mesrin.

EGLÉ: Azor. Wait. Wait.

MESRIN: Don't call him back. You have no need for him now that you have me.

EGLÉ: Yes, but I would love you more if I could have him as well. I don't want to lose anything.
(*Carise and Mesrou laugh.*)

EGLÉ: I don't see what's so amusing.

SCENE NINETEEN
Mesrou, Carise, Eglé, Mesrin, Adine, Azor.

ADINE: (*Laughing.*) There's the beautiful Eglé. If you ever want to see yourself again, you may come to me: I have your portrait. I obtained it without any difficulty.

EGLÉ: (*Throwing down Adine's portrait.*) Here's yours which I'm only too pleased to give back. It's not worth my keeping it.

ADINE: What? My portrait? Mesrin, what is she doing with my portrait?

MESRIN: I gave it to her.

EGLÉ: Azor, I wish to speak to you for a moment.

MESRIN: Why do you want to speak to him, Eglé? What about me?

ADINE: Come here, Mesrin, you seem to have taken leave of your senses.

SCENE TWENTY
Mesrou, Carise, Eglé, Mesrin, The Prince, Hermiane, Adine, Meslis, Dina, Azor.

HERMIANE: No. Stop this. Stop this outrage. I refuse to see any more, your Highness. I find Adine and Eglé intolerable. Why did you choose women who would display the most contemptible aspects of my sex?

EGLÉ: Who are all these people, Carise? They look very angry. I want to go away.
(*They all start to go.*)

CARISE: Stay here, all of you, and don't be frightened. These are all new friends and we must hear what they think. Ah, Dina, Meslis, you're here too. Good.

MESLIS: Hello, Carise. Look at all these new people, Dina.

DINA: Yes, but we have no need of them, do we?

MESLIS: No, we don't. There isn't a person here who can compare with you. Are these men or women, Carise?

CARISE: Both. The women are over there, and the men here. Look at the women, Meslis and if you see one who appeals to you more than Dina does, we'll give her to you.

EGLÉ: I could accept your friendship. What is your name?

MESLIS: My name is Meslis, but I have no friendship to offer you.

CARISE: Choose another woman, Meslis.

MESLIS: Thank you, Carise. They are all lovely but none of them interests me. There is only one Dina in this world.

DINA: That was beautifully said, Meslis.

CARISE: And you Dina, why don't you look at the men?

DINA: I've seen all there is to see. Let's go, Meslis.

HERMIANE: What an enchanting child. Let me look after her, your Highness.

THE PRINCE: Do. And I'll take care of Meslis.

DINA: We don't need anyone else. We only want to be together.

THE PRINCE: Have no fears, we won't separate you. Carise, set Dina and Meslis apart and I will decide what to do with the others. Hermiane, I'm afraid neither sex has grounds to condemn the other. Vices and virtues seem to have been equally distributed amongst them.

HERMIANE: No, your Highness, you must allow for a difference. The treachery of your sex is revolting. Men change for no reason at all and don't even try to excuse their behavior.

THE PRINCE: I admit that the conduct of your sex is more hypocritical and as such more decent. Women make a greater fuss over their conscience.

HERMIANE: Believe me, your Highness, this is no laughing matter. Let's go.

THE PRINCE: Yes, let us all go back to the court, and try once again to resolve this dispute.

END OF PLAY

Sorry

By Timothy Mason

TIMOTHY MASON Plays include *The Fiery Furnace* which starred Julie Harris; *Babylon Gardens*, with Timothy Hutton and Mary-Louise Parker; *The Less Than Human Club; Ascension Day; Only You; Before I Got My Eye Put Out; Bearclaw; Levitation* and *In A Northern Landscape*. Mason's plays have been produced in New York by Circle Rep, and by regional companies including the Actors Theatre of Louisville, Victory Gardens, Seattle Rep's Second Stage, Portland Stage, South Coast Repertory, Theatre 40 in Los Angeles, the Jungle Theatre in Minneapolis, and the Young Conservatory at San Francisco's A.C.T.

Mason has also written stage adaptations of young peoples' classics for The Children's Theatre Company of Minneapolis, including *How The Grinch Stole Christmas, The 500 Hats of Bartholomew Cubbins, Treasure Island, The Adventures of Tom Sawyer* and a dozen others.

He has won a W. Alton Jones Foundation grant, the Kennedy Center's Fund for New American Plays award, a playwriting fellowship from the National Endowment for the Arts, a Hollywood Drama-Logue Award, the Twin Cities Drama Critics Circle Award and a National Society of Arts and Letters Award.

CHARACTERS
    Pat, good-looking, in her 20s.
    Wayne, good-looking, in his 20s.

SETTING
    A small one-bedroom apartment in New York's East Village. The door to the hall, left, has a splintered hole in it, about three feet from the floor. The door on the right leads to the bathroom and the bedroom. The kitchen area is upstage, and features two tall windows in the upstage wall which look out over a courtyard to the back of the building beyond: fire escapes, lighted windows, a rooftop. Centerstage is a small dining room table, littered with newspapers, trade periodicals, notebooks, a can of Tab. There's a chest of drawers against the right wall and a television set somewhere.

TIME
    The Present

SORRY

August night, New York City, an apartment in the East Village.
Wayne sits in a chair, bleeding. Pat stands above him with a
pistol. Wayne wears black chinos, black high-topped tennis shoes,
and a black T-shirt. His right thigh is wrapped in a dark red
towel. Pat wears something for a hot night at home.

PAT: Honest to God, I am really sorry. (*Beat.*) Can I get you anything?
(*Beat.*) Shouldn't I be calling someone? I mean, really. (*Beat.*) Tea?
Toast? Have you eaten? (*Beat.*) You look like someone.

WAYNE: You aren't real, you can't be.

PAT: How's that chair? You could stretch out on the sofa, I wouldn't
mind, I'll put down newspapers. (*Beat.*) This is just like me, you
know that? This is exactly like me. God. What an idiot. I'm a
waitress. Actress really, but. (*Beat.*) I could make some tea, it'd be
no problem whatsoever. (*Beat.*) Earl Grey? Chamomile?

WAYNE: You just don't exist!

PAT: Mint?

WAYNE: Jesus.

PAT: Look, I was alone, I was scared. (*Beat.*) How do you feel now? Are
you feeling any better? You look a little better.

WAYNE: I feel like shit.

PAT: I know the feeling. Some days it's all I can do to get out of bed and
through that door.

WAYNE: Put the gun down.

PAT: Oh, my God, I didn't realize! Of course. Oh. I feel like such a fool.
You sure you don't want me to call an ambulance?

WAYNE: Yes! No! Do not. Call. Anyone.

PAT: So what's your name?

WAYNE: You're unreal.

PAT: I'm Pat. Aspirin! (*She starts for the bathroom door.*)

WAYNE: Put down the goddamned gun!

PAT: Just make yourself comfortable. (*Pat exits, still carrying the pistol.*)

WAYNE: Oh, boy. (*He explores his leg, tenderly.*) Ohhh, boy. (*He tries to*
stand.) Agggh! (*He falls back into the chair.*)

PAT: (*Calling from off.*) Two aspirin, coming right up!

WAYNE: Shit. Oh, shit.

(*Pat enters with a glass of water and a couple of aspirin.*)

PAT: I have the worst time swallowing these things, you wouldn't believe. Here you go.

(*Wayne turns his head away.*)

PAT: Go on, there's nothing to worry about, they're buffered.

WAYNE: Where's the gun?

PAT: Ah. I don't know, around here somewhere. Here's looking at you.

(*He takes the aspirin and the glass.*)

WAYNE: Aspirin, wow. (*He swallows the aspirin.*)

PAT: I grind them into powder and stir them into a glass of Tab. Tastes awful, but. (*She takes the glass from him.*) How are you feeling now?

WAYNE: I just took them, for Chrissake!

PAT: Hey, there, Mister, I *said* I was sorry.

WAYNE: You shot me!

PAT: So what am I supposed to do, kill myself?

WAYNE: It's an idea.

PAT: You don't mean that and you know it.

WAYNE: I've got to get out of here.

PAT: So how long have you been with the Little Brothers of Charity? (*Beat.*) They really call you that?

WAYNE: You're weird. You are so weird.

PAT: Talk about weird, you won't even go to the hospital.

WAYNE: It's a flesh wound.

PAT: Most wounds are. What's your name?

WAYNE: I just want to go home.

PAT: You can't even walk, for heaven's sake. What's your name? (*Beat.*)

WAYNE: Wayne.

PAT: You have got to be kidding.

WAYNE: Okay, that's it, I'm going. (*He tries to stand and falls back into the chair with a moan.*)

PAT: Take it easy.

WAYNE: What's wrong with Wayne?

PAT: Nothing, nothing. Nothing.

WAYNE: You know, you don't really *grow* on a person.

PAT: Okay, I'm sorry, I shouldn't have said anything.

WAYNE: Damn right!

PAT: Sorry!

WAYNE: Yeah, right. (*Pause.*)

PAT: It's just always struck me as a very wimpy sort of name.

WAYNE: Oh, you're making me feel great, you know that? You got a real knack for making a guy feel at home. You should put it down in a book. How to Meet Men.

PAT: What was I supposed to do? It's dark, I hear this noise outside my door ...

WAYNE: First date: get yourself a .45.

PAT: Oh, come on—it's just a little .22.

WAYNE: God, get me out of here.

PAT: Anytime you want. Wayne.

WAYNE: Believe me, lady, if I *could*. (*Beat.*)

PAT: How's that leg doing?

WAYNE: How do you think?

PAT: Let's see.

WAYNE: You keep away from me.

PAT: Attitude is going to get us nowhere. Now let's have a look at that leg. (*She begins to gently unwrap the towel from his thigh.*)

WAYNE: Ow!

PAT: What do you Little Brothers do, exactly?
(*Wayne whimpers softly.*)

PAT: You bring food to people, something like that? Meals On Wheels sort of thing? Oh, God, your leg is a mess.

WAYNE: Tell me about it.

PAT: I am so terribly sorry.

WAYNE: If you apologize one more time I swear I'll kill you.

PAT: I think the bleeding's stopped anyway, but it's hard to tell. Those pants are going to have to come off. (*Beat.*)

WAYNE: Not. On. Your. Life.

PAT: Look at you, dressed in black from head to toe, what was I supposed to think.

WAYNE: You didn't even see me, you shot right through the door!

PAT: I was holding it, it went off.

WAYNE: People like you should not have guns. People like you should not have anything! Forks!

PAT: Okay, *you* try living in this city.

WAYNE: I am, I am.

PAT: It's terrifying out there.

WAYNE: If you ask me, it's kind of scary right here.

PAT: The sound of a footstep behind you. A cough in the dark.

WAYNE: Bam! Another chest-cold victim bites the dust.

PAT: Look. Wayne. I am a woman alone.

WAYNE: It's no wonder. (*Beat.*)

PAT: This apartment has been broken into twice in the past six months. In the past two years I've had my purse snatched on the F train, the double R, the Lexington Avenue line, and the cross-town bus. And for the past month there's been some jerk on the roof across the courtyard, *staring*. With *binoculars*. At *me*. So if I'm just the littlest bit jumpy, *pardon me!*

WAYNE: Okay, okay. I'm sorry. You've had some bad breaks.

PAT: What I've had is a crime wave.

WAYNE: So you got yourself a gun.

PAT: My mother sent it. All the way from Seattle. That's where I'm from.

WAYNE: In the mail? That's illegal.

PAT: What other people do to me is illegal, what my mother does is blameless. What were you doing out in the hall, anyway?

WAYNE: I was trying to read the number on the door, lady—that's all.

PAT: The light out there's burned out.

WAYNE: I noticed.

PAT: So who were you looking for?

WAYNE: Not you.

PAT: Mr. Fischer? He used to get charity people. Someone came from the Synagogue twice a week, but he's dead now.

WAYNE: You plugged him, right?

PAT: You know, you're beginning to annoy me? I *liked* Mr. Fischer.

WAYNE: God. I feel weak.

PAT: Well, of course you do, you've lost a lot of blood.

WAYNE: How do you know it's stopped bleeding?

PAT: It's not dripping like it was before.

WAYNE: If I die here, lady, so help me …

PAT: The name is Pat and nobody's going to die, for goodness sake. And if you're so worried about it, why won't you go to the hospital?

WAYNE: Well, for one thing, what do you think would happen to you if I did? You got a permit for that thing?

PAT: It was Mother's.

WAYNE: Tell it to the judge, Annie Oakley.

PAT: So you're saying you're doing me a favor?

WAYNE: Damn right I am.

PAT: An act of charity.

WAYNE: Yes, as a matter of fact.

PAT: Well I can't tell you how grateful I am. (*Beat.*) You look pale.

WAYNE: I *feel* pale. How do you know he's looking at *you?*

PAT: Who?

WAYNE: The guy on the roof.

PAT: Every now and then he waves.

WAYNE: Maybe he's lonely.

PAT: Maybe *I'm* lonely, I don't take it to the rooftops.

WAYNE: Maybe he's just trying to get to know you.

PAT: Maybe it should occur to him to send flowers.

WAYNE: You sure the bleeding's stopped?

PAT: There's only one way to tell.

WAYNE: Oh, Lord.

PAT: Come on, come on. (*She starts to take off his tennis shoes.*) Do you really think I could be, like, arrested? For this?

WAYNE: If there is a God, yes.

PAT: I was protecting myself!

WAYNE: From what?

PAT: And you'd press charges against me?

WAYNE: This is why I'm here instead of there, because I wouldn't—get it?

PAT: Charity.

WAYNE: Why not?

PAT: I like your sneakers.

WAYNE: Thanks.

PAT: Can you stand?

WAYNE: I think so.

(*He does so, slowly. She begins to take off his trousers.*)

WAYNE: This is making me very uncomfortable.

PAT: So pretend I'm a nurse. Where'd you get them?

WAYNE: What?

PAT: Those hightops.

WAYNE: I don't know. That shop on First Avenue and St. Marks, right across from Spillacci's. (*Beat.*)

PAT: You live around here, don't you. (*Beat.*) Don't you.

WAYNE: Ow!

PAT: Don't try to change the subject.

WAYNE: It hurts!

PAT: Of course it hurts, you've been shot. So where do you live? (*She eases the trousers out from under him.*) I knew I'd seen you before. You live right here in the neighborhood, don't you.

WAYNE: So what?

PAT: So nothing. Your pants are finished, there's no getting out these stains.

WAYNE: Right.

PAT: Besides, there's a hole in them.

WAYNE: Right.

(*She looks at his bloody thigh.*)

PAT: Can't see a thing. You wait right there, I'll go get the alcohol.

(*She exits into the bathroom. Wayne sits and examines his thigh. Pat re-enters with a bottle of rubbing alcohol and a cotton swab.*)

WAYNE: You know, I really don't think it's so bad?

PAT: Really?

WAYNE: Yeah, I think maybe you just grazed me.

PAT: Oh, good!

WAYNE: Anyway, it hardly hurts at all anymore.

PAT: Great. Let me see. (*She daubs the thigh tenderly with the alcohol-soaked cotton.*)

WAYNE: *Aaaaaagggghhh!*

PAT: You've got to expect a little sting.

WAYNE: *Oh! Oh! Oh!*

PAT: Big baby.

WAYNE: Oh! Oh, God! Do you have any salt? Maybe you could rub some salt in it!

PAT: We're killing germs here, mister.

WAYNE: You're killing *me* here, lady!

PAT: Look at that. It's nothing. It's nothing. It's a scratch!

WAYNE: It's my body!

PAT: You have ruined two towels and a carpet for a *scratch!*

WAYNE: *Sorry!*

PAT: Where did all that blood come from?

WAYNE: Me!

PAT: What are you, some kind of bleeder?

WAYNE: Okay, I'm going. Now.

PAT: What do you plan to wear?

WAYNE: Oh, Lord.

PAT: You'd look great out there in your Fruit of the Looms.

WAYNE: They're not Fruit of the Looms.

PAT: What are they then?

WAYNE: Will you stop looking at my underwear!

PAT: I am not looking at your underwear!

WAYNE: You were too!

PAT: So big deal! You think this was all a plot in order to get a peek at your skivvies?

WAYNE: Just ... let me have something to wear out of here and we can forget about the whole thing.

PAT: Would you like a jumper or a plain cotton skirt?

WAYNE: You're not even funny.

PAT: You're not even civil.

WAYNE: Jeans, slacks ...

PAT: I'll take care of you, don't worry. (*She goes through his trousers pockets.*) Anything in here you want to keep?

WAYNE: Hey, get out of there!

PAT: Relax.

WAYNE: Give me those!

PAT: Keys; five-dollar bill, soggy; your cigarettes have had it; snapshot, also soggy. What a mess.

WAYNE: Give me that stuff.

PAT: I'm just going to dry it all out. (*She spreads the contents of his pockets on the table.*)

WAYNE: I want my things!

PAT: (*Looking at the snapshot.*) Who is this?

WAYNE: Give it here! (*Beat.*)

PAT: What is going on here? What the hell is going on?

WAYNE: Please, just …

PAT: This is me. This is a picture of me.

WAYNE: (*Weary.*) Oh, shit.

(*Pat begins to back slowly into the bathroom.*)

WAYNE: What are you doing? Look—calm down, it's no big deal.

(*Pat exits into the bathroom.*)

WAYNE: Are you getting me more aspirin?

(*She enters with the pistol.*)

WAYNE: I didn't think so.

PAT: Don't move.

WAYNE: I won't.

PAT: What the hell are you doing with a picture of me in your pocket!

WAYNE: Most girls would be flattered.

PAT: Little Brothers of Charity, God!

WAYNE: What are you going to do?

PAT: For starters, I am going to demand an explanation.

WAYNE: What are you going to do if I don't have one? (*Beat.*)

PAT: I don't know. (*Beat.*) What do you mean? You've got to have one!

WAYNE: I really don't feel very well.

PAT: Neither do I!

WAYNE: I'm sorry!

PAT: Don't be!

WAYNE: Do you think you could put the gun down?

PAT: I doubt it.

WAYNE: I figured. (*Beat.*) What's wrong with Wayne?

PAT: What?

WAYNE: You called me a wimp.

PAT: Brother. You really take the cake.

WAYNE: The one thing in my life I *wasn't* worried about, and you ruin it forever.

PAT: I want to know what you're doing here, understand?

WAYNE: I suppose you think John Wayne was a wimp.

PAT: Wayne was not his first name, *John* was his first name, *Duke* was his first name.

WAYNE: I don't see what difference that makes.

PAT: I'll give it to you in two words: Wayne Newton.

WAYNE: Well thanks a lot. You think it's nice to wreck a man's name for him? You think that's an act of kindness?

PAT: Sorry.

WAYNE: I'm afraid it's a little late for that.

PAT: Wait a minute. Wait a minute. Oh, boy. Oh, boy.

WAYNE: What?

PAT: Shut up, you! Stay right where you are! (*She moves to a bureau.*)

WAYNE: How did you get to be such a hostile person?
(*She rummages through the top drawer with one hand, the pistol in the other still pointed at Wayne.*)

WAYNE: Is that what they taught you back in Seattle? Or did you let the city do this to you?

PAT: Just shut up!

WAYNE: Charming. Winning. You've got a winning way about you.

PAT: (*She slams one drawer and opens another.*) I mean it!

WAYNE: You let the city do this to you, didn't you. You gave in. You let the violence of the city infect you. You're an infected person, Pat.

PAT: Wayne? Don't call me Pat.

WAYNE: So you had some bad breaks. The violence of the city touched you, and how did you respond? With more violence. It *is* possible to fight violence with compassion, you know. It is possible to live as a sensitive person in an insensitive environment.

PAT: (*Rummaging violently through a drawer.*) Where the fuck is it!

WAYNE: But no. You've given up your humanity and now you're playing by the city's rules. Congratulations.
(*Pat pulls a pair of binoculars from a drawer.*)

PAT: Gotcha!

WAYNE: Pat? What are you doing, Pat?

PAT: Shut up. (*She goes to him.*)

WAYNE: I don't understand, Pat. What's happened to us?

PAT: Hold them. (*She gives him the binoculars.*) Look through them.

WAYNE: Pat.

PAT: Do it!
(*He does.*)

PAT: Now wave, sucker.

WAYNE: (*A little wave.*) Hi. Remember me?

PAT: (*Holding the gun out in both hands.*) Bang! Bang, bang, bang, bang!

WAYNE: You're verbalizing your anger, this is good.

PAT: Bang!

WAYNE: Excuse me. Pat? Suggestion.

PAT: Bang!

WAYNE: Better you don't have a loaded gun in your hands when you're working through hostilities.

PAT: Bang!

WAYNE: I'm sorry you feel this way, Pat.

PAT: Oh, how I hate you.

WAYNE: Hate is an ugly word.

PAT: You terrified me!

WAYNE: We're all scared, every one of us. That's what this city does to people.

PAT: You're sick!

WAYNE: You want to spend some time in my moccasins before you say such a thing.

PAT: I wouldn't touch your creepy moccasins!

WAYNE: I can see we're not communicating.

PAT: You give me the creeps!

WAYNE: There's no point continuing this, you're not listening.

PAT: Peeping Tom! Voyeur!

WAYNE: Name-caller!

PAT: Sickness!

    (*Silence.*)

WAYNE: That was unkind and uncalled for. May I please have a pair of trousers?

PAT: (*Mimicking.*) May I please have a pair of trousers? Sorry, Wayne. Fresh out.

WAYNE: Oh, boy. You know, Socrates really hit it on the head.

PAT: *What?*

WAYNE: It's fascinating. How little a person's exterior reveals of her true self.

PAT: *Socrates?*

WAYNE: He also had a few words on the subject of the shrew.

PAT: You're going to Bellvue. Now. (*She goes to the telephone, still covering Wayne with the pistol.*)

WAYNE: God, how I fantasized about you. So pretty, so sexy, and yet I thought, so shy, so lonely. Ha! I thought maybe, just maybe, I had found someone special.

PAT: (*On the phone.*) Yes, please, the listing for Bellvue Hospital.

WAYNE: Someone wonderful.

PAT: (*On the phone.*) Outpatient, inpatient, how should I know? The number for lunatics. (*Beat.*) Yeah, well you have a real nice day yourself! (*She slams down the phone.*) All you get in this city is attitude.

WAYNE: Why don't you just call the police?

PAT: Good idea.

WAYNE: Nine-one-one.

PAT: Nine-one-one, right. (*She dials.*)

WAYNE: When you're done, I'd like to talk to them, too.

PAT: (*On the phone.*) Hello?

WAYNE: You see, I was shot by a neighbor with an unlicensed gun. (*Pause.*)

PAT: (*On the phone.*) Yes, I'm here. Oh, just … Keep up the good work. (*Beat.*) Well I'm sorry! (*She hangs up. She droops.*) God, it's hot. (*She wilts into a chair. Wayne and Pat look at each other. Long pause.*)

WAYNE: (*Finally.*) You should get out of the city in August.

PAT: I work.

WAYNE: Oh, yeah.

PAT: Although I don't know why, it's so slow this time of year you get nothing in tips.

WAYNE: I know.

PAT: Oh, yeah? You're a waiter?

WAYNE: Actor. But, yeah. When I'm between things.

PAT: What exactly are you between?

WAYNE: Well, nothing lately.

PAT: Right. Do you think one of those cigarettes would light?

WAYNE: Help yourself.

(*She fishes out a pink, damp cigarette from the pack.*)

PAT: I quit smoking two weeks ago.

WAYNE: I know.

PAT: God!

WAYNE: Sorry, sorry. I just … couldn't help noticing. I admired you for that.

PAT: Thanks.

WAYNE: This isn't going to make you start up again, is it?

PAT: We'll see. No. I don't think so. Want one?

WAYNE: See if yours lights first.

(*She lights the cigarette.*)

PAT: Gotcha. (*She savors an inhalation.*) Why? Why?

WAYNE: I guess … I guess I was lonely, it was hot, I started going up to the roof to cool off …

PAT: No, no. no. (*Taking another drag of the cigarette.*) Why does *this* have to be bad for your health? Why can't it be good for you?

WAYNE: Life's like that.

PAT: You're right, if I smoke this one I'll just light up another. You want it?

WAYNE: Actually, when I saw that you'd quit smoking, I did too.

PAT: So why do you carry cigarettes?

WAYNE: Willpower. That pack's two weeks old.

PAT: You quit because of me?

WAYNE: I thought if we ever got together, you'd prefer a nonsmoker.

PAT: Amazing.

WAYNE: I really don't do this, you know.

PAT: What?

WAYNE: *You* know.

PAT: Peek at girls through binoculars?

WAYNE: Honest to God, you're the only one. (*Pause.*)

PAT: How can I know if you're telling the truth?

WAYNE: I swear. (*Pause.*)

PAT: Geez, Wayne. Why didn't you just come over and knock on my door?

WAYNE: I did. You shot me. (*Pause.*)

PAT: You mean that's what you were ...

WAYNE: Tonight was the night.

PAT: Oh, God. (*Pause.*)

WAYNE: You can take day trips to Jones Beach, it's great, we both have Mondays off ...

PAT: How did you know Monday was my ... Forget I asked.

WAYNE: What do you say?

PAT: Let's just hold our horses here, shall we, mister?

WAYNE: Right. Sorry. (*Pause.*) I love Seattle.

PAT: You've been there?

WAYNE: Two months, Seattle Rep. I loved it.

PAT: They never cast me. (*Beat.*)

WAYNE: The pay wasn't so hot. (*Pause.*)

PAT: Where are you from, originally?

WAYNE: Shawnee Mission.

PAT: Where the hell is that?

WAYNE: Kansas.

PAT: Oh. Never heard of it.

WAYNE: Nobody has.

PAT: Kansas, huh?

WAYNE: Landlocked. First time I saw the Atlantic Ocean I fell in love with it. If I could live in the ocean, I would.

PAT: I grew up by the other one.

WAYNE: Do you swim?

PAT: Too cold around Seattle.

WAYNE: Oh, yeah. But you do?

PAT: Swim? From time to time.

WAYNE: Good. (*Pause.*)

PAT: Sexy?

WAYNE: What? Oh. Wow. Yes.

PAT: You're out of your mind.

WAYNE: You're not seeing anyone, are you.

PAT: You noticed.

WAYNE: Why aren't you?

PAT: Don't push it, Wayne.

WAYNE: Right. (*Beat.*)

PAT: I might have killed you.

WAYNE: Forget it.

PAT: I will not forget it! You could be dead right now! Or hideously ... Oh, God. One thing's for damn sure ... (*Picking up the pistol.*) ... the gun goes straight back to Mother.

WAYNE: You're not telling me you're going to put it in the mail?

PAT: Oh. No. I suppose not. (*She goes into the kitchen, steps on a pedal and the wastebasket opens.*)

WAYNE: You can't put a pistol down the chute.

PAT: Why not?

WAYNE: Might be a little rough on your super when he turns on the compactor.

PAT: Well what the hell am I supposed to ... (*She goes to the upstage windows and opens one.*)

WAYNE: You're going to let some little kid find it in the courtyard? (*She wheels on him.*)

PAT: *So make a suggestion!*

WAYNE: Looks like you're stuck with it.

PAT: I never want to see it again!

WAYNE: Once you let violence into your life it's hard to get it out.

PAT: You! You don't think what you've been doing to me is violent? With your binoculars? That's breaking and entering, Wayne!

WAYNE: I know, I know.

PAT: It's worse!

WAYNE: If I could possibly undo it all, start over, go out that door and come in again ... I like you.

PAT: (*Hollering.*) Well I like you, too, goddammit!

WAYNE: Honest?

PAT: Oh, shut up!

WAYNE: Right.

PAT: Now what am I going to do with this lousy gun?

WAYNE: The traditional thing for this neighborhood would be to throw it in the East River.

PAT: I could do that. I could do that.

WAYNE: Although it would be unfortunate if a cop saw you.

PAT: God. Oh, God.

WAYNE: Pat?

PAT: Wayne?

WAYNE: All those nights. Why didn't you just pull the shade? (*Pause.*)

PAT: What you are suggesting is obnoxious, totally. Obnoxious. I'll go get you a pair of pants. (*Pat exits into the bedroom. A moment later she re-enters, goes to the upstage windows and pulls the shades down violently. She exits again. She re-enters, carrying a pair of baggy painter's pants.*) It's not going to happen, we're not going to overcome a grotesque beginning and end up in each other's arms, okay? (*Beat.*) Just so that's clear.

WAYNE: Right.

(*She gives him the trousers, he turns his back to put them on.*)

WAYNE: It's about time for your rum and Tab.

PAT: What?

WAYNE: Every night about this time you pour a shot of rum into a glass of Tab, you turn on the TV, you watch the news, you turn off the TV, you write a letter or something, maybe it's a diary, I could never tell for sure, you wash the glass and then you turn off the lights and go to bed. (*Pause.*)

PAT: Are you *trying* to depress me?

WAYNE: No, no. Sorry. I *like* ritual.

PAT: Goodnight, Wayne.

WAYNE: Yeah. Well. Goodnight.

(*She opens the door for him.*)

PAT: (*Meaning the bullet-hole in the door.*) I'm going to have to get that fixed.

WAYNE: Oh. Yeah. I'm sorry.

PAT: No, *I'm* ... Good-bye, Wayne.

WAYNE: Good-bye, Pat.

(*He exits. She closes the door. There's a knock on the door. She opens it.*)

WAYNE: It's not my name, is it?

PAT: Good-bye, Wayne.

WAYNE: 'Cause I'll change it.

PAT: You don't have to change a thing, you just have to get out of here.

WAYNE: Right.

PAT: Now.

WAYNE: Right.

(*She slowly closes the door on him. She locks it several times. She goes to the refrigerator, takes out a can of Tab and a tray of ice cubes. She takes a bottle of rum from a cupboard and makes herself a rum and Tab. She takes it to the table. She turns on the television set and sits. She drinks.*)

NEWSCASTER: ... and Warner Wolff on sports.

(*She makes a dash for the TV and switches it off. She goes back to the table and sits. She opens a notebook and uncaps a pen.*)

PAT: It's a journal. (*She writes the day's date in the journal and stops. She caps the pen and closes the notebook. She takes her drink to the sink and pours it out. She begins to wash out the glass, then stops. She puts the glass down and goes into the bedroom. She re-enters, carrying two one-piece bathing suits. She regards them critically, first one, then the other. She shrugs. She lays them over a chair. She switches off the light and the stage is in darkness. Then she raises one of the window-shades and the room is lit by the glow of the city. She stands in silhouette, looking out anxiously. She droops, disappointed.*) What can I say? I'm sorry. (*She pulls down the shade, and the lights of the city disappear.*)

(*Two beats.*)

(*A knock on the door. Instantly, Pat switches on the light.*)

(*Blackout.*)

END OF PLAY

Love Lace

By Robert Patrick

ROBERT PATRICK's fifty plays in print include *My Cup Panneth Over, Mutual Benefit Life, Untold Decades,* and *Michelangelo's Models.* His *Kennedy's Children* won the Glasgow Citizens Theatre World Playwrighting Award. In honor of his pioneering play about Gay teenagers, two consecutive Manhattan Boro Presidents declared "Blue is for Boys" Weekends in Manhattan. He received the International Thespian Society's Founders Award "for services to theatre and to youth." His first novel, *Temple Slave,* is the only book about the origins of Off-Off Broadway theatre written by a participant. He welcomes correspondence at 1837 N. Alexandria Ave., #211, Los Angeles, CA 90027.

ORIGINAL PRODUCTION
Love Lace premiered at New York's W.P.A. Theatre in 1974, directed by Neil Flanagan, starring Jeremy Abbot and Sheri Burke.

LOVE LACE

The setting is a bare stage. A man and woman in modern dress enter.

HE: This place. This place is a dead-end street.

SHE: This place is an emergency ward where we bring people who throw fits in public places.

HE: This place is your Mafia hangout where you've brought me to rub me out because you're not supposed to fall in love with outsiders.

SHE: This place is a psychiatrist's office where I have to listen to your ravings.

HE: This place is a museum where I stand around as exhibit A, the first in your line-up of past works.

SHE: This place is a ladies' room in a swank nightclub where you, a weeping drunk blonde, have been brought by your girlfriend after an attack of the Martini maudlins.

HE: This place is the underground laboratory of a militant dyke organization where you've brought me to castrate me.

SHE: This place is a street corner where you stand around in a beanie yelling insults at every girl that passes.

HE: This place is a family therapy office where we get it all out throwing accusations at each other.

SHE: This place is a stalled elevator on the way to a divorce court where you make one last desperate try to win me back.

HE: This place is a party in a penthouse where you throw dry epithets at a cast-off gigolo.

SHE: This place is the waiting room at an expensive insane asylum where I wait helplessly for them to come and get you.

HE: This place is the waiting room at an expensive insane asylum where I have brought you and where you think you have brought me, causing me the pain that only a devout and puzzled lover can know as the only woman for him disintegrates before his eyes.

SHE: This place is a campus soda shop where the wittiest boy in Lit 101 wears himself out being clever to a new girl.

HE: This place is a torture-chamber in the basement of a slick-magazine skyscraper where you are trying to extract the secrets of my genius.

SHE: This place is a littered attic where a madman has brought a trusting fan whom he suddenly alcoholically menaces and murders.

HE: This place is a black bar where a jaded white lady goes for a few thrills with a vital stud from a member of a subjugated race.

SHE: This place is a World War I hospital where a gas-crazed lieutenant castigates and derides the nurse who has never heard such language before.

HE: This place is a dude ranch where a lady waiting for a divorce flirts with a wrangler while always clutching her plaited quirt.

SHE: This place is an expensive hotel suite where a girl trying to humor a passing lover finds herself requested to do sick, sado-masochistic games.

HE: This place is a gutter slum where a backstairs maid tries to wheedle her passionate, devoted admirer into flattering her fantasies of grandeur.

SHE: This place is a twenties Ziegfeld Follies revue where a baggy-pants comedian laces into a showgirl and honks his nose.

HE: This place is a midwestern motel where Humbert Humbert labors on the edge of neuralgia trying to amuse his pathetic, petty, uncomprehending Lolita.

SHE: This place is a Los Angeles bungalow where Joan Crawford slowly realizes that the helpless young man she has taken under her wing is in reality a deteriorating psychotic.

HE: This place is an English heath where Joan Fontaine is wracked with crippling suspicion about the marvelous man she will marry.

SHE: This place is a bad play about a brave woman realizing she has grown beyond a man whom she was cruel to let love her in the first place.

HE: This place is a gorgeous cliff beside a Big Sur sunset where Kim Novak fights her sincere passion for a man she was only out to trick and toy with.

SHE: This place is a Noel Coward drawing-room where two decent people, refined through suffering, meet for one last time and part wistfully like mature adults.

HE: This place is a Bernard Shaw parlor where a lovely and gracious matron seeks the kindest way to tell a young poet that she cannot accept his passion.

SHE: This place is a metropolitan cubbyhole where a working girl and an ambitious boy have tried very hard to be happy, but could find no suitable roles in which to comfort one another.

HE: This place is a famous landmark in the twenty-first century, with a plaque that says: "Her He and She, despite the beleaguering collapse of a corrupt culture, came to a new and fruitful understanding beyond all roles and all differences; here the battle of man and woman died in an historic compromise, and a new millennium was founded from a love that inspired the whole wailing world. Gloria in Excelsis Amo Perpetuum."

SHE: This place is a theater where we fell in love with one another as lead actors in a romantic play.

HE: This place is the dressing-room after that play where we found it was one another after all.

SHE: This place is a freeway motel where we went after the last performance and found that it was only the roles that we loved.

HE: This place is the chapel where we married one another in the strange cold kaleidoscopic light of a full moon through a florious rose window.

SHE: This place is a theater we have rented to act out the play again, only to find that our belief is gone.

HE: This place is a secret temple of Venus, where gossamer paisley hangings wave in the faint wind from strumming lutes, and a delicate perfumed fountain splashes and giggles like the multicolored houris who shuffle whispering about, serving our love, gossiping about our love.

SHE: This place is a whorehouse where Svengali hypnotizes Trilby, bringing her again and again to the verge of belief.

HE: This place is a primordial retreat, an immemorial cavern where a wounded wanderer stumbles to fall on his knees before the image of woman triumphant, gorgeous, muliebrious eternal, chthonic, conquering, bold.

SHE: This place is a quiet, small, safe nest away from a garbaged, gutted city, where a woman rests for a moment more, perhaps for the moments that make a few hours, with a tender man in whom there is no harm, to leave his life on the morning no matter what happens.

HE: This place is a quiet time machine, designed to bear one man and woman through the night until dawn, to leave them back where they started, forever reconciling frivolous differences in the quest of an untroubled unity, forever young, forevermore in love.

SHE: This place is a great repository of wisdom, where an opportunistic librarian seduces a poetry-struck youngster.

HE: This place is an interlaced forest glen, where a princess caresses a beggar, and finds she has disenchanted herself from cynicism, and he was her prince all along.

SHE: This place is a place of religious punishment, where a girl too proud and too callow is proved to herself to be human and needful and warm.

HE: This place is a place of psychedelic revelation, where great world-weaving patterns try themselves out like magical tapestries, and are tested by entangled lovers, and frayed and discarded until they find at last the proper patterning to cover and coddle and control them.

SHE: This place is a mess.

HE: This place is the modular, mystic beginning of order.

SHE: This place is a dell where lovers kneel.

HE: This place is a monument.

SHE: This place is a maze spun by a magician.

HE: This place is a nest built by a suitor.

SHE: This place is yours.

HE: This place is yours.

SHE: This place is ours.

HE: This place is cool.

SHE: This place is warm.

HE: This place is any place we truly want to be.

SHE: This place is where I want to be.

(*Curtain.*)

END OF PLAY

Aria Da Capo

A Play in One Act
By Edna St. Vincent Millay

EDNA ST. VINCENT MILLAY, (1892-1950) was born in Rockland, Maine, on February 22, 1892. She began writing early, her work being first published when she was 14 years old. She had published three books of poetry: *Renascence* (1917), *A Few Figs From Thistles* (1920); and *Second April* (1921), when she received the Pulitzer Prize for Poetry in 1923 for *The Harp-Weaver and Other Poems*. Millay was the first woman to be awarded this prize.

In addition to lyric and satiric poetry, Millay wrote over 100 sonnets, the libretto for an opera, and six works in dramatic form, one of which, *Aria da Capo*, is produced many times a year on stage and television and in numerous languages. Described as as "antiwar play," critics have called it "a devastating indictment of man's folly, his greed, his quarrels, his war-like games." Millay's later works reveal an increasing interest in social causes; she frequently wrote and spoke publicly on behalf of democracy and freedom.

The poet graduated from Vassar College in 1917 and later received several honorary degrees from other academic institutions. She was a member of the American Academy of Arts and Letters, and, in 1943 The Poetry Society of America awarded her a medal for her contribution to the humanities. Millay died on October 19, 1950.

ORIGINAL PRODUCTION
Aria da Capo was originally produced by the Provincetown Players, New York City, with the following cast:

Pierrot	Harrison Dowd
Columbine	Norma Millay
Cothurnus	Hugh Ferriss
Corydon	Charles Ellis
Thyrsis	James Light

CHARACTERS
Pierrot
Columbine
Cothurnus, Masque of Tragedy
Thyrsis (shepherd)
Corydon (shepherd)

SCENE
A Stage

Aria Da Capo

The curtain rises on a stage set for a Harlequinade, a merry black and white interior. Directly behind the footlights, and running parallel with them, is a long table, covered with a gay black and white cloth, on which is spread a banquet. At the opposite ends of this table, seated on delicate thin-legged chairs with high backs, are Pierrot and Columbine, dressed according to the tradition, excepting that Pierrot is in lilac, and Columbine in pink. They are dining.

COLUMBINE:
>Pierrot, a macaroon! I cannot *live*
>Without a macaroon!

PIERROT:
>My only love,
>You are *so* intense ... Is it Tuesday,
>Columbine?—
>I'll kiss you if it's Tuesday.

COLUMBINE:
>It is Wednesday,
>If you must know ... Is this my artichoke,
>Or yours?

PIERROT:
>Ah, Columbine, as if it mattered!
>Wednesday ... Will it be Tuesday,
>then, tomorrow,
>By any chance?

COLUMBINE:
>To-morrow will be—Pierrot,
>That isn't funny!

PIERROT:
>I thought it rather nice.
>Well, let us drink some wine and lose our heads

And love each other.

COLUMBINE:

Pierrot, don't you love

Me now?

PIERROT:

La, what a woman! how should I know?
Pour me some wine: I'll tell you presently.

COLUMBINE:

Pierrot, do you know, I think you drink too
much.

PIERROT:

Yes, I dare say I do ... Or else too little.
It's hard to tell. You see, I am always wanting
A little more than what I have,—or else
A little less. There's something wrong. My
dear,
How many fingers have you?

COLUMBINE:

La, indeed,

How should I know? It always takes me one
hand
To count the other with. It's too confusing.
Why?

PIERROT:

Why? —I am a student, Columbine;
And search into all matters.

COLUMBINE:

La, indeed?—

Count them yourself, then!

PIERROT:

No. Or, rather, *nay.*

'Tis of no consequence ... I am become
A painter, suddenly,—and you impress me—
Ah, yes!—six orange bull's-eyes, four green
pin-wheels,
And one magenta jelly-roll,—the title
As follows: *Woman Taking In Cheese From
Fire-Escape.*

COLUMBINE:

Well, I like that! So that is all I've meant
To you!

PIERROT:

Hush! All at once I am become
A pianist. I will image you in sound ...
On a new scale ... Without tonality ...
Vivace senza tempo senza tutto ...
Title: *Uptown Express at Six o'Clock.*
Pour me a drink.

COLUMBINE:

Pierrot, you work too hard.
You need a rest. Come on out into the garden,
And sing me something sad.

PIERROT:

Don't stand so near me!
I am become a socialist. I love
Humanity, but I hate people. Columbine,
Put on your mittens, child; your hands are cold.

COLUMBINE:

My hands are *not* cold!

PIERROT:

Oh, I am sure they are.
And you must have a shawl to wrap about you,
And sit by the fire.

COLUMBINE:

Why, I'll do no such thing!
I'm hot as a spoon in a teacup!

PIERROT:

Columbine,

I'm a philanthropist. I know I am,
Because I feel so restless. Do not scream,
Or it will be the worse for you!

COLUMBINE:

Pierrot,
My vinaigrette! I cannot *live* without
My vinaigrette!

PIERROT:

My only love, you are

So fundamental! … How would you like
 to be
An actress, Columbine?—I am become
Your manager.

COLUMBINE:

     Why, Pierrot, I can't act.

PIERROT:

Can't act! Can't act! La, listen to the woman!
What's that to do with the price of furs?—
 You're blonde,
Are you not? —you have no education, have
 you? —
Can't act! You under-rate yourself, my dear!

COLUMBINE:

Yes, I suppose I do.

PIERROT:

      As for the rest,
I'll teach you how to cry, and how to die,
And other little tricks; and the house will love
 you.
You'll be a star by five o'clock … That is,
If you will let me pay for your apartment.

COLUMBINE:

Let you? —well, that's a good one!
Ha! Ha! Ha!
But why?

PIERROT:

    But why? —well, as to that, my dear,
I cannot say. It's just a matter of form.

COLUMBINE:

Pierrot, I'm getting tired of caviar
And peacocks' livers. Isn't there something
 else
That people eat?—some humble vegetable,
That grows in the ground?

PIERROT:

    Well, there are mushrooms.

COLUMBINE:

       Mushrooms!

That's so! I had forgotten ... mush-
   rooms ... mushrooms ...
I cannot *live* with ... How do you like this
   gown?
PIERROT:
Not much. I'm tired of gowns that have the
   waist-line
About the waist, and the hem around the bot-
   tom,—
And women with their breasts in front of
   them!—
Zut and ehè! Where does one go from here!
COLUMBINE:
Here's a persimmon, love. You always liked
   them.
PIERROT:
I am become a critic; there is nothing
I can enjoy ... However, set it aside;
I'll eat it between meals.
COLUMBINE:
                              Pierrot, do you know,
Sometimes I think you're making fun of me.
PIERROT:
My love, by yon black moon, you wrong us both.
COLUMBINE:
There isn't a sign of a moon, Pierrot.
PIERROT:
                              Of course not.
There never was. "Moon's" just a word to
   swear by.
"Mutton!"—now *there's* a thing you can lay
   the hands on,
And set the tooth in! Listen, Columbine:
I always lied about the moon and you.
Food is my only lust.
COLUMBINE:
                              Well, eat it, then,
For Heaven's sake, and stop your silly
   noise!
I haven't heard the clock tick for an hour.

PIERROT:

It's ticking all the same. If you were a
      fly,
You would be dead by now. And if I were a
      parrot,
I could be talking for a thousand years!
      (*Enter* Cothurnus.)

PIERROT:

Hello, what's this, for God's sake? —What's
      the matter?
Say, whadda you mean? —get off the stage,
      my friend,
And pinch yourself,—you're walking in your
      sleep!

COTHURNUS:

I never sleep.

PIERROT:

                    Well, anyhow, clear out.
You don't belong on here. Wait for your own
      scene!
Whadda you think this is,—a dress rehearsal?

COTHURNUS:

Sir, I am tired of waiting. I will wait
No longer.

PIERROT:

                    Well, but whadda you going to do?
The scene is set for me!

COTHURNUS:

                                        True, sir; yet I
Can play the scene.

PIERROT:

                    Your scene is down for later!

COTHURNUS:

That, too, is true, sir; but I play it now.

PIERROT:

Oh, very well! —Anyway, I am tired
Of black and white. At least, I think I am.
      (*Exit Columbine.*)

PIERROT:
　　Yes, I am sure I am. I know what I'll do! —
　　I'll go and strum the moon, that's what I'll
　　　　do …
　　Unless, perhaps … you never can tell …
　　　　I may be,
　　You know, tired of the moon. Well, any-
　　　　way,
　　I'll go find Columbine … And when I find
　　　　her,
　　I will address her thus: *"Ehè*, Pierrette!"—
　　There's something in that.
　　　　　　　　(*Exit Pierrot.*)

COTHURNUS:
　　　　　　　　　　　　You, Thyrsis! Corydon!
　　Where are you?

THYRSIS: *(off stage)*
　　　　　　　　Sir, we are in our dressing-room!

COTHURNUS:
　　Come out and do the scene.

CORYDON: *(off stage)*
　　　　　　　　　　You are mocking us!—
　　The scene is down for later.

COTHURNUS:
　　　　　　　　　　　　That is true;
　　But we will play it now. I am the scene.
　　(*Seats himself on high place in back of stage.*)
　　(*Enter Corydon and Thyrsis.*)

CORYDON:
　　Sir, we were counting on this little hour.
　　We said, "Here is an hour, —in which to think
　　A mighty thought, and sing a trifling song,
　　And look at nothing." —And, behold! the hour,
　　Even as we spoke, was over, and the act begun,
　　Under our feet!

THYRSIS:
　　　　　　　　Sir, we are not in the fancy
　　To play the play. We had thought to play it
　　　　later.

CORYDON:

Besides, this is the setting for a farce.
Our scene requires a wall; we cannot build
A wall of tissue-paper!

THYRSIS:

We cannot act
A tragedy with comic properties!

COTHURNUS:

Try it and see. I think you'll find you can.
One wall is like another. And regarding
The matter of your insufficient mood,
The important thing is that you speak the lines,
And make the gestures. Wherefore I shall
    remain
Throughout, and hold the prompt-book. Are
    you ready?

CORYDON-THYRSIS: (*Sorrowfully.*)

Sir, we are always ready.

COTHURNUS:

Play the play!
(*Corydon and Thyrsis move the table and chairs to one side out of the
way, and seat themselves in a half-reclining position on the floor.*)

THYRSIS:

How gently in the silence, Corydon,
Our sheep go up the bank. They crop a
    grass
That's yellow where the sun is out, and black
Where the clouds drag their shadows. Have
    you noticed
How steadily, yet with what a slanting eye
They graze?

CORYDON:

As if they thought of other things.
What say you, Thyrsis, do they only question
Where next to pull? —Or do their far minds
    draw them
Thus vaguely north of west and south of
    east?

THYRSIS:

One cannot say ... The black lamb wears

    its burdocks
As if they were a garland,—have you noticed?
Purple and white—and drinks the bitten
    grass
As if it were a wine.

CORYDON:

                                  I've noticed that.
What say you, Thyrsis; shall we make a song
About a lamb that thought himself a shepherd?

THYRSIS:

Why, yes!—that is, why,—no. (I have for-
    gotten my line.)

COTHURNUS: (*Prompting.*)

"I know a game worth two of that."

THYRSIS:

Oh, yes ... I know a game worth two of
    that!
Let's gather rocks, and build a wall between
    us;
And say that over there belongs to me,
And over here to you!

CORYDON:

                       Why,—very well.
And say you may not come upon my side
Unless I say you may!

THYRSIS:

                     Nor you on mine!
And if you should, 'twould be the worse for you!
    (*They weave a wall of colored crêpe paper ribbons from the centre front
    to the centre back of the stage, fastening the ends to Columbine's chair
    in front and to Pierrot's chair in the back.*)

CORYDON:

Now, there's a wall a man may see across,
But not attempt to scale.

THYRSIS:

                  An excellent wall.

CORYDON:

Come, let us separate, and sit alone
A little while, and lay a plot whereby
We may outdo each other.

(*They seat themselves on opposite sides of the wall.*)

PIERROT: (*Off stage.*)

> *Ehè* Pierrette!

COLUMBINE: (*Off stage.*)
My name is Columbine! Leave me alone!

THYRSIS: (*Coming up to the wall.*)
Corydon, after all, and in spiteof the fact
I started it myself, I do not like this
So very much. What is the sense of saying
I do not want you on my side of the wall?
It is a silly game. I'd much prefer
Making the little song you spoke of making,
About the lamb, you know, that thought himself
A shepherd! —what do you say?
> (*Pause.*)

CORYDON: (*At wall.*)
(I have forgotten the line.)

COTHURNUS: (*Prompting.*)
"How do I know this isn't a trick?"

CORYDON:
Oh, yes … How do I know this isn't a
    trick
To get upon my land?

THYRSIS:
> Oh, Corydon,
You *know* it's not a trick. I do not like
The game, that's all. Come over here, or
    let me
Come over there.

CORYDON:
> It is a clever trick
To get upon my land. (*Seats himself as before.*)

THYRSIS:
> Oh, very well!

(*Seats himself as before. To himself.*)
I think I never knew a sillier game.

CORYDON: (*Coming to wall.*)
Oh, Thyrsis, just a minute! —all the water
Is on your side the wall, and the sheep are
    thirsty.
I hadn't thought of that.

THYRSIS:

                                                   Oh, hadn't you?

CORYDON:
  Why, what do you mean?

THYRSIS:

                                 What do I mean? —I mean
That I can play a game as well as you can.
And if the pool is on my side, it's on
My side, that's all.

CORYDON:
                         You mean you'd let the sheep
Go thirsty?

THYRSIS:
                Well, they're not my sheep. My sheep
Have water enough.

CORYDON:
                Your sheep! You are mad, to call them
Yours—mine—they are all one flock! Thyrsis,
    you can't mean
To keep the water from them, just because
They happened to be grazing over here
Instead of over there, when we set the wall up?

THYRSIS:
  Oh, can't I? —wait and see! —and if you try,
To lead them over here, you'll wish you hadn't!

CORYDON:
  I wonder how it happens all the water
Is on your side ... I'll say you had an eye
    out
For lots of little things, my innocent friend,
When I said, "Let us make a song," and you said,
"I know a game worth two of that!"

COLUMBINE: (*Off stage.*)
                               Pierrot,
D'you know, I think you must be getting old,
Or fat, or something—stupid, anyway!—
Can't you put on some other kind of collar?

THYRSIS:
  You know as well as I do, Corydon,
I never thought of anything of the kind.
Don't you?

CORYDON:

I *do* not.

THYRSIS:

Don't you?

CORYDON:

Oh, I suppose so.

Thyrsis, let's drop this,—what do you say?—
  it's only
A game, you know ... We seem to be forget-
  ting
It's only a game ... a pretty serious game
It's getting to be, when one of us is willing
To let the sheep go thirsty for the sake of it.

THYRSIS:

I know it, Corydon.
(*They reach out their arms to each other across the wall.*)

COTHURNUS: (*Prompting.*)

"But how do I know?—"

THYRSIS:

Oh, yes ... But how do I know this isn't a
  trick
To water your sheep, and get the laugh on me?

CORYDON:

You can't know, that's the difficult thing
  about it,
Of course, —you can't be sure. you have to
  take
My word for it. And I know just how you feel.
But one of us has to take a risk, or else,
Why, don't you see? —the game goes on for-
  ever!...
It's terrible, when you stop to think of it ...
Oh, Thyrsis, now for the first time I feel
This wall is actually a wall, a thing
Come up between us, shutting you away
From me ... I do not know you any more!

THYRSIS:

No, don't say that! Oh, Corydon, I'm willing
To drop it all, if you will! Come on over

And water your sheep! It is an ugly game.
I hated it from the first ... How did it start?
CORYDON:
I do not know ... I do not know ...
   I think
I am afraid of you! —you are a stranger!
I never set eyes on you before! "Come over
And water my sheep," indeed! —They'll be
   more thirsty
Than they are now before I bring them over
Into your land, and have you mixing them up
With yours, and calling them yours, and trying
   to keep them!
                    (*Enter Columbine.*)
COLUMBINE: (*To Cothurnus.*)
   Glummy, I want my hat.
THYRSIS:

                              Take it, and go.

COLUMBINE:
   Take it and go, indeed! Is it my hat,
   Or isn't it? Is this my scene, or not?
   Take it, and go! Really, you know, you two
   Are awfully funny!
                    (*Exit Columbine.*)
THYRSIS:

                         Corydon, my friend,
   I'm going to leave you now and whittle me
   A pipe, or sing a song, or go to sleep.
   When you have come to your senses, let me
      know.
   (*Goes back to where he has been sitting, lies down
   and sleeps.*)
   (*Corydon, in going back to where he has been
   sitting, stumbles over bowl of colored confetti and
   colored paper ribbons.*)
CORYDON:
   Why, what is this? —Red stones—and purple
      stones—
   And stones stuck full of gold! —The ground is

full
Of gold and colored stones! ... I'm glad the
    wall
Was up before I found them! Otherwise,
I should have had to share them. As it is,
They all belong to me ... Unless—(*He
    goes to wall and digs up and down the length
    of it, to see if there are jewels on the other side.*)
    None here—
None here—none here —They all belong to
    me! (*Sits.*)

THYRSIS: (*Awakening.*)
How curious! I thought the little black lamb
Came up and licked my hair; I saw the wool
About its neck as plain as anything!
It must have been a dream. The little black
    lamb
Is on the other side of the wall, I'm sure. (*Goes
    to wall and looks over. Corydon is seated
    on the ground, tossing the confetti up into the
    air and catching it.*)
 Hello, what's that you've got there, Corydon?

CORYDON:
Jewels.

THYRSIS:
        Jewels? —And where did you ever get them—?

CORYDON:
Oh, over here.

THYRSIS:
                You mean to say you found them,
By digging around in the ground for them?

CORYDON: (*Unpleasantly.*)

                                    No, Thyrsis,
By digging down for water for my sheep.

THYRSIS:
Corydon, come to the wall a minute, will you?
I want to talk to you.

CORYDON:

I haven't time.
I'm making me a necklace of red stones.

THYRSIS:

I'll give you all the water that you want
For one of those red stones,—if it's a good one.

CORYDON:

Water? —what for? —what do I want of water?

THYRSIS:

Why, for your sheep!

CORYDON:

My sheep? —I'm not a shepherd!

THYRSIS:

Your sheep are dying of thirst.

CORYDON:

Man, haven't I told you
I can't be bothered with a few untidy
Brown sheep all full of burdocks? —I'm a mer-
    chant.
That's what I am! —And if I set my mind to it
I dare say I could be an emperor!
(*To himself.*) Wouldn't I be a fool to spend
    my time
Watching a flock of sheep go up a hill,
When I have these to play with? —when I have
    these
To think about? —I can't make up my mind
Whether to buy a city, and have a thousand
Beautiful girls to bathe me, and be happy
Until I die, or build a bridge, and name it
The Bridge of Corydon, —and be remembered
After I'm dead.

THYRSIS:

Corydon, come to the wall,
Won't you? —I want to tell you something.

CORYDON:

Hush!
Be off! Be off! Go finish your nap, I tell you!

THYRSIS:
  Corydon, listen: if you don't want your sheep,
  Give them to me.
CORYDON:
                            Be off! Go finish your nap!
  A red one—and a blue one—and a red one—
  And a purple one. —give you my sheep, did
      you say?—
  Come, come! What do you take me for, a fool?
  I've a lot of thinking to do,—and while I'm
      thinking,
  The sheep might just as well be over here
  As over there ... A blue one—and a red one—
THYRSIS:
  But they will die!
CORYDON:
                        And a green one—and a couple
  Of white ones, for a change.
THYRSIS:
                                    Maybe I have
  Some jewels on my side.
CORYDON:
                              And another green one—
  Maybe, but I don't think so. You see, this rock
  Isn't so very wide. It stops before
  It gets to the wall. It seems to go quite deep,
  However.
THYRSIS: (*With hatred.*)
                    I see.
COLUMBINE: (*Off stage.*)
                          Look, Pierrot, there's the moon!
PIERROT: (*Off stage.*)
  Nonsense!
THYRSIS:
          I see.
COLUMBINE: (*Off stage.*)
                    Sing me an old song, Pierrot,—
  Something I can remember.

PIERROT: (*Off stage.*)

Your mind is made of crumbs—like an escallop
Of oysters,—first a layer of crumbs, and then
An oyster taste, and then a layer of crumbs.

THYRSIS: (*Searching.*)

I find no jewels ... but I wonder what
The root of this black weed would do to a man
If he should taste it ... I have seen a sheep
    die,
With half the stalk still drooling from its mouth.
'Twould be a speedy remedy, I should think,
For a festered pride and a feverish ambition.
It has a curious root. I think I'll hack it
In little pieces ... First I'll get me a drink;
And then I'll hack that root in little pieces
As small as dust, and see what the color is
Inside. (*Goes to bowl on floor.*) The pool is very
    clear. I see
A shepherd standing on the brink, with a red
    cloak
About him, and a black weed in his hand ...
'Tis I. (*Kneels and drinks.*)

CORYDON: (*Coming to wall.*)

                    Hello, what are you doing, Thyrsis?

THYRSIS:

Digging for gold.

CORYDON:

                            I'll give you all the gold
You want, if you'll give me a bowl of water.
If you don't want too much, that is to
    say.

THYRSIS:

Ho, so you've changed your mind? —It's differ-
    ent,
Isn't it, when you want a drink yourself?

CORYDON:

Of course it is.

THYRSIS:

                    Well, let me see ... a bowl

Of water,—come back in an hour, Corydon.
I'm busy now.
CORYDON:

                    Oh, Thyrsis, give me a bowl
Of water! —and I'll fill the bowl with jewels,
And bring it back!
THYRSIS:

                  Be off, I'm busy now.
(*He catches sight of the weed, picks it up and
looks at it, unseen by Corydon.*)
Wait! —Pick me out the finest stones you
    have ...
I'll bring you a drink of water presently.
CORYDON: (*Goes back and sits down, with the jewels
before him.*)
A bowl of jewels is a lot of jewels.
THYRSIS: (*Chopping up the weed.*)
I wonder if it has a bitter taste.
CORYDON:
There's sure to be a stone or two among
    them
I have grown fond of, pouring them from one
    hand
Into the other.
THYRSIS:

             I hope it doesn't taste
Too bitter, just at first.
CORYDON:

               A bowl of jewels
Is far too many jewels to give away
And not get back again.
THYRSIS:

                          I don't believe
He'll notice. He's too thirsty. He'll gulp it
    down
And never notice.
CORYDON:

             There ought to be some way
To get them back again ... I could give

him a necklace,
And snatch it back, after I'd drunk the water,
I suppose ... Why, as for that, of course, a
    necklace ...
(*He puts two or three of the colored tapes together
and tries their strength by pulling them, after
which he puts them around his neck and pulls
them, gently, nodding to himself. He gets up and
goes to the wall, with the colored tapes in his
hands.*)
(*Thyrsis in the meantime has poured the pow-
dered root—black confetti—into the pot which
contained the flower and filled it up with wine
from the punch-bowl on the floor. He comes
to the wall at the same time, holding the bowl of
poison.*)

THYRSIS:
Come and get your bowl of water, Corydon.

CORYDON:
Ah, very good! —and for such a gift as that
I'll give you more than a bowl of unset stones.
I'll give you three long necklaces, my friend.
Come closer. Here they are.
(*Puts the ribbons about Thyrsis' neck.*)

THYRSIS: (*Putting bowl to Corydon's mouth.*)
                          I'll hold the bowl
Until you've drunk it all.

CORYDON:
                             Then hold it steady.
For every drop you spill I'll have a stone back
Out of this chain.

THYRSIS:
                        I shall not spill a drop.
(*Corydon drinks, meanwhile beginning to strangle Thyrsis.*)

THYRSIS:
Don't pull the string so tight.

CORYDON:
                       You're spilling the water.

THYRSIS:
You've had enough—you've had enough—stop

pulling
The string so tight!
CORYDON:

                    Why that's not tight at all ...

   How's this?
THYRSIS: (*Drops bowl.*)
                    You're strangling me! Oh, Corydon!
   It's only a game! —and you are strangling me!
CORYDON:
   It's only a game, is it? —Yet I believe
   You've poisoned me in earnest! (*Writhes and pulls the strings tighter,
      winding them about Thyrsis' neck.*)
THYRSIS:

                                        Corydon! (*Dies.*)

CORYDON:
   You've poisoned me in earnest ... I feel so
      cold ...
   So cold ... This is a very silly game ...
   Why do we play it? —let's not play this game
   A minute more ... let's make a little song
   About a lamb ... I'm coming over the wall,
   No matter what you say,—I want to be near
      you ...
   (*Groping his way, with arms wide before him, he
   strides through the frail papers of the wall without
   knowing it, and continues seeking for the wall
   straight across the stage.*)
   Where is the wall? (*Gropes his way back, and
      stands very near Thyrsis without seeing him;
      he speaks slowly.*) There isn't any wall,
   I think. (*Takes a step forward, his foot touches
      Thyrsis' body, and he falls down beside him.*)
   Thyrsis, where is your cloak? —just give me
   A little bit of your cloak!. . . (*Draws corner
   of Thyrsis' cloak over his shoulders, falls across
   Thyrsis' body and dies.*)
   (*Cothurnus closes the prompt-book with a bang,
   arises matter-of-factly, comes down stage, and
   places the table over the two bodies, drawing down
   the cover so that they are hidden from any actors on*

*the stage, but visible to the audience, pushing in
their feet and hands with his boot. He then
turns his back to the audience, and claps his hands
twice.)*

COTHURNUS:

Strike the scene! (*Exit Cothurnus. Enter Pierrot and Columbine.*)

PIERROT:

Don't puff so, Columbine!

COLUMBINE:

                      Lord, what a mess
This set is in! If there's one thing I hate
Above everything else,—even more than getting
    my feet wet—
It's clutter! —He might at least have left the
    scene
The way he found it … don't you say so,
    Pierrot?
(*She picks up punch bowl. They arrange chairs
as before at ends of table.*)

PIERROT:

Well, I don't know. I think it rather diverting
The way it is. (*Yawns, picks up confetti bowl.*)

                           Shall we begin?

COLUMBINE: (*Screams.*)

                                  My God!
What's that there under the table?

PIERROT:

                        It is the bodies
Of the two shepherds from the other play.

COLUMBINE: (*Slowly.*)

How curious to strangle him like that,
With colored paper ribbons.

PIERROT:

                          Yes, and yet
I dare say he is just as dead. (*Pauses. Calls.*)
    Cothurnus!
Come drag these bodies out of here! We can't
Sit down and eat with two dead bodies lying
Under the table! … The audience wouldn't
    stand for it!

COTHURNUS: (*Off stage.*)
  What makes you think so? —Pull down the
    tablecloth
  On the other side, and hide them from the house,
  And play the farce. The audience will forget.
PIERROT:
  That's so. Give me a hand there, Columbine.
  (*Pierrot and Columbine pull down the table*
  cover in such a way that the two bodies are hidden
  from the house, then merrily set their bowls back
  on the table, draw up their chairs, and begin the
  play exactly as before.)
COLUMBINE:
    Pierrot, a macaroon—I cannot *live*
  Without a macaroon!
PIERROT:
                      My only love,
  You are *so* intense! ... Is it Tuesday,
    Columbine?—
  I'll kiss you if it's Tuesday. (*Curtains begin to*
    close slowly.)
COLUMBINE:
                     It is Wednesday,
  If you must know ... Is this my artichoke
  Or yours?
PIERROT:
         Ah, Columbine, as if it mattered!
  Wednesday ... Will it be Tuesday, then to-
    morrow,
  By any chance? ...
    (*Curtain.*)

CURTAIN

AUTHOR'S NOTE

So great is my vexation always, when reading a play, to find its progress constantly being halted and its structure loosened by elaborate explanatory parentheses, that I resolved when I should publish *Aria da Capo* to incorporate into its texts only those explanations the omission of which might confuse the reader or lend a wrong interpretation to the lines. Since, however, *Aria da Capo* was written not only to be read but also to be acted, and being conscious that the exclusion of the usual directions, while clarifying the play to the reader, may make it bare of suggestions and somewhat baffling to the producer, I am adding here some remarks which have been found of value in preparing it for presentation on the stage.

Since the production of *Aria da Capo* by the Provincetown Players, I have received a great many letters from the directors of little theatres, asking for copies of it with a view to producing it. Very often, after I send the play, I receive a letter in reply asking for some suggestions for its presentation, and enclosing direct questions on points that have been difficult. It occurred to me that it would be reasonable to make up a sort of informal prompt-book to send about with the play; and it is that which is printed below. It will be found incomplete, and uneven, in some instances unnecessarily detailed, in others not sufficiently so; all of which is due to the fact that it was put together loosely, from answers to chance questions, rather than logically, as an entity in itself.

SUGGESTIONS FOR THE PRODUCTION OF
ARIA DA CAPO

SETTING:

The setting required is simple:— a grey curtain, a long black table, two slender black high-backed chairs, and a raised platform.

Instead of wings and back-drop the Provincetown Players cleverly utilized painted screens, the heights varying from 6 to 10 feet, these being set right and left of the stage in such manner as to give the effect of depth and distance.

The table, six feet long and two feet wide, has thin legs and is painted black.

When Peirrot and Columbine enter in the final scene, it is not necessary that the table which Cothurnus had replaced shall entirely conceal the bodies of Thyrsis and Corydon. Pierrot and Columbine must ignore them until the lines indicate their discovery, no matter how they may have fallen.

Particular attention must be given to the chairs in this set. They are used to construct the tissue-paper wall, and, although delicate, should be heavy enough to remain solid and steady, up and down stage, without the possibility of an upset when Corydon strides through the wall.

Near the footlights (actors' left) are two sofa pillows, used to represent the rocks against which the shepherds lean. On the left of the stage have another pillow, which Thyrsis places under his head when he lies down to sleep. Use cloth or crêpe paper for these pillows, and have them of spotted black and white material, or of any gay color except red or blue.

Cothurnus occupies a chair upon a platform, up-stage, centre, with two or three steps surrounding it on three sides. Drape this with plain heavy black cloth.

The table covering is important. Its width is equal to that of the added height and width of the table. As it must be moved to cover the bodies of Thyrsis and Corydon, it should be of sufficient weight to prevent slipping. It will be well to experiment with this, to ensure proper performance.

The cover should have black and white spots and striped ends.

The table is set as follows: two large wooden bowls (at least seven inches high and fourteen inches in diameter). One is placed at each end of the table. That at Columbine's end should contain persimmons, pomegranates, grapes and other bright exotic fruits. Pierrot's bowl has confetti and colored paper ribbons, the latter showing plainly over the edge. (If Columbine uses practical macaroons, put them into this bowl.)

Near Columbine, place a practical uncooked artichoke; have this of good size, and nail it to a wooden standard, painted black. At both places there are tall white wooden goblets.

In the centre of the table there should be a curious, grotesque, but very gay flower, standing upright in a pot of wood or heavy paper, which will not break when Thyrsis drops it. Concealed at the root of this plant there should be a small sack of black confetti, to be used in the "poison scene."

The table should be set with nothing but these articles, and yet give the appearance of bounty and elegance.

Place the table parallel with the footlights,—the long side toward the audience.

Columbine's chair is at the actors' right, and Pierrot's opposite— Columbine's hat hangs from her chair-top. Both chairs are festooned with tissue-paper ribbons, at least ten feet long, to be used later by the shepherds to represent their wall. These must be of such a texture as to break readily when Corydon walks through, and a pre-arranged transverse tear or two will assist in the prompt breakage when he does so.

PROPERTIES:

Two white wooden bowls, one filed with fruits and the other with confetti and paper ribbons,—one ribbon to be of cotton or silk, in order to be not too easily broken by Corydon when strangling Thyrsis.

Two tall white wooden goblets.

One artichoke nailed to a standard.

One flower in paper or wooden pot, the root wrapped with black crêpe paper (or use confetti).

Black and white tablecloth.

Macaroons.

Boots and prompt-book for Cothurnus (large flat black book).

Also, if desired, mask of Tragedy for Cothurnus.

Crêpe or tissue streamers of different colors, including no red or blue, for wall.

COSTUMES:

PIERROT: Lavender or lilac satin, preferable a blue-lavender. Care should be taken that the lavender does not turn pink under the stage lights. Pierrot's costume is the conventional smock with wide trousers, with black crepe paper rosettes on the smock, wide white tarleton ruff. Black evening pumps with black rosettes may be worn. Black silk skull-cap.

COLUMBINE: Tight black satin bodice cut very low, with straps over the shoulders, quite like the modern evening gown: very full tarleton skirts of different shades of pink and cerise, reaching to the knees: ruffled bloomers of apple-green tarleton, the ruffles showing below the skirts: black silk stockings and black ballet slippers, laced with green. Hat of lavender crêpe paper, with streamers of gay colors—including, however, no clear red or blue. Hat should be small and very smart—not a *shepherdess* hat. Columbine should be made up to suggest a doll. As originally interpreted she had short light hair, standing out busily all over her head. Long hair should be rolled under to give a *bobbed* effect, or could be arranged in obvious caricature of some extreme modern style, but must look attractive, and must be blonde.

COTHURNUS: Plain toga of dull purple in some heavy, unreflecting material which will fall into large folds, lined with sombre flame-color; a garment with large purple sleeves, of which only the sleeves were visible, was worn under the toga,—but the effect should be classical; heavy boots should be worn, as nearly as possible like the tragic Roman buskin; one end of the great toga is tied into a rough hood which covers the actor's head; a mask may be worn, but it is often difficult to speak through, and, if desired, the actor's face may be made up to represent a mask of Tragedy.

THYRSIS AND CORYDON: These costumes in striking contrast to the elegance of those of Pierrot and Columbine, should be very simple, and very roughly made; short tunics of outing-flannel or some such material—fastened loosely over one shoulder,—one shoulder, as well as most of the back and breast exposed. Legs bare, or swathed from the knee to the ankle in rough strips of the same material. Sandals. Cloaks of heavier, cheap material fastened to the tunics in such a way that they will appear to be simply flung over the shoulder, but actually fastened very cleverly in order to avoid tripping the shepherds, who are continually sitting down on the floor and getting up again.

Thyrsis wears a dark grey tunic and cloak of raw bright red,—but not a turkey-red, as this color will kill the blue of Corydon's cloak. Corydon wears tunic of light grey and cloak of brilliant blue. There must be no red or blue used anywhere in the entire play excepting in the blue and red of these two cloaks. The two shepherds must be so strong and vivid in every way that when Columbine comes in and says, "Is this my scene or not?" it will seem to the audience that it is she, not the shepherds, who is hopelessly out of the scene.

CHARACTERS

PIERROT: Pierrot sees clearly into existing evils and is rendered gaily cynical by them; he is both too indolent and too indifferent to do anything about it. Yet in several lines of the play his actual happiness is seen,—for instance, "Moon's just a word to swear by," in which he expresses his conviction that all beauty and romance are fled from the world. At the end of the play the line, "Yes, and yet I dare say he is just as dead," must not be said flippantly or cynically, but slowly and with much philosophic concentration on the thought. From the moment when Columbine cries, "What's that there under the table?" until Pierrot calls, "Cothurnus, come drag these bodies out of here!" they both stand staring at the two bodies, without moving in any way, or even lifting their eyes. (This same *holding* of the play is used several times also by the shepherds,—for instance, always during the off-stage interpolations, they stand either staring at each other across the wall, or maintaining whatever other position they may have had when the off-stage voice begins speaking, until the interruption is over, when they resume their drama quite as if nobody had spoken.) Columbine's "How curious to strangle him like that" is spoken extremely slowly, in a voice of awe, curiosity, and horror. For a moment the two characters seem almost to feel and be subdued by the tragedy that has taken place. They remain standing very quietly while Cothurnus speaks his final lines off stage, and for a moment after he has said, "The audience will forget"; then very slowly raise their eyes and exchange glances, Pierrot nods his head curtly and says, "That's so"; they set their bowls gaily back on the table, and the play begins again.

Pierrot in such lines as "Ah, Columbine, as if it mattered!" speaks with mock saccharine tenderness; but in such lines as "If you were a fly you would be dead by now!" although he speaks very gaily his malice must be apparent almost even to her; Columbine bores him to death. When he says, "I'll go and strum the moon!" he is for the instant genuinely excited and interested; he is for this moment like a child, and is happy.

COLUMBINE: Pretty and charming, but stupid; she never knows what Pierrot is talking about, and is so accustomed to him that she no longer pretends to understand him; but she is very proud of him, and when he speaks she listens with trustful admiration. Her expression, "I cannot live without" this or that, is a phrase she uses in order to make herself more attractive, because she believes men prefer women to be useless and extravagant; if left to herself she would be a domestic and capable person.

COTHURNUS: This character should be played by a tall and imposing figure which a tremendous voice. The voice of Cothurnus is one of the most important things in the acting play. He should have a voice deeper than the voice used by any of the other persons, should speak weightily and with great dignity, but almost without intonation, and quite without feeling, as if he had said the same words may times before. Only in his last speech may he be permitted a comment on the situation. This speech should be spoken quite as impressively as the others and fully as slowly.

CORYDON AND THYRSIS: These two characters are young, very simple, and childlike; they are acted upon by the force that sits on the back of the stage behind them. More and more as their quarrel advances they begin to see that something is wrong, but they have no idea what to do about it, and they scarcely realize what is happening, the quarrel grows so from little things into big things. Corydon's first vision of the tragedy is in "It's terrible when you stop to think of it." Thyrsis' first vision comes when he looks into the pool; in seeing the familiar reflection he is struck by the unfamiliarity of one aspect of it, the poisonous root; for the first time he realizes that this man who is about to kill with poisoned water his most beloved friend, is none other than Thyrsis *himself,* —"Tis I!" The personalities of Thyrsis and Corydon are not essentially different. They develop somewhat differently, because of the differing circumstances.

When Columbine goes out for the first time she takes with her her artichoke and her wine-glass, also a couple of macaroons, which she nibbles, going out. This helps to get the table cleared. The other articles are removed by the shepherds when they prepare the stage for their scene, in this manner: at the cue "Sir, we are always ready...Play the play!", Corydon and Thyrsis come down-stage, Corydon to Pierrot's end of the table, and Thyrsis to Columbine's; simultaneously, first, they set back the chairs against the wall,

Pierrot's left front, Columbine's right front; next they remove the two big bowls and set them in symmetrical positions on the floor, left front and right front, in such a way that the bowl of confetti may be the mine of jewels for Corydon, and the bowl of fruits, the punch-bowl, may represent the pool of water for Thyrsis; then, taking the table by the two ends, they set it back against the wall, right; next, while Corydon places the two pillows from the left wall on the floor to represent rocks in their pasture, Thyrsis removes from the table everything that is left on it except the table-cloth,—this should be only Pierrot's wine-goblet and the flower in its pot. (The flower is to represent later the poisonous weed which Thyrsis finds, the wine-goblet a drinking-cup beside the pool, the flower-pot a bowl in which to mix the poison and bring it to Corydon.) The two shepherds do this setting of their stage swiftly and silently, then seat themselves at once, in easy but beautiful postures, and remain for a moment looking off as if at their sheep while a complete silence settles over the stage and house,—a *pastoral* silence, if it is possible to suggest it—before they begin to speak.

When Columbine comes in, looking for her hat, she picks up the hat from her chair, now in the centre of the stage near the footlights, in a direct line with Pierrot's, which is centre back, just in front of Cothurnus,—the shepherds having set them in these positions, back to back, in order to have their aid in weaving the wall. After taking her hat, Columbine stands looking at the shepherds to see what is going on. They do not look at her. After a moment Thyrsis, slowly, with his eyes steadfastly on Corydon's, says, "Take it, and go." When Columbine comes in in the final scene, she is wearing the hat. She takes it off, however, as she sits down again at the table, so that the second beginning of the play may recall as vividly as possible to the audience the first beginning.

The Open Road
A One-Act Play
By Brad Slaight

BRAD SLAIGHT is a Los Angeles based actor-comic-writer. He has been on staff and written jokes and sketch material for numerous television shows and radio programs including: *The Tonight Show (NBC); The Sunday Comics (FOX); Into The Night (ABC); Evening at the Improv (A&E); Haywire! (FOX); Cutler Radio Network (SYNDICATED)*, as well as a script for the sitcom *Just the Ten of Us (ABC)*. Recently *National Lampoon* contracted Brad to create special comedy material (350 jokes) for a CD-Rom computer program. He had also written several stage plays, including *Sightings* and *High Tide* and *Class Action*, which received their world premiere at the Tony Award winning American Conservatory Theater in San Francisco. In addition to writing, Brad is a popular actor and stand-up comic who works extensively on TV and in clubs throughout the country. His many television and film credits include *The Young and the Restless, Married...With Children, Unsolved Mysteries*, and *Freshman Dorm*. He was recently voted "Comedian of the Year" by *Playboy.*

CHARACTERS

Amanda Sommers:
The Mother. Amanda loves her husband and her son, but feels that they are both slipping away from her. She believes that people change for the better when they are led, rather than pushed. Amanda is the kind of Mother everyone wishes to have. Strong. Sympathetic. Supportive.

Jack Sommers:
The Father. Jack was once a dreamer, but has long since buckled under to the pressures of responsibility. Tries to do the right thing for his family, even if they don't feel it is the right thing. Jack watches the evening news every night, and it throws him into heated tirades. Jack has a hard time accepting that there are others in the world who don't think and feel the same way he does.

Allen Sommers:
The Son. Just a few weeks ago Allen was a typical seventeen-year-old, wandering aimlessly through life. He enjoyed baseball games, his CD player, and surfing the "net." That was then, this is tonight. The profound change that comes over him may not last long, but it will affect his life forever. He transcends rebellion.

THE OPEN ROAD

The modern living room of the Sommers family. Amanda Sommers, the mother, sits on the couch, reading a book. She pauses occasionally to think about what she has just read. Her literary moment is interrupted by the sound of a car door being slammed shut. Amanda hides the book in a nearby sewing basket and begins to straighten up the living room.

VOICE *(O.S.)*: Damn it Carson! That's the second time this week your kid left his bike in my driveway. *(Pause.)* Well, he's your kid and that makes you responsible!
(The back door slams and Jack Sommers, the father, blusters into the living room. He throws his briefcase and overcoat in a heap, then crosses stage left, looking off into another room.)
AMANDA: You're home early dear.
JACK: What's wrong with him?
AMANDA: I guess he just doesn't care about his bike. The whole family is like that.
JACK: Not Carson's kid. I don't care about Carson's kid. I'm talking about our kid...Allen. What's wrong with him?
AMANDA: Nothing is wrong with Allen.
JACK: What did the doctor say?
AMANDA: What doctor?
(Amanda crosses over and picks up his coat, to avoid answering the question.)
JACK: Dr. Tyler! I was hoping he would have called by now.
AMANDA: Why would Dr. Tyler call?
JACK: Don't do this to me, Amanda.
AMANDA: Do what, Jack?
JACK: There you go again. You're acting like there is nothing wrong, when you know damn well that there is.
(Jack starts to light up a cigarette, Amanda crosses to him and takes it away. Hands him some gum.)

AMANDA: You're doing so well, don't blow it now. Remember what they told you at the clinic . . .

JACK & AMANDA: "When the urge to smoke is gnawing at you, grab some gum and start to chew."

AMANDA: I really don't know why you're so upset.

JACK: I think you do.

AMANDA: I think I don't.

JACK: *(Calmer.)* All right, maybe you don't. Is Allen here?

AMANDA: Yes, he got home before I did. He's in his room.

(Jack leads her to the couch and sits her down, in preparation for bad news.)

JACK: He went over the edge today.

AMANDA: Who did?

JACK: Allen.

AMANDA: Allen went over the edge?

JACK: It shouldn't come as a big surprise. It's been building up for three weeks now.

AMANDA: I really don't know what you are talking about, Jack. Besides, I have to get dinner ready. *(She starts off, Jack stops her with his voice.)*

JACK: Don't try to cover for him, Amanda. It's too late for that now.

AMANDA: He's just going through a phase. That's all.

JACK: A phase?

AMANDA: Yes, all teenagers do. It's part of growing up.

JACK: Amanda, our son thinks he's WALT WHITMAN. I'd say that's more than just a phase.

AMANDA: He doesn't think he's Walt Whitman, he just emulates him. There's nothing wrong with that.

JACK: It's your sister Sheila's fault.

AMANDA: Sheila?

JACK: She's the one who sent him that book of poetry for his birthday, "SPEARS OF GRASS."

AMANDA: *(Correcting him.)* "Leaves of Grass."

JACK: Whatever. His birthday was three weeks ago. That's when all this crazy stuff started.

AMANDA: I admit that book made quite an impression on Allen, but I don't see any harm in that. Walt Whitman was, and still is, a very respected man. One of America's greatest poets. And a real free spirit, did you know that his poems were banned from many libraries because...

JACK: Take the blinds off, Amanda. We have a real problem here.

AMANDA: You're making too much of this.

JACK: I don't think so, you didn't see what he did today. *(Jack crosses to the phone and dials.)*

AMANDA: Who are you calling?

JACK: There is something wrong with our son and I intend to find out what it is. *(Into phone.)* Dr. Tyler Please. *(Pause.)* This is Jack Sommers. *(Pause.)* No, wait…you don't need my records. *(Pause; to Amanda.)* I'm on hold. Music is playing.

AMANDA: Do you recognize the song?

JACK: Recognize the song? No, I…*(Into phone.)* Dr. Tyler? Hello. *(Pause.)* Yes, I'm fine. *(Pause.)* No, I haven't had a cigarette in over three months. Listen, did Allen come in to see you today? *(Pause.)* Yes, I sent him over. *(Pause.)* That's right, he was wearing a big floppy hat and a very loose suit. *(Pause.)* What do you mean he's all right? No fever? Rapid heart rate? *(Pause; dramatic.)* Any sign of drugs?

AMANDA: Jack!

JACK: You sure? *(Pause.)* Did you do any blood tests? *(Pause.)* No need to? Well, you're the Doc. *(Pause.)* Yeah, 'bye. *(Jack hangs up.)*

JACK: He says Allen is fine.

AMANDA: You see.

JACK: Oh, what does Tyler know, anyway. He's a quack.

AMANDA: I really think that you're making a big deal out of nothing.

JACK: Well, I don't.

AMANDA: Actually, I think it's kind of cute.

JACK: So did I…the first week! I didn't think anything of it. I mean, what's wrong with a seventeen-year-old walking around quoting poetry. There's a lot worse things.

AMANDA: Exactly.

JACK: I had no problem with that, although I would have preferred to hear some poetry that was a little more modern, you know, stuff that rhymed.

AMANDA: Not all poetry rhymes, Jack.

JACK: I know that, but that's the kind I like. And quit trying to distract me.

AMANDA: I'm not trying to distract you.

JACK: Like I said, the first week was fine. But the second week…that's when I noticed how much Allen was changing. He wasn't just quoting Walt Whitman, he was talking like him. You know, that old style kind of talk, half talking—half preaching.

AMANDA: I like that kind of talk, it's so romantic.

JACK: I started getting confused, I couldn't distinguish what was poetry and what was his own words. And then when he came down to work after school, he started talking like that in the mail room. Needless to say, if it's one thing that Garnett Enterprises doesn't appreciate is a part-time mail room clerk that speaks free verse. He even talked to some of our clients that way.

AMANDA: I didn't know he was doing it at work.

JACK: I told Mr. Michaels that Allen was in a play at school and he was just practicing his lines.

AMANDA: That was very clever of you.

JACK: But this last week *(Jack shakes his head and crosses to the bar to get a drink.)*

AMANDA: What happened, Jack?

JACK: I couldn't cover up anymore. It was awful. Not only was Allen the laughing stock of the company, but I am too. Guilty through genetics. Everyone thinks he's crazy. And I can't blame them for thinking that.

AMANDA: You shouldn't worry so much about what other people think.

JACK: And then today when he showed up for work dressed like that. Wearing that stupid hat...I didn't know what to do. He was so serious. Didn't even care that people stared at him. So I sent him over to Doc Tyler. I know he's only an M.D., but I was hoping that it was a virus or something.

AMANDA: *(Consoling.)* You did the right thing.

JACK: And then Porter, that jerk in our sales department...He had the nerve to come up to me, in front of everyone, and ask me what was wrong with Allen. I'm sure he was the "elected spokesman."

AMANDA: And what did you tell that jerk Porter?

JACK: I calmly explained that my son thinks he's a nineteenth-century poet...then finished my coffee and came home as fast as I could to strangle Allen for putting me through that.

AMANDA: Seems to me that you are the one with the problem.

JACK: *(Incredulous.)* Me?

AMANDA: You send your son to the doctor to make sure he's all right, then you can't wait to get home to abuse him.

JACK: Don't pull that psychology garbage with me, Amanda. Our son is a nut case and your sister Sheila is to blame.

AMANDA: Don't blame Sheila for everything that goes wrong with our family. Ever since she spilled that dessert on you at the picnic you have blamed her for *(The argument is cut short by the entrance of Allen, the son. He wears a loose fitting, oversized wool suit and a white silk shirt, which is open at the throat. He sports a fake, yet impressive, long flowing white beard. All of this is topped off by a large floppy hat.)*

JACK: Here he is…our son, Walt. *(Allen runs to Jack and hugs him. He speaks in an old style monotonic metered speech pattern.)*

ALLEN: O Father, I embrace you as I would a new day.
O Father, who when I was young would
Walk and hold me gently at your hand.
O Father, who begot me with your seed.
O Father, whose strong limbs carried me.
O Father, who…

JACK: O Allen, that's enough. *(Allen pulls a copy of "Leaves of Grass" from his pocket and begins reciting.)*

ALLEN: *(Reading Whitman.)*
"I celebrate myself and sing myself,
And what I assume you shall assume
For every atom belonging to me
As good belongs to you."

JACK: We don't want to hear it Allen.

AMANDA: *(To Jack.)* Speak for yourself. *(To Allen.)* Allen, your father and I want to have a little talk with you. *(Jack crosses over and looks at Allen.)*

JACK: Hey, the beard is new. You didn't have that on earlier today. Nice touch, fruitcake.

AMANDA: Jack, please. *(To Allen.)* Allen, sit down on the couch for a moment and talk with us. *(She leads Allen to the couch, they sit. Jack stands looking at Allen.)*

ALLEN: *(Reading Whitman.)*
"I loafe and invite my soul,
I lean and loafe at my ease
Observing a spear of summer
Grass."

JACK: Looks more like you've been smoking a spear of summer grass.

AMANDA: Jack!

ALLEN: *(Reading Whitman.)*
"Born here of parents born here from
Parents the same, and their parents
The same,"

AMANDA: You see Jack, he knows we're his parents. That's a good sign.

JACK: How proud that makes me feel. *(Allen begins to explore his surroundings.)*

ALLEN: O Couch, that held me when I was young
O Furrowed table with teething marks.
O Carpet new, a stranger in our home
O Welcomed stranger, my feet will feel the
Follicles of your friendly soul.

JACK: *(To Amanda.)* Was that him, or was that Whitman?

AMANDA: I think that was him. He usually reads from the book when he's quoting the actual poetry.

JACK: *(Sarcastic.)* It's nice to know that we didn't raise a plagiarist.

AMANDA: *(To Allen.)* Allen, your father and I are a little bit concerned about you lately.

JACK: No, not concerned. We're out of our freakin' minds with fear that you have blown a major gasket!

AMANDA: Jack, please. *(To Allen.)* Allen, are you Allen Sommers, or are you Walt Whitman?

ALLEN: *(Reading Whitman.)*
"I exist as I am, that is enough,
If no other in the world
Be aware I sit content,
And if each and all
Be aware I sit content."

JACK: *(Angry.)* Answer your mother, Allen!

ALLEN: *(Reading Whitman.)*
"I am the poet of the body and I am the
Poet of the soul,
I am the poet of the woman the same as the man,
And I say it is as great to be a woman
As to be a man,
And I say there is nothing greater than
The mother of men."

AMANDA: That was nice.

JACK: Great, now he wants to be a woman. He's more confused than I thought.

AMANDA: I don't think he meant it that way.

JACK: *(To Allen.)* Are you Walt Whitman?

ALLEN: *(Reading Whitman.)*

"Walt Whitman, a kosmos, of Manhattan
The son,
Turbulent, fleshy, sensual, eating
Drinking and breeding,"

JACK: Dear God, he thinks he is. He really thinks he is! And you watch your language, we'll have none of that breeding stuff around here.

AMANDA: But what about Allen Sommers? Aren't you really Allen Sommers?

ALLEN: And I am that, too.

I am Allen of this house.
Born here these four walls
Born here to these people
Born of this skin, this air
All forming what I am
Allen of this world
Behold what you see, I am Allen
And Allen is within us all

AMANDA: *(To Jack.)* You see, Jack. I told you he was all right.

JACK: All right? All right? Look at him. That's not our son. Does he look like our son? *(Amanda pulls down on the fake beard, which is held by an elastic strap, revealing Allen's face.)*

AMANDA: Yes, that's Allen.

JACK: Does he sound like our son? You know, the kid who just a few weeks ago walked in the front door and said to us, "check out my car, it's like too brutal!"

AMANDA: I understand what he says now more than I did a few weeks ago. That's an improvement. *(Amanda pats Allen on his knee in loving encouragement.)*

JACK: I don't believe this. *(Allen stands to his feet.)*

ALLEN: Mother and Father, such talks can we have

Let us exchange the words that for so many years
Have recessed in hollow caves.
Let us speak of things long hidden in our hearts;
Our words swelling up in the eddies of the soul.
Let me walk with you
Let me talk with you.

AMANDA: He sure is good at that.

JACK: *(To Allen.)* Wait right here. *(Jack runs off stage. Amanda helps Allen adjust his beard. She looks him over with pride.)*

AMANDA: You look so distinguished, so grown up. *(Jack enters, holding two tickets in his hand.)*

JACK: Look, Allen. Two tickets for tonight's Dodger game.

AMANDA: I thought you were going to the game with Bernie.

JACK: I was, but I'd rather go with my son, Allen. My normal baseball loving boy. *(To Allen.)* Allen, why don't you go change your clothes. Put on some jeans and a sweatshirt and we'll go to the game. We'll go cheer on the "big blue wrecking crew." How about that? *(Allen takes a beat and looks at the ticket that Jack has just handed him.)*

ALLEN: *(Reading Whitman.)*
"Urge and urge and urge,
Always the procreant urge of
The world."

JACK: What the hell does that have to do with the Dodgers?

ALLEN: Always the urge of victory,
Men and urge and victory.
The newness of the day cannot be
Outdone by the spiked heels of
The barbarian.

JACK: Well, that certainly clears it up for me. *(Jack takes the ticket back, crosses over to a chair and sits.)*

AMANDA: Allen, what would you like for dinner. Is there anything I can make for you? How about a meat loaf? You just love my meat loaf.

JACK: How about a nut loaf?

ALLEN: Loaf...loafe? *(Reading Whitman.)*
"Loafe with me on the grass,
Loose the stop from your throat,
Not words, not music or rhyme I want,
Not custom or lecture,
Not even the best,
Only the lull I like, the hum of
Your valved voice."

AMANDA: That's beautiful.

JACK: Don't encourage him.

AMANDA: *(To Allen.)* I'm not very good at translating poetry, I only got a C+ in English...so you'll have to tell me, Allen, was that last little verse pro or con my meat loaf? *(Allen's eyes brighten, not in response to his Mother's question, but to something that he sees outside. He crosses to the window and looks out.)*

AMANDA: Allen?

JACK: Allen, get away from the window. The neighbors might see you.

AMANDA: Allen?

JACK: Allen, do you hear me?

ALLEN: *(Chanting Whitman.)*
"I hear america singing . . .
I hear america singing . . .
I hear america singing . . ."

JACK: *(To Amanda.)* He's flipping out. *(Allen pulls a wild flower from his jacket and gives it to Amanda; he continues chanting to himself.)*

AMANDA: Oh, Allen. It's beautiful. I don't think that you have ever given me a flower before.

(Allen begins to read from the book, but he loses the Whitmanesque accent. He lifts his eyes from the book and looks deep into Amanda's eyes. He quotes Walt Whitman, but on a very personal level.)

ALLEN: *(Quoting Whitman.)*
"Stop this day and night with me and you
Shall possess the origin of all poems,
You shall possess the good of the earth
And sun, (there are millions of suns left,)"

(Allen extends his arms to Amanda. She accepts him, at arms length, and there is a moment of realization between the two of them.)

JACK: I've had about enough of this. I've done everything right. I tried to be calm. I've called the doctor. I offered my companionship and my Dodger tickets. I've done everything a concerned father should. But now you leave me no choice. *(Jack interrupts their moment; he leads Allen towards his room.)*

JACK: You are still living in my house and you will abide by my wishes. *(Firmly.)* As your father, I command you to go into your room, change those ridiculous clothes, and come back out here to have dinner with us, your parents. *(Jack removes Allen's big floppy hat and starts to take the book away from him. There is a bit of a struggle and Allen regains control of the book. He then calmly hands the book to Jack.)*

ALLEN: *(Quoting Whitman.)*
"Are you the new person drawn toward me?
To begin with take warning,

I am surely far different from
What you suppose;
  Do you suppose you will find
In me your ideal?"
(Allen exits.)

JACK: *(To Amanda.)* Was that Whitman?

ALLEN *(O.S.)*: Page one hundred nineteen. *(Amanda takes the book from Jack and looks at the bottom of page one hundred nineteen.)*

AMANDA: There it is...*(Reads Whitman.)*
"Are you the new person drawn..."

JACK: Now don't you start doing it, too. *(She hands the book to Jack, he waves it away. He spits out his gum and unwraps another piece, shoving it into his mouth.)*

JACK: Now I think we're finally getting somewhere. I didn't mean to be rough on him, but it was for his own good.

AMANDA: He's a good boy, Jack.

JACK: Most of the time, but he still needs my guidance and experience.

AMANDA: I kinda liked the change.

JACK: Change? It was more like a disfigurement. You don't understand these kids today, Amanda. I do. They don't appreciate hard work and responsibility. They're all dreamers now. I want better than that for Allen.

AMANDA: Yes, we wouldn't want Allen to have any dreams.

JACK: Don't twist it Amanda. You always have to twist it.

AMANDA: Your dreams and my dreams might not be right for Allen. He's a sensitive boy who needs *(Jack is not listening to her, he has other things on his mind.)*

JACK: I think we can skip the meat loaf tonight. We'll get a couple of Dodger Dogs at the game. Lots of mustard. Allen takes after me in that respect, loves lots of mustard on his Dodger Dog.

AMANDA: Whatever you say, Jack.
(Allen enters. He has not changed anything. Instead he has added a blanket roll, which is slung over his shoulder. He also carries a walking stick. Amanda crosses to him, gives him back the book of poetry.)

JACK: I thought I told you to change your clothes.

AMANDA: Are you leaving us Allen?

JACK: He's not going anywhere.

ALLEN: *(Quoting Whitman.)*
"Afoot and light-hearted I take to the

Open road,
Healthy, free, the world before me,
The long brown path before me
Leading wherever I choose."
(Allen starts for the door, Jack intervenes.)
JACK: Okay, Allen. Maybe I came on too strong. Let's talk about this.
Now don't fight me *(Allen struggles for a moment, finally pushing Jack out of his way. He opens the door and pauses for a moment.)*
ALLEN: *(Quoting Whitman.)*
"Unscrew the locks from the doors!
Unscrew the doors themselves from
Their jambs!"
JACK: Allen, it's that stupid book. It brainwashed you. Your Aunt Sheila never liked you. She sent you that book to corrupt you. To make you turn against me.
AMANDA: *(To Jack.)* Sheila didn't send him that book…I did.
JACK: What?
AMANDA: Sheila sent him pillow cases. I gave him the book.
JACK: Pillow cases?
AMANDA: With little "choo choo" trains embroidered on them. She still thinks that Allen is nine years old. *(Jack is stunned. Amanda crosses to Allen.)*
AMANDA: *(To Allen.)* The open road is waiting, Allen. Explore it, discover it, live it. And when you come back, we will be here for you. *(Allen looks at her for a moment and then at Jack, who is still trying to sort all of this out.)*
ALLEN: *(Quoting Whitman.)*
"One hour to madness and joy! O furious! O confine me not!
(What is it that frees me so
In storms? What do my shouts
Amid lightnings and raging
Winds mean?)"
(Allen takes a deep breath and then exits out the door. Amanda shuts it behind him.)
(Long pause.)
JACK: *(To Amanda.)* Why? Why did you give him that book?
AMANDA: Because he had your eyes, Jack.
JACK: My eyes?

AMANDA: I never told you this before, but I married you because of your eyes. They were so bright and adventurous. There were lots of men in my life, but when I met you and saw your eyes...I knew that I could be happy with you.

JACK: That doesn't make any sense.

AMANDA: When Allen was born and they placed him in my arms, I looked first at his eyes and I was so happy because he had them, too.

JACK: So I've got nice eyes, Allen has nice eyes...What does that have to do with anything?

AMANDA: *(Continuing.)* And with Allen came responsibility. A family. That scared you. And it changed you. *(She looks hard at Jack.)* I remember a day, as clear as I will remember today, we were sitting at a picnic table at Meyer's Lake, looking out over the water as the sun set. Allen was sitting between us and I felt so content. I wanted the moment to go on forever. I reached over for the security of your arm, to hold you close and you pulled away from me. You pulled away because you just had to look at your watch. You just had to check the time. *(Pause.)* I looked into your eyes and I noticed that they were no longer bright, no longer adventurous, and no longer full of life. Your eyes were only empty. And it was then that I knew I had lost you.

JACK: There's nothing wrong with keeping track of the time, of being on a schedule. I won't apologize for being a responsible man. I've always taken pride in my punctuality. *(Pause.)* Just what is your point, Amanda. *(Amanda crosses to the window and looks out.)*

AMANDA: The years continued and Allen grew up. With you on his back all the time.

JACK: On his back?

(Amanda crosses back to Jack.)

AMANDA: Counting the moments of his life like you do the seconds on your watch. Signing him up for Little League, making him take a paper route so he could learn a sense of business, getting him a job at your company after school so he could prepare for his future. Tick, tick, tick. Allen's life ticked by like the measured beats of his father's clock. And his eyes grew dimmer and dimmer. Just like yours.

JACK: You're speaking in riddles.

AMANDA: I think you know exactly what I'm talking about, Jack.

JACK: And that little book of poems is suppose to bring him back to his senses? That's Dr. Amanda's remedy for an emotionally abused boy?

AMANDA: Walt Whitman gave him a spark. Something to think about. Something to dream about. *(Jack crosses over to the window.)*

JACK: And the neighbors something to talk about. He's still in the front yard.

AMANDA: What's he doing?

JACK: Talking to a squirrel. That's not a spark, Amanda, that's a full scale explosion. *(Jack crosses to the couch and sits heavily.)*

JACK: How did I become the bad guy here?

AMANDA: Try to understand, Jack.

JACK: This is going to blow my chances for a promotion. Twenty-seven years I sink into that company. Working hard, making suggestions, putting out one hundred and ten per cent…and after all that, the only thing I'll be remembered for is that I'm Walt Whitman's father.

(Amanda crosses to her sewing basket and removes the book she was reading before Jack came home. She sits next to Jack and hands him the book.)

JACK: What's this?

AMANDA: A present. From me.

JACK: A book?

AMANDA: A very special book. *(He hands it back to her.)*

JACK: Oh, no. I don't like Walt Whitman, never did.

AMANDA: It's not Walt Whitman. *(She hands it to him, once again.)*

JACK: *(Reading cover.)* "The Collected Essays of Henry David…" *(Not sure how to pronounce it.)* Thore-You?

AMANDA: It's pronounced "Thore-O." Henry David Thoreau.

JACK: I'd rather have a fishing pole.

AMANDA: Read the essay called "Civil Disobedience." *(Jack opens the book and looks at the index, finds the essay that Amanda requested. He looks at Amanda and then down at the book. Jack begins reading some of it to himself.)*

JACK: "Civil Disobedience"…Well, at least it isn't poetry. *(Jack reads some more, turns a couple of pages. He starts to become interested. Amanda snuggles up to him on the couch.)*

AMANDA: Read it out loud, Jack.

JACK: Amanda, I don't see how this…

AMANDA: Please? *(She gives him a look so sweet that it causes Jack to smile. He begins to read out loud.)*

JACK: *(Reading Thoreau.)* "The mass of men serve the state thus, not as men-mainly, but as machines, with their bodies." *(Jack begins to become excited about what he is reading and as he continues, his emotions build, as if he is the embodiment of Thoreau. His eyes are bright and his voice is assured. Amanda enjoys his newfound enthusiasm.)*

JACK: *(Reading Thoreau.)* "They are the standing army, and the militia, jailers, constables, posse comitatus, etc. In many cases there is no free exercise whatever of the judgement, or of the moral sense; but they put themselves on a level with wood and earth and stones; and wooden men can perhaps be manufactured that will serve the purpose as well. Such command no more respect than men of straw or a lump of dirt." *(Jack continues to read out loud, but it is silent to the audience. His lips move, as if in reading, but no words are heard. From the back of the audience we can hear Allen.)*

ALLEN *(O.S.): (Quoting Whitman.)*
"Here, take this gift,
I was reserving it for some hero,
Speaker, or general,
One who should serve the good old cause,
The great idea, the
Progress and freedom of the race,
Some brave confronter of despots,
Some daring rebel;
But I see that what I was reserving
Belongs to you just as much
As to any."
(Jack continues to read to Amanda as the lights fade to black.)

END OF PLAY

Cleveland
By Mac Wellman

Poet and playwright MAC WELLMAN was born in Cleveland and is a resident of New York City. Recent productions include: *Tallahassee* (with Len Jenkin); *Swoop* and *Dracula* at Soho Rep; *The Hyacinth Macaw* at Primary Stages; *The Land of Fog and Whistles* (as part of the Whitney/Philip Morris' "Performance on 42nd" series); and *A Murder of Crows* (at Primary Stages and elsewhere). He has received numerous honors, including both N.E.A. and John Simon Guggenheim Fellowships. In 1990 he received a Village Voice Obie (Best New American Play) for *Bad Penny, Terminal Hip* and *Crowbar*. In 1991 he received another Obie for *Sincerity Forever*. Two collections of his plays have recently been published: *The Bad Infinity* (PAJ/Johns Hopkins University Press) *Two Plays* (Sun & Moon). Sun & Moon also published *A Shelf in Woop's Clothing*, his third collection of poetry, and two novels: *The Fortuneteller* (1991) and *Annie Salem* (1995).

ORIGINAL PRODUCTION

Cleveland was originally produced at BACA in association with Cement in October 1986. It was directed by Anne Bogart with the following cast:

Panda Hands	Mark Austin
Marta	Melissa Cooper
Kate	Catherine Coray
Man, Mr. Barfly	Ryan Cutrona
Mother	Elzbieta Czyzewska
Bertha	Karen Evans-Kandel
Losin' Susan	Zivia Flomenhaft
Joan	Joan Macintosh
Narrator	Nicky Paraiso
Griselda	Mary Shultz

CHARACTERS

Joan, a high school girl with a secret
her Mother, with a secret of her own
a Man, a neighborly Trotskyite
Susan, Losin' Susan and Joan's other pals:
    Marta, Kate,Bertha,and Griselda
Richard, alias Panda Hands, Joan's date to the prom
Mister Barfly, a teacher at a fashionable boy's school in Cleveland
The Mayor of Cleveland, a man in a difficult fix
and a strange Man, with a wand

SETTING

Cleveland takes place in Cleveland during the prom season and in the dreamtime of Joan. An asterisk (*) indicates an overlap of lines. A Note on Mirandan Whispertalk: only consists of consonants, except for an occasional ending. Mainly sibilants and fricatives. Vowels are free. "C" is pronounced like "ch" in church.

CLEVELAND

SCENE 1

*Joan in a pool of light. Writing in her diary. Her Mother reading
it aloud, simultaneously, in another pool of light. Nice music plays.*

MOTHER: Dear Diary. I feel like I'm losing
my mind. Like Losin' Susan.
I feel sure Johnny will ask me
to the prom. Johnny on the Spot.
If not him, then Panda Hands.
I will end it all if he does.
I do not wish to go to the prom
because since we have lost all
our money we are no longer
fashionable. As we once were.
Ahead lies a life of meaningless
drudgery and not the glitter and
champagne of high society. Sigh.
I do not love Johnny. But I do
love Jimmy. In my secret heart
of hearts. Sigh. Jimmy the Door.
Way to my dreams. I'm not sure
I want that. My dreams scare me ...
Jimmy goes to the Boys Prep School
and I go to the Catholic Girls School.
Our Lady of the Bleeding Knuckle.
Our Lady of the Runny Nose.
A chasm of religion divides us.
And he will not ask me to the
Prom. Yes, because I am not
fashionable. If Mother could read
this she would know, yes, all
my unclean thoughts. To tell
the truth, dear diary, I feel
quite fed up with life since Dad

died and did not go to Heaven.
Strange things are afoot in the heavens …
(*Mother looks puzzled. Joan whistles her song from Scene Seven.*)
MOTHER: I dreamed last night I was
Pope Joan. And a Trotskyite, like Dad.

SCENE 2

The kitchen. Mother is trying to unclog the sink with a plunger.
The sink makes strange noises. Joan is trying to do her homework
at the kitchen table. More nice music.

JOAN: Mother, how can I concentrate on my homework
with you making that noise?
MOTHER: I'm sorry dear. It doesn't drain.
Mr. Barfly the plumber was supposed
to come fix it, but he never did.
JOAN: But I'm trying to do my homework.
MOTHER: Joanie, there's nothing I can do. (*Pause.*)
JOAN: Mother, what's the largest moon in the
solar system?
MOTHER: Why, Triton, dear. A moon of Neptune.
Not a very hospitable place. My, this
sink is hopeless. Miranda's much prettier.
JOAN: Thanks. Mr. Delaplane's science class is
really hard. (*Loud crash outside.*)
JOAN: What's that noise?
MOTHER: (*Going to look.*) Just some commotion in the street.
JOAN: Who is Pope Joan? Bet you don't know.
MOTHER: Haven't the faintest, dear.
(*Phone rings.*)
JOAN: Oh, God, what if it's Panda Hands asking
me to the prom?
(*Rings.*)
MOTHER: I thought we weren't fashionable enough
to be invited.
(*Rings.*)
JOAN: Well, I still want to go. It depends. You
get it.
MOTHER: Silly girl.

(*She gets the phone.*) Hello? No, he's dead. That's right. Dead. No, we don't need any. Thank you. Good-bye.

(*Hangs up. Pause.*) Well, it wasn't Panda Hands.

(*Knock at the door.*)

MOTHER: Who could that be?

JOAN: If it's Panda Hands I'm not here.

MOTHER: (*At door.*) Yes? Can I help you?

(*A Man enters.*)

MAN: Lady. Your front porch. It ah. Fell into the street. Somebody's underneath. In a car. One of those imports. Squashed flat.

MOTHER: Oh, how terrible. Well, come in.

MAN: Thanks. All you can see is the hubcap.

MOTHER: The phone's right there.

JOAN: Mother?

MOTHER: It's all right, Joanie. The front porch fell into the street and it seems there's a car underneath.

MAN: What's the police number?

MOTHER: Haven't the faintest.

(*He reads it off the phone and dials.*)

JOAN: Mother, what if Jimmy asks me and not Panda Hands?

MOTHER: Then I expect you should go. Even if we're not fashionable.

MAN: No one answers at the Police. Strange. (*Hangs up.*)

MOTHER: That is strange.

JOAN: Very strange. Hey, can I go look?

MOTHER: If you're very careful.

(*Joan skips out.*)

MAN: I'll call the wrecking company. You got a Yellow Pages?

MOTHER: Sure, right here. (*Shows him. Goes to the sink and plunger.*) You know, I think I want to go back to school. Learn a skill. I'm tired of being a drudge. And since my husband died. It's rough being alone.

MAN: You're young to be a widow.

MOTHER: He was a Trotskyite.

MAN: (*On phone.*) Acme Wrecking? Yeah, part of a house's fallen

across River Road near Willoughby. Traffic's
already backed up pretty far. And I think
there's someone trapped underneath. Yeah,
in a car. (*Hangs up.*)

MOTHER: He was a Trotskyite.

MAN: So am I. Thanks, lady.
(*He goes out. She goes back to the sink. Joan enters.*)

JOAN: Oh, you should see it. Everything's all
smashed. It's really neat. Say, do you
suppose someone's dead under all that
pile of rubble?

MOTHER: Could be, darling. Could be. Wash up, it's
dinner time.

JOAN: If Jimmy calls I'm here. If Johnny calls
I'm not. If Panda Hands calls I'm dead.

MOTHER: Yes, dear. (*Pause.*)
You know, Joanie. I think I want to go back to school.

JOAN: You'd be a great student. And I'll do the
grocery shopping. We'll trade.
(*They giggle.*)

MOTHER: So. What's the biggest moon in the solar
system?

JOAN: Miranda.

MOTHER: Miranda's the prettiest. Triton's the biggest.

JOAN: Darn. Well you tell me who is Pope Joan.

MOTHER: Never heard of her.
(*They giggle.*)

JOAN: I want to be like Pope Joan. Only I want
to be a Trotskyite.

MOTHER: This sink is disgusting.
(*The Man enters again.*)

MAN: Lady, can I use the phone again?

MOTHER: Sure.
(*He dials. Pause.*)

JOAN: If he's on the phone all the time,
how's Jimmy going to call me?

MOTHER: Ever think it might be Panda Hands?
(*They giggle. Blackout.*)

SCENE 3

The same. The Man is using the plunger now. Mother looks on philosophically. More nice music. Joan's daydreaming. A lengthy pause.

MAN: Jesus, lady, what'd you put down here, cement?

MOTHER: I'm afraid some bones got stuck. Last week.
Rather large game fowl.

(*Five of Joan's friends enter. The Man continues plunging.*)

MARTA: Guess who lucked out and got Jimmy?

SUSAN: Jimmy the Door!

KATE: Losin' Susan here.

SUSAN: It's on account of I can cha cha.

(*They laugh.*)

BERTHA: I got Jewel Rude Dude. He's such an elegant
dresser.

GRISELDA: Very neat.

MARTA: What about you, Joan?

JOAN: No one's called yet.

SUSAN: You end up with Johnny on the Spot.

JOAN: No way, Santa Fe.

KATE: Oh, yes. I foresee it. Written in the sky.

GRISELDA: Sorry, he asked me.* I thought you knew.

MARTA: Sneaky. Sneaky* secret keeper.

KATE: Well that leaves me and you and*
you know who invited me? Guess!

MARTA: I shall be out of town. Thank God.

JOAN: Fiji Three Eyes.

KATE: Who's that?

MARTA: I'm really not interested.* I'm going away
for a college weekend. At Denison. Party school.

KATE: You shouldn't call him that.

BERTHA: But he's so cute.

GRISELDA: The name's not cute.

SUSAN: Last prom before I move* to Albuquerque.

JOAN: Who cares?

MARTA: That leaves you. (*To Joan.*)

KATE: Guess!

GRISELDA: That leaves only* Panda Hands.

SUSAN: Oh, Jimmy and I shall bop the night away.

MARTA: Groan.

JOAN: Groan indeed.

GRISELDA: Coming to cheerleader practice?

JOAN: No, our porch fell off.

KATE: I wondered what all that garbage was
in the street.

BERTHA: Come on. Let's get going.

GRISELDA: Okay. Okay. If it's got to be it's got to be.
Johnny on the Spot.* Yech.

KATE: So. No one wants to know* who invited me?

BERTHA: (*To Griselda.*) You got any gum?

MARTA: If I had any gum I wouldn't give it to you.

SUSAN: That leaves only* Panda Hands.

JOAN: That leaves only Panda Hands. Yech.

SUSAN: Too gross for words.
(*They laugh. The Man stops plunging.*)

MAN: Well it's pretty much cleared. I guess.
(*The Girls trail out. Joan with them.*)

SUSAN: So long, Mrs. P.

MOTHER: Bye bye, Susie. Have fun. Don't be too late,
Joanie.

MAN: (*Sits wearily.*) Howzabout you and me go down to
party headquarters and lift a few?

MOTHER: What about the front porch?

MAN: It's not going anywhere. Say, what's
your name?

MOTHER: You wouldn't believe me if I told you.

MAN: Try me.
(*They laugh. She approaches.*)

SCENE 4

*Mother is back at the sink with the plunger. Joan enters whistling
a bit of her song. The Mother suddenly stops plunging.*

JOAN: I thought that guy fixed the sink.

MOTHER: He did. For a while. It's the thing in there that
grinds stuff up. It's strange.

JOAN: At least most of the wreckage is gone from
the street.

MOTHER: How was practice?

JOAN: Nifty. Anyone call?

MOTHER: Nope. No one ever calls anymore. (*Pause.*)
Why is it so dark out today?

JOAN: That time of year, Mom. Honestly … (*Pause.*)
Mom, why don't you ever talk about it?

MOTHER: About what?

JOAN: You know. Dad. All that stuff.
(*Her Mother goes back to the plunger.*)

JOAN: I know we're not fashionable.
Okay, Mom, but. But Christ. There's
a limit. You could talk.
(*Pause.*) I mean it looks as though I'll be going
to the prom with old Panda Hands himself,
but I'll go. I don't hold it all inside.
(*Her Mother stops plunging. Pause.*)

MOTHER: I would like just once to do something original. Just once is all
I ask. Even if we're not fashionable anymore.

JOAN: Mom, don't talk like that.

MOTHER: Maybe go back to school. Earn
valuable career credits. An exciting
career in robotics may await me.

JOAN: Mom, please talk to me.

MOTHER: That nice man who fixed the drain-
pipe was a Trotskyite like your father.
It makes me nervous …

JOAN: Mom, I don't care if we're not
fashionable. I love you.
(*Pause. Her Mother sits.*)

MOTHER: Well. All right. We were in New York
for the party congress. We had
just met the Mayor of Cleveland.
Of course he wasn't a Trotskyite.
He was far too fashionable for that.
A fine, big man he was, with a
fine, big, round head. He said
to your father: "Fine work. That
report on solid waste." Then he
introduced himself to me. It was

an awkward moment because, of
course, your father had no idea
what the Mayor was talking about.
It seems he was at the wrong hotel.
"We're Trotskyites," we said. "My
apologies," he said. "May I buy you
a drink?" And he did. One of those
elegant little sidewalk cafes. Lovely.
(*A sad moment.*) We were sitting on the sidewalk. Or,
rather, at a table on the sidewalk. And
your father leaned over to make a point
and spilled his espresso. As he moved
forward with the saucer in his other
hand the heel snapped off his shoe and
well he slid back into the chair. Of
course the coffee got over everyone.
And the chair leg broke and, it was
quite remarkable, he did a nice,
little, wholly unintentional back
flip into the street. I shall never
forget the sight of his shoes, the
soles of them, as they lifted high
into the air. He was trying to save
the cup, poor dear. But it shattered
in the street, and then the first car
ran over it. And the saucer which had
been undamaged miraculously up to that
point. He was a quite fastidious man.
The second car ran over your father.
Quite a large car. A limo, I think.
"My word," said the Mayor. What a
strange thing to say. Of course he was
dead. Your father, I mean. That's about it.
More coffee?

JOAN: At least now I know. The truth.

MOTHER: Yes. That's the least of it. Now you know.

(*She goes back to the plunger. The phone rings. Joan gets it.*)

MOTHER: Panda Hands.

JOAN: Oh. Hi. Sure. I guess.

(She grimaces to her Mother. Black.)

SCENE 5

Joan's dream. Dressed in red as a Trotskyite Antipope. Losin'
Susan, a blue Antipope, lies in an open coffin. The others are,
respectively: Marta, black; Griselda, white; Bertha, green; Kate,
yellow. Barfly is Joan's Swiss Guard. He carries an halberd.

JOAN: Are we prepared, Barfly?

BARFLY: Yes, excellency.

JOAN: Bring them in.

BARFLY: Singly? Or together? Excellency?

JOAN: En masse. We might as well deal
with them all at once.
(Barfly goes. Returns with the others. They arrange themselves about
the room. Pause.)

JOAN: Bertha, you look well.

MARTA: No need for small talk, Joan.

KATE: What are the conditions you propose?

JOAN: Ah, Griselda, I hear you are fully recovered.

GRISELDA: Tolerably.

BERTHA: What is to be the final disposition
of the Matriarchate of Cordoba?
Merged with Cadiz?

JOAN: Not quite.

KATE: And Tunis, Carthago, Malta?

JOAN: That depends on your decision, my dear.

KATE: My decision! It is not apparent from my
information that your decision to summon
this conclave, this silence of Antipopes,
has been informed to the minutest degree
by a regard for my opinion.

MARTA: Be still, Kate.

GRISELDA: Hibernia? What of Hibernia?

BERTHA: Macedonia. The Sanjak of Novi Bazaar?

MARTA: And what of the Eastern Matriarchates?
We who provide a buffer between you all
and the Turks? Have you considered
the possible consequences?

JOAN: Of course, Marta. of course.

MARTA: Now that Diotima has passed on …

JOAN: You are referring to Losin' Susan …

SUSAN: (*Who sits up in her coffin.*) I don't want to move to Albuquerque. (*Lies down.*)

KATE: That isn't Latin. Is it Ladino?

BERTHA: Be still, dear.

JOAN: I have called this Silence of Antipopes because there is a traitor in our midst.

BERTHA: Explain yourself.

JOAN: If you allow* me.

MARTA: Preposterous.

GRISELDA: Let Joan speak. (*Pause.*) There. Go on.

BERTHA: All this beating around the bush is tiresome.

JOAN: I suspect one of you of fomenting an anti-reformation.

KATE: No!

BERTHA: Impossible.

GRISELDA: How can this be?

JOAN: It is true. These (*She shows the document.*) are a set of 496 Antitheses concerning our canons of heteroclite unorthodoxy. Found nailed to the door by one of my Swiss Guards, Jimmy. Someone of you has sought a codification of the undreamed of, the unspoken, and the unthinkable. It is signed with a crow's feather. Thus.

MARTA: It's a hoax.

KATE: Yes. Joan, must it be? (*Weeps.*)

GRISELDA: Griselda, please.

KATE: No, you're Griselda. I'm Kate.

GRISELDA: Sorry.

BERTHA: So emotional …

MARTA: I don't trust you, Joan. Are you accusing one of us, and if so, which? If you have charges present them. I have my Nuncios and Legates with me. In the antechamber …

JOAN: That will not be necessary, Marta.

MARTA: I knew it was a mistake to come. This is a trap.

JOAN: Be quiet. (*Pause.*) In at least 98 of the aforementioned 496 antitheses there is incontrovertible evidence of the Mirandan heresy.

(*Gasps.*)

KATE: Impossible.

GRISELDA: That was stamped out centuries ago.

KATE: How can you be so sure?

JOAN: There are numerous quotations in the demotic script of Whispertalk, the Mirandan cipher.

BERTHA: If that is true then perhaps you are the author of these documents. You are, after all, the world's leading expert on Whispertalk ...

GRISELDA: Be still, let her speak.

JOAN: I cannot tell who it is.

MARTA: Of course not.

JOAN: Therefore I have taken steps, with sadness, but also with a firm sense of determination and duty, to abolish all of your matri-archates. From now on there is only one Antipope, and I am she.

(*Barfly bars door.*)

MARTA: I knew it.

GRISELDA: But Joan, how can you be capable of this?

MARTA: Damn you, Griselda, for ever talking me into attending this silence. I was foolish ever to trust a Trotskyite Antipope. My fastness at Antioch could have held out forever against her rhinodraconopeds.

KATE: Will you ransom us?

BERTHA: Sorry, Joan. A legion of my best fusiliers are deployed in the Great Hall, just beyond those doors. If I blow on this Anti-papal secret clerical dog whistle they will rush to our defense.

JOAN: Two legions of my Swiss Guard surround the palace grounds, Bertha. You have no choice but to renounce your powers and accept me as the supreme Antipontiff.

(*Pause.*) You see, Bertha, all your fusiliers are dead.

BERTHA: I don't believe you.

(Joan snaps her fingers. Barfly opens the doors to the Great Hall. Joan points down the corridor.)

BERTHA: I still don't believe you.

JOAN: You are aware, I presume, of the symptoms
of ergotic poisoning?

(All look down the corridor and gasp.)

MARTA: Demon.

JOAN: Twitching and quaking.

SUSAN: *(Sitting up in her coffin.)* I don't want to move to Albuquerque.

KATE: Be quiet, fool. Your character would never say
that.

(Susan lies down.)

JOAN: Diotima here was the guardian of the Glassy
Sphere. With her voices at my command
I do not need your approval. My word is
law. Whichever one of you is the Mirandan
agent I don't know. It hardly matters.
The ransom will be a million obuluses. Each.

GRISELDA: Each?

KATE: Each! But that's absurd.

MARTA: You'll never get away with this, Joan.

JOAN: Except for you, Marta. You will remain here
till the next intersection of the Seven Cosmic
Circles. Then Diotima's disembodied voice
will tell us who is behind all this heretical
Whispertalk. It may be a long time.

KATE: But we trusted you, Joan.

BERTHA: I never trusted her.

MARTA: Oh, what a fool I am.

(Blackout.)

SCENE 6

The next day. The kitchen again. Mother at the table intently reading a college catalogue. Joan preparing herself an after school snack.

JOAN: The prom's tomorrow.

MOTHER: You must be very excited.

JOAN: What's that?

MOTHER: Catalogue for Polytechnical College.

JOAN: (*Reading over her shoulder.*)
"Human Body Fluid and Advanced Polymerization."
Golly, Mom.

MOTHER: Just looking at what courses are
available.

JOAN: Gee, when you said you wanted to go
back to school I thought you meant
something like Business I or Creative
Writing.

MOTHER: How was cheerleader practice today?

JOAN: Fine. Learned some new tricks. (*Pause.*)
Only. Mom.

MOTHER: Yes, dear.

JOAN: I had a kind of bad dream last night.

MOTHER: I shouldn't have told you. So explicitly.

JOAN: No, it wasn't about Dad. It was something
else.

MOTHER: The sink is fixed again. There's fresh coffee.

JOAN: It was all kinda confused. All about
Pope Joan and stuff.

MOTHER: I have to mend your dress for the prom.
Why don't you try it on?
(*She goes out for the dress.*)

JOAN: (*Off.*) Mr. Delaplane said you know a lot about
astronomy but that nobody knows the
orbital eccentricity of Triton. It's
too far away.

MOTHER: I knew it. I should never have told you the
details. About your father's death.

JOAN: Was it ever fashionable to be a
Trotskyite?

MOTHER: Yes, dear. Once it was very fashionable.
(*She enters in a bright red prom dress. Her Mother sets about mending
a hem. Pause.*)

JOAN: How come you know so much about astronomy?

MOTHER: And we were personal acquaintances of the
Mayor. If things had only worked out a
little differently. We might still be
fashionable.

JOAN: Mom, would you tell me something?

MOTHER: Our kitchen sink might not have been stopped up. Our front porch might not have. Fallen into the street. Poor dear, you know they haven't tcmbbd the body yet.

JOAN: What? What did you say?

MOTHER: Slip of the tongue. They haven't identified his body yet.

(*Pause.*)

JOAN: Have you seen that man? Again?

MOTHER: What man?

JOAN: The man that fixed the sink.

MOTHER: Once. Briefly. But it won't happen again. (*Pause. Mother finishes her mending.*)

JOAN: Did you sleep with him?

MOTHER: What do you want from me? Do I tell you how to live your life? No, damn it. Is that how they teach you to think at that fancy Catholic school? Just because we're Trotskyites and you feel socially embarrassed. Just because we were once fashionable but aren't anymore. Just because I want so desperately, once in my life, to do something, anything, original ...

JOAN: Okay. Okay. Just curious. (*Pause.*)

MOTHER: He's had an accident. Very serious one. He won't be back. (*Pause.*)

JOAN: Mother, who are you?

MOTHER: Another cup of coffee?

JOAN: Really. (*Pause.*)

MOTHER: Since you ask. My name is Bqbqpstu, Emissary of Larav, Empress of the Sshhs, who live on the world you call Miranda, a moon of Uranus. Very, very far away. I'm here on a secret mission.

(*Her aspect becomes strange and unearthly.*)

My world, Miranda, is in danger. Triton sleepstickers and stickwalkers. Hammer-headed and creased foot spluch.

The rain skies up and the suns dump on
fells. That and the rats. They sqssqu
and shake. Badass hocus pocus. Snsps. Pssps.
Qvspt. Xxp. Tsspppcqtsm! Sks. Polymers.
Xxxxxs. Plplp. Qsssp. Sskllpc. Hssssssp.
O. Ppbbppsspc.

JOAN: I knew it, pure Whispertalk.
You should know. I am immune to the
subtle poison of Whispertalk.

MOTHER: What, who are you, to know our way?

JOAN: What did you do with father?

MOTHER: (*Holding up a clear glass vial.*)
Only the purest spinal fluid for the wind
machines of Larav. Empress Larav.

JOAN: Dad? And Mr. Barfly, too? You fiend.

MOTHER: Mr. Barfly. And the man who fixed the sink.
And Mr. Delaplane next. And then the Mayor
of Cleveland. And soon you, my dear.
Qssssmssssssplxmnsxsxsssxku!

JOAN: (*Squaring off.*) Xtr. Tr. Rqnrhrdtt. C!

MOTHER: Tritonian? I suspected. Show your glide
wave number and fight.

JOAN: I am Becky Brighteye, girl space-cop and
I'm taking you back to Triton, world that
you and your kind have despoiled. With
your wind machines and inverted energy
schemes. All of it Xxqmmmntnp, as you
say it in your dialect.

MOTHER: Once I get your time feather, you're finished.

JOAN: Try and get it.
(*They fight.*)

JOAN: Qqkwvll. Llllgpppvmvptzc.

MOTHER: Hsstu. Psspmpsstmpt. Ptzc.

JOAN: Bhtsspssbh.

MOTHER: Filthy girl. I should've scwwpsst you in
your sleep. Sleep hsp.

JOAN: Tsstssttp to you. What's your real name
before I take your feather. (*She defeats her Mother.*)

MOTHER: Inglefinger. Fourth Dyad. Tenth moeity.

JOAN: One of the unclean ones? That's how desperate
you are.

MOTHER: Wolfling, we'll destroy you yet.

JOAN: I've got a hot pllptpccclpu waiting for me.
In a small apple grove in Indiana. Then it's
clear sailing back home. With your time feather.
You'll be out cold for a week.

MOTHER: No, no. (*Faints.*)
(*Joan drags her halfway off. Her feet remain visible. Doorbell rings.
Richard (Panda Hands) enters, dressed formally. He wears panda
gloves and carries her corsage.*)

PANDA HANDS: Hi, Joanie. I heard someone whispering. So
I didn't come in. So I just stood outside.
Here's your corsage.

JOAN: Oh, that's beautiful, Richard. But the prom's
tomorrow night.

PANDA HANDS: The fifteenth. That's what it says on the
card. That's tonight. Gee, what's wrong
with your mother?

JOAN: One of her fainting spells. Don't worry.
Let me just get my coat.

PANDA HANDS: Like my gloves?
(*She puts on her coat.*)

PANDA HANDS: Shouldn't we, like, call the doctor?

JOAN: You warm up the car. I'll be right out. It's all right.

PANDA HANDS: I'll go warm up the car. Okay? (*He goes. Pause.*)

JOAN: Fthr. Fthr. Qskmpplptu. Pxp.

MOTHER: (*Groaning.*) Glpglpmpa. Gld. Dddd.
(*She holds up a strange feather. Joan snatches it in triumph. Panda
Hands re-enters.*)

JOAN: Shall we go.

PANDA HANDS: Golly. Sure. What's that?
(*Points to the feather. She puts it in her purse.*)

JOAN: Skip it.
(*Blackout.*)

SCENE 7

*The prom. In the Men's Room. Nice prom music in the
background. The Mayor of Cleveland, a chaperone, stands to one
side. His head is wedged in the towel machine. He is formally
attired. A strange Man enters with a wand.*

MAN: I am the Imperial Fsqqtu for Becky Brighteye.
I think I deserve better than this. Plopped
down on a contemptible third-rate planet.
Populated by third-string coat hangers and
hat racks. When I talk to one of you
you say many things, but all you ever
mean is "I believe in pop music. I believe
everything I hear on the radio." In my earthly
aspect I perform a boring and meaningless
task over and over. All your solutions to
problems are simpleminded. You want to
look inside things, but the insides
of most things are the same. One, two.
On, off. Boy, girl. Cat, dog. All
the same and very boring. Pleasure is
on the surface. Pleasure is not boring.
On my world people go mad from excessive
happiness, which you would never understand.
Nor would you ever understand what a Fsqqtu
is, which is why I am not going to explain.
When the screws from the big bank come to
close this circus down they'll show fire
and say: "We've come. We're taking everything
you've got." I wanted to build a system,
to perfect an art. And look what I've got.
Out of control *stuff,* a rat shoot at the
county dump, an endless prospect of indigest-
ible cheese. (*He shudders.*)
On this world one can deduce nothing
on the basis of looking at the sky.
That is not so where I come from.
Everything depends upon the sky.
I would like, yes, I would very much
like to talk about the sky. But you
would not understand. So ...
(*Pause.*) I glide the way and skin the smooth, in case
any more Mirandans show up. This is the Men's
Room of Panda Prep. The prom, remember? If you
listen carefully you can hear music in the

background. Cheesy band. Golden oldies, in
the local argot.
That's the Mayor of Cleveland. A chaperone.
He's drunk. Looks like he got his head caught
in the towel machine. How'd he manage that?
I haven't a clue. Sh. I hear people coming.
Sh.
(*Backs into a stall and disappears. Losin' Susan enters. Realizes her
mistake and exits. Panda Hands enters. Urinates. Washes hands. Exits.
Returns. Does a doubletake. Re-exits. Pause. Re-enters with Joan.*)

PANDA HANDS: Will you get a load of that?

JOAN: What's wrong with him?

PANDA HANDS: It's the Mayor. Looks like he's had an accident.
  (*A teacher, Mr. Barfly, enters.*)

BARFLY: Pardon me. (*He exits hurriedly. Re-enters.*)
  Hey. What's going on here?

PANDA HANDS: Sorry, Mr. Barfly. Sir. It's the Mayor.

BARFLY: The Mayor. Why so it is.

JOAN: He's stuck.

BARFLY: How the devil'd he do that?

JOAN: Beats me.

BARFLY: What are you doing in here young lady?

JOAN: We were looking for him. He got drunk
  and threw up in the punch bowl.

BARFLY: The Mayor?

JOAN: Sad to say.

BARFLY: Tony, what are you doing in there?
  (*Muffled noises from the Mayor.*)

PANDA HANDS: What do we do Mr. Barfly?

BARFLY: This has to be done discreetly. A lot of
  fashionable people are out there.

JOAN: It sure calls for discretion. Maybe we can
  find a crowbar in the custodian's room.

PANDA HANDS: This is too much. (*He exits.*)

BARFLY: Young lady what are you staring at?

JOAN: It's pretty amazing if you think about it.

BARFLY: Watch the door. No one must know.

JOAN: Discretion. Right. (*Someone tries to enter. She blocks the door.*) You
  can't come in.

BARFLY: No, no, no. Don't do that.

JOAN: You said I should watch the door.

BARFLY: Where's Richard?

JOAN: Went for a crowbar. Or a more appropriate tool. A Phillips screwdriver perhaps.

BARFLY: This is ridiculous.

JOAN: I find it very interesting.

BARFLY: Could be the ruin of a fine public figure.

JOAN: Never been in the Men's Room before.

BARFLY: Tony, are you all right? For Christ's sake what happened?

JOAN: This sure is a fashionable school.
I go to Our Lady of the Bleeding Knuckle.

BARFLY: Why don't you be quiet?

JOAN: Just trying to lighten the mood. Sorry.

BARFLY: Where'd he go?

JOAN: You mean Panda Hands.

BARFLY: Richard.

JOAN: Beats me. Maybe he went home. We call him Panda Hands because he paws all the girls.

BARFLY: Tony, help is coming.

JOAN: That band sucks, doesn't it?

BARFLY: Why don't you go away?

JOAN: This is a fascinating experience.
Wouldn't miss it for the world.
(*Panda Hands enters with the rest of the girls.*)

GRISELDA: Oh, look!

KATE: Wow!

SUSAN: What's wrong with him?

PANDA HANDS: Everybody's looking for you, Mr. Barfly.

BERTHA: I've never been in the Men's Room before.
(*The door opens.*)

A MALE VOICE: (*Off.*) Sorry.
(*Closes. Reopens.*)
Hey, what's going on here?
(*The girls hold the door shut.*)

BARFLY: (*To Richard.*) Would you get them out of here?
Did you bring a screwdriver?

PANDA HANDS: This was all I could find. (*It's a hammer.*)

BARFLY: What good is that? Go find a screwdriver.
A Phillips screwdriver.

PANDA HANDS: But where?

BARFLY: Look. Use your imagination, Richard.
(*Panda Hands exits.*)

JOAN: Quite remarkable, isn't it.

KATE: Very.

SUSAN: Never seen anything like it.

KATE: That band's lousy, isn't it.

BERTHA: The pits.

GRISELDA: This sure is a fashionable place. Did
you see all the ivy outside?

SUSAN: He threw up all over everything. Really gross.

BARFLY: He's the Mayor. Remember. Show some respect.

SUSAN: (*To mayor.*) Sorry, sir.

BARFLY: (*To Joan.*) And you. Keep an eye on that door.

KATE: Want some gum?

JOAN: Sure.

BERTHA: Is there a party after the prom?

GRISELDA: Who knows?

SUSAN: Jimmy the Door's such a good dancer.

GRISELDA: Johnny on the Spot's stepped all over
my feet. See.

KATE: Wow. That's awful.

BERTHA: Can I have a stick of gum?
(*Kate doesn't reply.*)

JOAN: Mr. Barfly, sir, do you have a relative
who's a plumber?

BARFLY: Why, yes, do you know him?

JOAN: We had some trouble with our kitchen sink.
(*Muffled sounds from the Mayor.*)

BARFLY: Easy now, Tony, we'll have you out of there
in a jiffy.

JOAN: Sir, Mr. Barfly, what if we greased his head
with a stick of butter? I'm sure we could
find a stick of butter.

BARFLY: Very funny.

BERTHA: I'm bored. (*She goes out.*)

KATE: Let's go back to the dance.

BARFLY: Not a word of this to anyone. Promise.

GRISELDA: Sure.

BARFLY: I mean it.

KATE: Mum's the word.

SUSAN: I've never met a real Mayor before.

GRISELDA: Good night, Mr. Mayor. Good luck!

SUSAN: Good-bye, Joan. See you soon.

JOAN: Bye.

(*They troop out except for Joan, Mr. Barfly, and of course the Mayor.*)

BARFLY: What are you staring at young lady?

JOAN: (*In a strange voice.*) Maybe you should go help Richard and
the others find an appropriate tool.

BARFLY: Yes, maybe you're right, young lady.

(*He gets up to go. Pause.*)

Oh, would you do me a favor and don't mention
my cousin the plumber? Around here. That's
not a very fashionable profession. (*He goes. Long pause.*)

JOAN: Don't worry
Mister Mayor. I'll stand watch over you.
You had a kind word for my father
even though he was a Trotskyite
and you being a fashionable Mayor
and Public Figure and all in all
quite the thing. Everyday despair
gets to a person when they're trapped
by the limits of their ecosystems ...
Back home in Skyeyesqll the air's
so thick you could stir it with
a spoon. My real father's an Xylmn.
They don't have Xylmns here, and I
guess it would take too long to explain
what that is and you've got problems
of your own. Enemies of our Way
have tried to force the issue.
Inglefinger, my fake mother, got
more than she bargained for. We're
a tough people. We never look back
and when we do a thing we do it right.
Still, Triton's not much to look at.
Old Queen Larav needs the spinal fluid

for her wind machines. Out that far
if you don't keep the air in motion
it freezes up. And that's a sticky
situation. I can tell you. I know.
Isn't this corsage nice? Richard's
a nice boy. Panda Hands. Not a bad
dancer. There are more of them
around here. Mirandans, I mean. I'll
be one of the missing. Others will take
my place. Uranus, our sister planet,
has a pretty, velvet ring, black as coal.
It glitters in the night sky like black
pearls. I sing and dance a lot. On my
days off. Would you believe I'm nearly
five-hundred thousand years old. A Pisces.
Mr. Mayor, I like Cleveland and well
I'll miss school. Our Lady of the
Bleeding Knuckle. Our Lady of the
Runny Nose. There aren't any Catholics
on Triton. No Trotskyites either.
We have a different way of doing things.
We keep whatever daylight reaches us in
these little stone jars. Sometimes the
whole Plain of Qqqsmsmccctu is covered
with them. Our enemies on Miranda are
pretty dumb. We've almost got them beat.
Another few centuries at most they say.
I'll miss my girlfriends, especially
Losin' Susan. She's a riot. I think
she's still a virgin. Who knows?
But Inglefinger's right. Miranda's
a prettier place than Triton. That's
why we want it. Our rhinodraconopeds
need it for grazing. Tough shit, you
Mirandans! I figured out my Pope
Joan dream. It was about how worried
I was about the prom and feeling bad
because I got stuck with old Panda Hands.
You want to hear some Whispertalk?
"Skrxxsx. Kxrs. Bkssxx. Xs. Bkxxxllxxxllmnnmcc ... "

That's the first line of a poem about the Sea
of Kxrs. Frozen methane. Looks a little like
Lake Erie. Panda Hands will want to go and
make out behind the shopping center.
But I'm gonna tell him I want to go to
Indiana. Will he ever be excited! A
pllptptcccplpu's there waiting to take me
home. You ever seen a time feather? This (*Holds it up.*)
is one. Pretty isn't it? I'll tell you a secret.
I don't love Jimmy the Door anymore. Want to
hear one of our songs?
(*She sings a strange song.*)
In the land of Tlpccc
the trees grow upside down,
but nobody knows they do.
(*Pause.*) Tlpccc, that's like China. On the other side
of the world. Get it?
(*She whistles a refrain. Panda Hands enters.*)
PANDA HANDS: Was that you singing?
I didn't know you could sing.
I got a screwdriver, a Phillips screwdriver.
JOAN: Richard, I've got a great idea.
You want to go for a drive?
(*Blackout.*)

END OF PLAY

A NOTE ON PRODUCTION
At the B.A.C.A. production (1986) a Narrator (the strange Man of
Scene Seven) introduced all the scenes and gave most of the stage
directions. Anne Bogart's direction involved, therefore, a thorough and
ongoing response to these as an integral part of the author's text.
Therefore, for the adventurous, these introductory scenic texts are given
in order, below. The Narrator's text in Scene Seven is identical in both
versions. For those who prefer a more conventional staging the original
configuration of the play is reproduced as a basic text.

SCENE: 1
NARRATOR: Welcome to the theater. X all the way to X', a whole hell of
a way. You ever wonder what the world'd be like if a circle were

defined as a round straight line with a hole in the middle? Joan and her mother live in Cleveland. Joan writes in her diary. Later her mother sneaks a look at what her daughter has written. Far away in the land of Tlpccc, it is said there are no secrets between mother and daughter. Music plays. It is "nice" music.

SCENE: 2

NARRATOR: Scene Two. The kitchen. The mother is trying to unclog the sink with a plunger. The sink makes strange noises. Joan is trying to do her homework at the kitchen table. More nice music. Far away, the Plain of Qqqsmccctu is littered with little stone jars filled with light.

SCENE: 3

NARRATOR: Scene Three. The same as before. The kitchen. The man is using the plunger now. The mother looks on philosophically. More nice music. Joan is daydreaming. A long pause. As heavy with meaning as a herd of grazing rhinodraconopeds.

SCENE: 4

NARRATOR: Scene Four. The mother is back at the sink, with the plunger. Joan enters, singing a bit of her strange song.

SCENE: 5

NARRATOR: Scene Five. Darkness. A wind of other worlds. Far away and far ago. Joan's dream. She is dressed as a Trotskite Antipope. Losin' Susan, a blue Antipope lies in an open coffin. The other Antipopes are, respectively: Marta, black; Griselda, white; Bertha, green; Kate, yellow. Mister Barfly is now Joan's Swiss Guard. He carries an halberd. The room is full of lethal whispers.

SCENE: 6

NARRATOR: Next day. Again the kitchen. The mother is seated at the table reading a college catalogue. Joan is preparing an after-school snack. The snack is an unusually grotesque sandwhich. On the wall there is a picture of the Massacre of Innocents. Prehaps at Skyeyesqll. The picture is tilted. How odd!

The Happy Journey
to Camden and Trenton
By Thornton Wilder

THORNTON WILDER (1897–1975) had a lifelong fascination with the one-act play as a dramatic form and great success with his own shorter works. Even today, almost a century after his birth, such Wilder plays as *The Long Christmas Dinner* and *The Happy Journey from Camden to Trenton* remain staples of the one-act repertoire.

Wilder often conceived of his one-acts as discrete pieces of a larger scheme. As an undergraduate, for example, he wrote a series of *Three–Minute Plays for Three Persons*. In 1956 he began working on several one-acts that became part of a projected cycle of fourteen plays depicting the Seven Deadly Sins and the Seven Ages of Man. Sadly, Wilder completed only six plays in this ambitious project—two "ages" and four "sins"—of which *The Wreck on the Five-Twenty-Five*, portraying the sin of Sloth, is one.

With Lillian Gish and Hiram Sherman in leading roles, the play received its world premier in 1957 in West Berlin as part of the celebration surrounding the dedication of that city's new Congress Hall. Although the play received favorable notices, Wilder never again permitted it to be produced or even to be published.

In October 1994, nearly four decades after the first draft had been completed, *The Wreck of the Five-Twenty-Five* was finally published in *The Yale Review* (Volume 82, Number 4). Readers interested in the history of this work as well as details about the fate of the other "sins" and "ages," are referred to the Introductory Note by Donald Gallup, Thornton Wilder's Literary Executor, in that publication.

Thornton Wilder, recognized as one of this country's most distinguished men of letters, was born in Madison, Wisconsin in 1897. After growing up in China and California, he attended Oberlin and Yale for his baccalaureate studies. After college, he spent a year studying archaeology in Rome. From that experience came his first novel, *The Cabala* (1926). He later taught French at Lawrenceville School in New Jersey, and English at the University of Chicago. In 1927 he wrote *The Bridge of San Luis Rey*, a novel which won the Pulitzer Prize and turned him overnight into a leading writer. His other novels included *The Woman of Andros*, *Heaven's My Destination*, *Ides of March* and *The Eighth Day*. His last novel, *Theophilus North*, was published in 1973.

Today, Thornton Wilder is perhaps better known from his plays, among them the Pulitzer Prize winning *Our Town* (1938) and *The Skin of Our Teeth* (1943). Wilder's *The Matchmaker* (1954), a great success with the actress Ruth Gordon, served as the basis of the hit musical *Hello Dolly!* starring Carol Channing. He also collaborated on two operas, one composed by Paul

Hindemith. Collections of his essays and journals have been published since Wilder's death in Hamden, Connecticut in 1975. Currently, research is being conducted on such topics as his long friendship with Gertrude Stein and his consuming interest in the work of James Joyce.

CHARACTERS
> The Stage Manager
> Ma Kirby
> Arthur (13)
> Caroline (15)
> Pa (Elmer) Kirby
> Beulah (22)

THE SCENE
No scenery is required for this play. The idea is that no place is being represented. This may be achieved by a gray curtain backdrop with no side pieces; a cyclorama; or the empty bare stage.

THE HAPPY JOURNEY
TO CAMDEN AND TRENTON

All directions are given from the actor's Right and Left.
As the curtain rises the Stage Manager is leaning lazily against the
proscenium pillar at the Left. He is smoking. Arthur is playing
marbles down Center in pantomime. Caroline is way up Left
talking to some girls who are invisible to us. Ma Kirby is anxiously
putting on her hat (real) before an imaginary mirror up Right.

MA: Where's your pa? Why isn't he here? I declare we'll never get
started.

ARTHUR: Ma, where's my hat? I guess I don't go if I can't find my hat.
(*Still playing marbles.*)

MA: Go out into the hall and see if it isn't there. Where's Caroline gone
to now, the plagued child?

ARTHUR: She's out waitin' in the street talkin' to the Jones girls.—I just
looked in the hall a thousand times, Ma, and it isn't there (*He spits
for good luck before a difficult shot and mutters:*) Come on, baby.

MA: Go and look again, I say. Look carefully.
(*Arthur rises, reluctantly, crosses Right, turns around, returns swiftly to
his game Center, flinging himself on the floor with a terrible impact
and starts shooting an aggie.*)

ARTHUR: No, Ma, it's not there.

MA: (*Serenely.*) Well, you don't leave Newark without that hat, make up
your mind to that. I don't go on journeys with a hoodlum.

ARTHUR: Aw, Ma!
(*Ma comes down Right to the footlights, pulls up an imaginary
window and talks toward the audience.*)

MA: (*Calling.*) Oh, Mrs. Schwartz!

THE STAGE MANAGER: (*Down Left. Consulting his script.*) Here I am,
Mrs. Kirby. Are you going yet?

MA: I guess we're going in just a minute. How's the baby?

THE STAGE MANAGER: She's all right now. We slapped her on the back
and she spat it up.

MA: Isn't that fine!—Well, now, if you'll be good enough to give the cat a saucer of milk in the morning and the evening, Mrs. Schwartz, I'll be ever so grateful to you.—Oh, good afternoon, Mrs. Hobmeyer!

THE STAGE MANAGER: Good afternoon, Mrs. Kirby, I hear you're going away.

MA: (*Modest.*) Oh, just for three days, Mrs. Hobmeyer, to see my married daughter, Beulah, in Camden. Elmer's got his vacation week from the laundry early this year, and he's just the best driver in the world.

(*Caroline comes down stage Right and stands by her mother.*)

THE STAGE MANAGER: Is the whole family going?

MA: Yes, all four of us that's here. The change ought to be good for the children. My married daughter was downright sick a while ago—

THE STAGE MANAGER: Tchk—tchk—tchk! Yes. I remember you tellin' us.

MA: (*With feeling.*) And I just want to go down and see the child. I ain't seen her since then. I just won't rest easy in my mind without I see her. (*To Caroline.*) Can't you say good afternoon to Mrs. Hobmeyer?

CAROLINE: (*Lowers her eyes and says woodenly,*) Good afternoon, Mrs. Hobmeyer.

THE STAGE MANAGER: Good afternoon, dear.—Well, I'll wait and beat these rugs until after you're gone, because I don't want to choke you. I hope you have a good time and find everything all right.

MA: Thank you, Mrs. Hobmeyer, I hope I will.—Well, I guess that milk for the cat is all, Mrs. Schwartz, if you're sure you don't mind. If anything should come up, the key to the back door is hanging by the ice-box.

CAROLINE: Ma! Not so loud.

ARTHUR: Everybody can hear yuh.

MA: Stop pullin' my dress, children. (*In a loud whisper.*) The key to the back door I'll leave hangin' by the ice-box and I'll leave the screen door unhooked.

THE STAGE MANAGER: Now have a good trip, dear, and give my love to Beuhly.

MA: I will, and thank you a thousand times. (*She lowers the window, turns up stage and looks around. Caroline goes Left and vigorously rubs her cheeks. Ma occupies herself with the last touches of packing.*) What can be keeping your pa?

ARTHUR: (*Who has not left his marbles.*) I can't find my hat, Ma.

(*Enter Elmer holding a cap, up Right.*)

ELMER: Here's Arthur's hat. He musta left it in the car Sunday.

MA: That's a mercy. Now we can start.—Caroline Kirby, what you done to your cheeks?

CAROLINE: (*Defiant-abashed.*) Nothin'.

MA: If you've put anything on 'em, I'll slap you.

CAROLINE: No, Ma, of course I haven't. (*Hanging her head.*) I just rubbed'm to make'm red. All the girls do that at High School when they're goin' places.

MA: Such silliness I never saw. Elmer, what kep' you?

ELMER: (*Always even-voiced and always looking out a little anxiously through his spectacles.*) I just went to the garage and had Charlie give a last look at it, Kate.

MA: I'm glad you did. (*Collecting two pieces of imaginary luggage and starting for the door.*) I wouldn't like to have no breakdown miles from anywhere. Now we can start. Arthur, put those marbles away. Anybody'd think you didn't want to go on a journey to look at yuh. (*They go out through the "hall." Ma opens an imaginary door down Right. Pa, Caroline and Arthur go through it. Ma follows, taking time to lock the door, hang the key by the "ice-box." They turn up at an abrupt angle, going up stage. As they come to the steps from the back porch, each arriving at a given point, starts bending his knees lower and lower to denote going downstairs, and find themselves in the street. The Stage Manager moves from the Right the automobile. It is Right Center of the stage, seen partially at an angle, its front pointing down Center.*)

ELMER: (*Coming forward.*) Here, you boys, you keep away from that car.

MA: Those Sullivan boys put their heads into everything.

(*They get into the car. Elmer's hands hold an imaginary steering wheel and continually shift gears. Ma sits beside him. Arthur is behind him and Caroline is behind Ma.*)

CAROLINE: (*Standing up in the back seat, waving, self-consciously.*) Good-bye, Mildred. Good-bye, Helen.

THE STAGE MANAGER: (*Having returned to his position by the Left proscenium.*) Good-bye, Caroline. Good-bye, Mrs. Kirby. I hope y'have a good time.

MA: Good-bye, girls.

THE STAGE MANAGER: Good-bye, Kate. The car looks fine.

MA: (*Looking upward toward a window Right.*) Oh, good-bye, Emma! (*Modestly.*) We think it's the best little Chevrolet in the world.— (*Looking up toward the Left.*) Oh, good-bye, Mrs. Adler!

THE STAGE MANAGER: What, are you going away, Mrs. Kirby?

MA: Just for three days, Mrs. Adler, to see my married daughter in Camden.

THE STAGE MANAGER: Have a good time.

(*Now Ma, Caroline, and the Stage Manager break out into a tremendous chorus of good-byes. The whole street is saying good-bye. Arthur takes out his pea shooter and lets fly happily into the air. There is a lurch or two and they are off.*)

ARTHUR: (*Leaning forward in sudden fright.*) Pa! Pa! Don't go by the school. Mr. Biedenbach might see us!

MA: I don't care if he does see us. I guess I can take my children out of school for one day without having to hide down back streets about it.

(*Elmer nods to a passerby.*)

MA: (*Without sharpness.*) Who was that you spoke to, Elmer?

ELMER: That was the fellow who arranges our banquets down to the Lodge, Kate.

MA: Is he the one who had to buy four hundred steaks?

(*Pa nods.*)

MA: I declare, I'm glad I'm not him.

ELMER: The air's getting better already. Take deep breaths, children.

(*They inhale noisily.*)

ARTHUR: (*Pointing to a sign and indicating that it gradually goes by.*) Gee, it's almost open fields already. "Weber and Heilbronner Suits for Well-dressed Men." Ma, can I have one of them some day?

MA: If you graduate with good marks perhaps your father'll let you have one for graduation.

(*Pause. General gazing about, then sudden lurch.*)

CAROLINE: (*Whining.*) Oh, Pa! Do we have to wait while that whole funeral goes by?

(*Elmer takes off his hat. Ma cranes forward with absorbed curiosity.*)

MA: (*Not sharp and bossy.*) Take off your hat, Arthur. Look at your father.—Why, Elmer, I do believe that's a lodge-brother of yours. See the banner? I suppose this is the Elizabeth branch.

(*Elmer nods. Ma sighs: Tchk—tchk—tchk. The children lean forward and all watch the funeral in silence, growing momentarily more solemnized. After a pause, Ma continues almost dreamily but not sentimentally:*)

MA: Well, we haven't forgotten the funeral that we went on, have we? We haven't forgotten our good Harold. He gave his life for his country, we mustn't forget that. (*There is another pause; with cheerful resignation.*) Well, we'll all hold up the traffic for a few minutes some day.

THE CHILDREN: (*Very uncomfortable.*) Ma!

MA: (*Without self-pity.*) Well, I'm "ready," children. I hope everybody in this car is "ready." And I pray to go first, Elmer. Yes.
(*Elmer touches her hand.*)

CAROLINE: Ma, everybody's looking at you.

ARTHUR: Everybody's laughing at you.

MA: Oh, hold your tongues! I don't care what a lot of silly people in Elizabeth, New Jersey, think of me.—Now we can go on. That's the last.
(*There is another lurch and the car goes on.*)

CAROLINE: (*Looking at a sign and turning as she passes it.*) "Fit-Rite Suspenders. The Working Man's Choice." Pa, why do they spell Rite that way?

ELMER: So that it'll make you stop and ask about it, Missy.

CAROLINE: Papa, you're teasing me.—Ma, why do they say *"Three Hundred Rooms Three Hundred Baths"*?

ARTHUR: *"Miller's Spaghetti: The Family's Favorite Dish."* Ma, why don't you ever have spaghetti?

MA: Go along, you'd never eat it.

ARTHUR: Ma, I like it now.

CAROLINE: (*With gesture.*) Yum-yum. It looked wonderful up there. Ma, make some when we get home?

MA: (*Dryly.*) "The management is always happy to receive suggestions. We aim to please."
(*The children scream with laughter. Even Elmer smiles. Ma remains modest.*)

ELMER: Well, I guess no one's complaining, Kate. Everybody knows you're a good cook.

MA: I don't know whether I'm a good cook or not, but I know I've had practice. At least I've cooked three meals a day for twenty-five years.

ARTHUR: Aw, Ma, you went out to eat once in a while.

MA: Yes. That made it a leap year.
(*The children laugh again.*)

CAROLINE: (*In an ecstasy of well-being puts her arms around her mother.*) Ma, I love going out in the country like this. Let's do it often, Ma.

MA: Goodness, smell that air, will you! It's got the whole ocean in it.— Elmer, drive careful over that bridge. This must be New Brunswick we're coming to.

ARTHUR: (*After a slight pause.*) Ma, when is the next comfort station?

MA: (*Unruffled.*) You don't want one. You just said that to be awful.

CAROLINE: (*Shrilly.*) Yes, he did, Ma. He's terrible. He says that kind of thing right out in school and I want to sink through the floor, Ma. He's terrible.

MA: Oh, don't get so excited about nothing, Miss Proper! I guess we're all yewman beings in this car, at least as far as I know. And, Arthur, you try and be a gentleman.—Elmer, don't run over that collie dog. (*She follows the dog with her eyes.*) Looked kinda peakèd to me. Needs a good honest bowl of leavings. Pretty dog, too. (*Her eyes fall on a billboard at the Right.*) That's a pretty advertisement for Chesterfield cigarettes, isn't it? Looks like Beulah, a little.

ARTHUR: Ma?

MA: Yes.

ARTHUR: (*"Route" rhymes with "out."*) Can't I take a paper route with the Newark *Daily Post*?

MA: No, you cannot. No, sir. I hear they make the paper boys get up at four-thirty in the morning. No son of mine is going to get up at four-thirty every morning, not if it's to make a million dollars. Your *Saturday Evening Post* route on Thursday mornings is enough.

ARTHUR: Aw, Ma.

MA: No, sir. No son of mine is going to get up at four-thirty and miss the sleep God meant him to have.

ARTHUR: (*Sullenly.*) Hhm! Ma's always talking about God. I guess she got a letter from Him this morning.

MA: (*Outraged.*) Elmer, stop that automobile this minute. I don't go another step with anybody that says things like that. Arthur, you get out of this car.

(*Elmer stops the car.*)

MA: Elmer, you give him a dollar bill. He can go back to Newark by himself. I don't want him.

ARTHUR: What did I say? There wasn't anything terrible about that.

ELMER: I didn't hear what he said, Kate.

MA: God has done a lot of things for me and I won't have Him made fun of by anybody. Get out of this car this minute.

CAROLINE: Aw, Ma,—don't spoil the ride.

MA: No.

ELMER: We might as well go on, Kate, since we've got started. I'll talk to the boy tonight.

MA: (*Slowly conceding.*) All right, if you say so, Elmer.

(*Elmer starts the car.*)

ARTHUR: (*Frightened.*) Aw, Ma, that wasn't so terrible.

MA: I don't want to talk about it. I hope your father washes your mouth out with soap and water.—Where'd we all be if I started talking about God like that, I'd like to know! We'd be in the speak-easies and night-clubs and places like that, that's where we'd be.

CAROLINE: (*After a very slight pause.*) What did he say, Ma? I didn't hear what he said.

MA: I don't want to talk about it.

(*They drive on in silence for a moment, the shocked silence after a scandal.*)

ELMER: I'm going to stop and give the car a little water, I guess.

MA: All right, Elmer. You know best.

ELMER: (*Turns the wheel and stops; as to a garage hand.*) Could I have a little water in the radiator—to make sure?

THE STAGE MANAGER: (*In this scene alone he lays aside his script and enters into a role seriously.*) You sure can. (*He punches the left front tire.*) Air all right? Do you need any oil or gas? (*Goes up around car.*)

ELMER: No, I think not. I just got fixed up in Newark.

(*The Stage Manager carefully pours some water into the hood.*)

MA: We're on the right road for Camden, are we?

THE STAGE MANAGER: (*Coming down on Right side of car.*) Yes, keep straight ahead. You can't miss it. You'll be in Trenton in a few minutes. Camden's a great town, lady, believe me.

MA: My daughter likes it fine,—my married daughter.

THE STAGE MANAGER: Ye'? It's a great burg all right. I guess I think so because I was born near there.

MA: Well, well. Your folks still live there?

THE STAGE MANAGER: (*Standing with one foot on the rung of Ma's chair. They have taken a great fancy to one another.*) No, my old man sold the farm and they built a factory on it. So the folks moved to Philadelphia.

MA: My married daughter Beulah lives there because her husband works in the telephone company.—Stop pokin' me, Caroline!—We're all going down to see her for a few days.

THE STAGE MANAGER: Ye'?

MA: She's been sick, you see, and I just felt I had to go and see her. My husband and my boy are going to stay at the YMCA. I hear they've got a dormitory on the top floor that's real clean and comfortable. Had you ever been there?

THE STAGE MANAGER: No. I'm Knights of Columbus myself.

MA: Oh.

THE STAGE MANAGER: I used to play basketball at the Y though. It looked all right to me. (*He reluctantly moves away and pretends to examine the car again.*) Well, I guess you're all set now, lady. I hope you have a good trip; you can't miss it.

EVERYBODY: Thanks. Thanks a lot. Good luck to you.

(*Jolts and lurches.*)

MA: (*With a sigh.*) The world's full of nice people.—That's what I call a nice young man.

CAROLINE: (*Earnestly.*) Ma, you oughtn't to tell 'm all everything about yourself.

MA: Well, Caroline, you do your way and I'll do mine.—He looked kinda pale to me. I'd like to feed him up for a few days. His mother lives in Philadelphia and I expect he eats at those dreadful Greek places.

CAROLINE: I'm hungry. Pa, there's a hot dog stand. K'n I have one?

ELMER: We'll all have one, eh, Kate? We had such an early lunch.

MA: Just as you think best, Elmer.

(*Elmer stops the car.*)

ELMER: Arthur, here's half a dollar.—Run over and see what they have. Not too much mustard either.

(*Arthur descends from the car and goes off stage Right. Ma and Caroline get out and walk a bit, up stage and to the Left. Caroline keeps at her mother's Right.*)

MA: What's that flower over there?—I'll take some of those to Beulah.

CAROLINE: It's just a weed, Ma.

MA: I like it.—My, look at the sky, wouldya! I'm glad I was born in New Jersey. I've always said it was the best state in the Union. Every state has something no other state has got.

(*Presently Arthur returns with his hands full of imaginary hot dogs which he distributes. First to his father, next to Caroline, who comes forward to meet him, and lastly to his mother. He is still very much cast down by the recent scandal, and as he approaches his mother says falteringly:*)

ARTHUR: Ma, I'm sorry. I'm sorry for what I said. (*He bursts into tears.*)

MA: There. There. We all say wicked things at times. I know you didn't mean it like it sounded.

(*He weeps still more violently than before.*)

MA: Why, now, now! I forgive you, Arthur, and tonight before you go to bed you ... (*She whispers.*) You're a good boy at heart, Arthur, and we all know it.

(*Caroline starts to cry too. Ma is suddenly joyously alive and happy.*)

MA: Sakes alive, it's too nice a day for us all to be cryin'. Come now, get in.

(*Crossing behind car to the right side, followed by the children.*)

MA: Caroline, go up in front with your father. Ma wants to sit with her beau.

(*Caroline sits in front with her father. Ma lets Arthur get in car ahead of her; then she closes door.*)

MA: I never saw such children. Your hot dogs are all getting wet. Now chew them fine, everybody.—All right, Elmer, forward march.

(*Car starts. Caroline spits.*)

MA: Caroline, whatever are you doing?

CAROLINE: I'm spitting out the leather, Ma.

MA: Then say: Excuse me.

CAROLINE: Excuse me, please. (*She spits again.*)

MA: What's this place? Arthur, did you see the post office?

ARTHUR: It said Laurenceville.

MA: Hhn. School kinda. Nice. I wonder what that big yellow house set back was.—Now it's beginning to be Trenton.

CAROLINE: Papa, it was near here that George Washington crossed the Delaware. It was near Trenton, Mama. He was first in war and first in peace, and first in the hearts of his countrymen.

MA: (*Surveying the passing world, serene and didactic.*) Well, the thing I like about him best was that he never told a lie.

(*The children are duly cast down. There is a pause. Arthur stands up and looks at the car ahead.*)

MA: There's a sunset for you. There's nothing like a good sunset.

ARTHUR: There's an Ohio license in front of us. Ma, have you ever been to Ohio?

MA: No.

(*A dreamy silence descends upon them. Caroline sits closer to her father, toward the Left; Arthur closer to Ma on the Right, who puts her arm around him, unsentimentally.*)

ARTHUR: Ma, what a lotta people there are in the world, Ma. There must be thousands and thousands in the United States. Ma, how many are there?

MA: I don't know. Ask your father.

ARTHUR: Pa, how many are there?

ELMER: There are a hundred and twenty-six million, Kate.

MA: (*Giving a pressure about Arthur's shoulder.*) And they all like to drive out in the evening with their children beside'm. Why doesn't somebody sing something? Arthur, you're always singing something; what's the matter with you?

ARTHUR: All right. What'll we sing? (*He sketches:*)
"In the Blue Ridge Mountains of Virginia,
On the ... "
No, I don't like that any more. Let's do:
"I been workin' on de railroad
(*Caroline joins in.*)
All de liblong day.
(*Ma sings.*)
I been workin' on de railroad
(*Elmer joins in.*)
Just to pass de time away.
Don't you hear de whistle blowin',", etc.
(*Ma suddenly jumps up with a wild cry and a large circular gesture.*)

MA: Elmer, that signpost said Camden. I saw it.

ELMER: All right, Kate, if you're sure.
(*Much shifting of gears, backing, and jolting.*)

MA: Yes, there it is. Camden—five miles. Dear old Beulah. (*The journey continues.*) Now, children, you be good and quiet during dinner. She's just got out of bed after a big sorta operation, and we must all move around kinda quiet. First you drop me and Caroline at the door and just say hello, and then you men-folk go over to the YMCA and come back for dinner in about an hour.

CAROLINE: (*Shutting her eyes and pressing her fists passionately against her nose.*) I see the first star. Everybody make a wish.
Star light, star bright
First star I seen tonight.
I wish I may, I wish I might
Have the wish I wish tonight.
(*Then solemnly.*) Pins. Mama, you say "needles."
(*She interlocks little fingers with her mother across back of seat.*)

MA: Needles.

CAROLINE: Shakespeare. Ma, you say "Longfellow."

MA: Longfellow.

CAROLINE: Now it's a secret and I can't tell it to anybody. Ma, you make a wish.

MA: (*With almost grim humor.*) No, I can make wishes without waiting for no star. And I can tell my wishes right out loud too. Do you want to hear them?

CAROLINE: (*Resignedly.*) No, Ma, we know'm already. We've heard'm. (*She hangs her head affectedly on her left shoulder and says with unmalicious mimicry:*) You want me to be a good girl and you want Arthur to be honest-in-word-and-deed.

MA: (*Majestically.*) Yes. So mind yourself.

ELMER: Caroline, take out that letter from Beulah in my coat pocket by you and read aloud the places I marked with red pencil.

CAROLINE: (*Laboriously making it out.*) "*A few blocks after you pass the two big oil tanks on your left ...* "

EVERYBODY: (*Pointing backward.*) There they are!

CAROLINE: " *... you come to a corner where there's an A and P store on the left and a firehouse kittycorner to it ...* " (*They all jubilantly identify these landmarks.*) " *... turn right, go two blocks, and our house is Weyerhauser St. Number 471.* "

MA: It's an even nicer street than they used to live in. And right handy to an A and P.

CAROLINE: (*Whispering.*) Ma, it's better than our street. It's richer than our street. Ma, isn't Beulah richer than we are?

MA: (*Looking at her with a firm and glassy eye.*) Mind yourself, Missy. I don't want to hear anybody talking about rich or not rich when I'm around. If people aren't nice I don't care how rich they are. I live in the best street in the world because my husband and children live there. (*She glares impressively at Caroline a moment to let this lesson sink in, then looks up, sees Beulah off Left and waves.*) There's Beulah standing on the steps lookin' for us.

(*Beulah enters from Left, also waving. They all call out: "Hello, Beulah—hello." Presently they are all getting out of the car, except Elmer, busy with brakes.*)

BEULAH: Hello, mama. Well, lookit how Arthur and Caroline are growing.

MA: They're bursting all their clothes.

BEULAH: (*Crossing in front of them and kissing her father long and affectionately.*) Hello, Papa. Good old papa. You look tired, Pa.

MA: Yes, your pa needs a rest. Thank Heaven, his vacation has come just now. We'll feed him up and let him sleep late. (*Elmer gets out of car and stands in front of it.*)

MA: Pa has a present for you, Loolie. He would go and buy it.

BEULAH: Why, Pa, you're terrible to go and buy anything for me. Isn't he terrible?

(*Stage Manager removes automobile.*)

MA: Well, it's a secret. You can open it at dinner.

BEULAH: (*Puts her arm around his neck and rubs her nose against his temple.*) Crazy old pa, goin' buyin' things! It's me that ought to be buyin' things for you, Pa.

ELMER: Oh, no! There's only one Loolie in the world.

BEULAH: (*Whispering, as her eyes fill with tears.*) Are you glad I'm still alive, Pa? (*She kisses him abruptly and goes back to the house steps.*)

ELMER: Where's Horace, Loolie?

BEULAH: He was kep' over a little at the office. He'll be here any minute. He's crazy to see you all.

MA: All right. You men go over to the Y and come back in about an hour.

BEULAH: Go straight along, Pa, you can't miss it. It just stares at yuh.

(*Elmer and Arthur exit down Right.*)

BEULAH: Well, come on upstairs, Ma, and take your things.—Caroline, there's a surprise for you in the back yard.

CAROLINE: Rabbits?

BEULAH: No.

CAROLINE: Chickins?

BEULAH: No. Go and see.

(*Caroline runs off stage, down Left.*)

BEULAH: There are two new puppies. You be thinking over whether you can keep one in Newark.

MA: I guess we can.

(*Ma and Beulah turn and walk way up stage Right. The Stage Manager pushes out a cot from the Left, and places it down Left on a slant so that its foot is toward the Left. Beulah and Ma come down stage Center toward Left.*)

MA: It's a nice house, Beulah. You just got a *lovely* home.

BEULAH: When I got back from the hospital, Horace had moved everything into it, and there wasn't anything for me to do.

MA: It's lovely.

(*Beulah sits on the cot, testing the springs.*)

BEULAH: I think you'll find this comfortable, Ma. (*Beulah sits on down stage end of it.*)

MA: (*Taking off her hat.*) Oh, I could sleep on a heapa shoes, Loolie! I don't have no trouble sleepin'. (*She sits down upstage of her.*) Now let me look at my girl. Well, well, when I last saw you, you didn't know me. You kep' saying: *When's Mama comin'? When's Mama comin'?* But the doctor sent me away.

BEULAH: (*Puts her head on her mother's shoulder and weeps.*) It was awful, Mama. It was awful. She didn't even live a few minutes, Mama. It was awful.

MA: (*In a quick, light, urgent undertone.*) God thought best, dear. God thought best. We don't understand why. We just go on, honey, doin' our business. (*Then almost abruptly.*) Well, now, (*stands up*) what are we giving the men to eat tonight?

BEULAH: There's a chicken in the oven.

MA: What time did ya put it in?

BEULAH: (*Restraining her.*) Aw, Ma, don't go yet. (*Taking her mother's hand and drawing her down beside her.*) I like to sit here with you this way. You always get the fidgets when we try and pet yuh, Mama.

MA: (*Ruefully, laughing.*) Yes, it's kinda foolish. I'm just an old Newark bag-a-bones. (*She glances at the backs of her hands.*)

BEULAH: (*Indignantly.*) Why, Ma, you're good-lookin'! We always said you were good-lookin'.—And besides, you're the best ma we could ever have.

MA: (*Uncomfortable.*) Well, I hope you like me. There's nothin' like bein' liked by your family.—(*Rises.*) Now I'm going downstairs to look at the chicken. You stretch out here for a minute and shut your eyes. (*She helps Beulah to a lying position.*) Have you got everything laid in for breakfast before the shops close?

BEULAH: Oh, you know! Ham and eggs.

(*They both laugh. Ma puts an imaginary blanket over Beulah.*)

MA: I declare I never could understand what men see in ham and eggs. I think they're horrible.—What time did you put the chicken in?

BEULAH: Five o'clock.

MA: Well, now, you shut your eyes for ten minutes.

(*Ma turns, walks directly upstage, then along the back wall to the Right as she absent-mindedly and indistinctly sings:*)
"There were ninety and nine that safely lay
In the shelter of the fold ... "
(*And The Curtain Falls.*)

END OF PLAY

The Stonewater Rapture
By Doug Wright

To Bruce and Catherine, who know the terrain.

DOUG WRIGHT's plays include *The Stonewater Rapture, Interrogating the Nude, Dinosaurs, Lot 13: The Bone Violin, Watbanaland, Wildwood Park*, and a musical, *Buzzsaw Berkeley*, with songs by Michael John LaChiusa. His new play *Quills*, based on the life of the Marquis de Sade, was recently awarded the Kesselring Prize and opened at New York Theater Workshop in November 1995. His work has been performed at the Yale Repertory Theater, the WPA Theater, Lincon Center Theater, the Mark Taper Forum New Work Festival, The Woolly Mammoth Theater, and The McCarter Theater, among others. Television scripts include four pilots for producer Norman Lear, and a three-hour adaptation of *The Arabian Nights* for Hallmark Entertainment. He was named a McKnight Fellow for 1995\6, and is a past recipient of the William I. Bradley Fellowship at Yale University, the Charles MacArthur Fellowship at the Eugene O'Neill Theater Center, an HBO Fellowship in playwriting, and the Alfred Hodder Fellowship at Princeton University. He received a bachelor's degree from Yale University in 1985, and an MFA in playwriting from NYU in 1987, and is a member of the Dramatists Guild, the Writer's Guild East, and New York Theater Workshop. He has taught playwriting at Princeton University.

ORIGINAL PRODUCTION

The Stonewater Rapture was originally produced by the Yale University Dramatic Association in New Haven, Connecticut on October 6, 1983. It was directed by Doug Wright with the following cast:

Whitney . . . . Dan Kael
Carlyle . . . . Stephanie Simpson

The Stonewater Rapture was presented by American Stage Directions at the Borderline Theatre, in Edinburgh, Scotland on August 13, 1984. It was directed by Steven Ullman with the following cast:

Whitney . . . . Christopher Strand
Carlyle . . . . Ann Osmond

The Stonewater Rapture was originally published in The Best Short Plays, 1987 edited by Ramon Delgado.

CHARACTERS

Carlyle, eighteen and pretty
Whitney, the same age and rather pensive

The Stonewater Rapture

Setting: Part of the living room and the entire porch of a small, white frame house in a West Texas town. The area of the porch is surrounded by trees and shrubbery. It is well kept and even charming with a few potted plants and possibly a porch swing. A pair of plaster kittens play on a nearby tree. Indoors, the house is simply and cleanly furnished. The slipcovers are hand sewn, covering faded upholstery and there are a few needlepoint pillows on the couch and on the chairs, and a few small pettipoint pictures of flowers and cocker spaniels hanging on the walls. There is a magazine rack containing such publications as Family Circle, Better Homes and Gardens, Parents Magazine *and a wide variety of religious material. The familiar bearded portrait of Christ hangs over the mantel, and a sumptuous leather-bound Bible sits on its own stand.*

It is dusk and the sky is awash with streaks of stormy blue and orange. Stars are barely visible. There is the buzz of insects and in the distance the soothing sound of wind. The porch light is on, and Whitney enters, followed by Carlyle. As they talk, they enter the house, flip on the lights and settle themselves on the couch.

SCENE ONE

CARLYLE: Whitney, Ted Pewter was the only other boy who had a chance and he's guilty of the sin of pride. Look at the way he blow dries his hair.

WHITNEY: I don't want to be president.

CARLYLE: How do you think that makes me feel?

WHITNEY: I'm glad you got secretary. Carlyle, I'm not going to be a preacher.

CARLYLE: Getting president doesn't mean you have to be a preacher.

WHITNEY: You want to see something?

(*Whitney crosses to the desk and pulls out a thin stack of papers. He hands it to Carlyle.*)

CARLYLE: You didn't tell me you were applying to seminary school! Whitney, I think that's wonderful. Look. You typed all the answers.

WHITNEY: My Dad filled it out for me. He wrote all the essays to make sure I wouldn't tell them I was Hindu or something. Now all it needs is my signature, then it goes in the mail, and *wham!* I'm behind a pulpit.

CARLYLE: They might not accept you.

WHITNEY: I was just voted president of the Youth Ministry. It's the kiss of death.

CARLYLE: It doesn't mean you'll get in. It takes a lot more to be a good preacher. You have to be blessed with strength and faith and love for your fellow man …

WHITNEY: There's something more.

CARLYLE: What?

WHITNEY: You have to be a good public speaker. I suck.

CARLYLE: You're not so awful.

WHITNEY: You saw me this afternoon.

CARLYLE: You knew if you won, you'd have to make a speech. You should've had one ready.

WHITNEY: I did. My father gave me this whole five-page speech on the positive power of prayer in adolescence. It was right in my back pocket. But you saw. I practically fainted, all because of the word "puberty." I couldn't stand up there and say "puberty" in front of all those ladies. They would've choked on their egg salad. I suck.

CARLYLE: Then they probably won't take you.

WHITNEY: They'll take me. I make all A's and my uncle is on the board.

CARLYLE: Mama says you have the calling.

WHITNEY: Dad says there are only two honorable professions in the world: carpentry and preaching. I made him a tie rack for his birthday and the wood split. That's my calling.

CARLYLE: Where are your folks?

WHITNEY: Cleaning up after the picnic. Then they're teaching that singles seminar on "Finding a Mate Through God." Dad says a lot of nice bachelors show up. He thinks your mom should give it a try.

CARLYLE: Can we go out on the porch?

WHITNEY: It's hotter than hell and there are mosquitoes.

CARLYLE: You shouldn't have me over if your parents aren't here.

(*She leads him out onto the porch.*)

WHITNEY: We've been seeing each other for two months now and I'm still afraid I'll get a face full of tear gas if I brush up against your knee.

CARLYLE: Whitney, I've made a list of the things we should start doing. (*Whitney groans.*) First, we're going to start making those Wednesday night sing-a-longs at the nursing home mandatory attendance for the whole group. I feel stupid singing all by myself. It keeps the old people from joining in. They think it's a solo. Miss Willoughby, she tries to help out, but whenever she sings it's always the wrong song. I could be singing the Doxology, and she still thinks it's "Indian Love Call." It embarrasses everybody, but she refuses to wear her hearing aid. Second, I'm sick and tired of the way some people come to the Fellowship parties for the food and not the faith. It makes us look bad. Part of that is your responsibility. If you'd try harder to attract people at school ...

WHITNEY: I was going to go out for the football team, but that's shot to hell now. I can't be at practice and Bible Study at the same time.

CARLYLE: Your legs are too skinny. You'd get bulldozed.

WHITNEY: They are not.

CARLYLE: You could soak your feet in a Coke bottle.

WHITNEY: Cut it out. I've been eating more.

CARLYLE: Let me see.

WHITNEY: No.

CARLYLE: Come on. Please.

WHITNEY: Uh-uh.

CARLYLE: You told me you hated football. I don't know why you want to play now.

WHITNEY: Everybody plays.

CARLYLE: Who?

WHITNEY: Arthur Horrishill and Michael MaCaffey.

CARLYLE: But they're mean to you.

WHITNEY: No, they're not.

CARLYLE: Yesterday they put Vaseline all over your steering wheel.

WHITNEY: It was a joke.

CARLYLE: You zigzagged all the way home.

WHITNEY: It was funny. Anyway, if I was on the team, do you think they'd do that?

CARLYLE: But you're better than they are. Mama says you're the only decent boy for miles. She'd rather talk to you than most people her own age. She says boys like Arthur and Michael have one-track minds that lead straight to hell, and knives where their flesh should be, but not you.

WHITNEY: Thanks.

CARLYLE: Which brings us to the third thing on my list.

WHITNEY: What?

CARLYLE: Thelma Peeler.

WHITNEY: What about her?

CARLYLE: You mean you don't know?

WHITNEY: How would I?

CARLYLE: Your friend Michael MaCaffey took advantage of her.

WHITNEY: Michael wouldn't be seen with Thelma. He's captain of the team.

CARLYLE: What's worse, he did it on a dare. Arthur Horrishill took a pool, and the whole team bet he couldn't do it. They ended up paying him fifty dollars.

WHITNEY: Somebody started a rumor, and you believed it.

CARLYLE: It's true. He got her so drunk she didn't know her own name. I know she has pimples and those orthopedic shoes. But he did it just the same.

WHITNEY: Did what? Kiss her through her mustache?

CARLYLE: Made her pregnant. Michael wouldn't even offer to make it right. His family just gave her family money for one of those operations. Well, she wasn't about to let them kill it, so she ran away and now there are patrol cars looking all over the state for her. Can't you just see her clomping along the roadside in those big black shoes? They'll catch her in a minute and then her parents'll send her back to that detention home, after they cut the baby out. And it wasn't even her fault. It was his. Mama says he's damned without a chance. Anyway, I think the Youth Ministry should take up a collection to pay for the birth of that baby.

WHITNEY: If the kid looks anything like his mother, the first thing it'll need is a clean shave.

CARLYLE: Stop. Don't be ugly. And don't go thinking Michael MaCaffey is any great shakes just because he's captain of the team.

WHITNEY: Is that the list?

CARLYLE: We have to choose the verses for next Sunday's meeting.

WHITNEY: You can.

CARLYLE: You have to help. You're president.

WHITNEY: My Dad probably rigged the election. Ted should've gotten it.

CARLYLE: You don't want it because you're lazy.

WHITNEY: I don't want it because the guys'll think I'm a fairy. Ted should've gotten it because he is one.

CARLYLE: He's always at Sunday School and he always wins the Old Testament Crossword Puzzle Contest.

WHITNEY: He hangs around the grammar school and feels up the fifth grade boys.

CARLYLE: He'd never do that. Not in Stonewater. He'd be in jail.

WHITNEY: He gives them dollars. They buy cigarettes.

CARLYLE: Let he who is without sin cast the first stone.

WHITNEY: I don't feel up fifth grade boys.

CARLYLE: You're talking about it. That's pretty bad.

WHITNEY: You're welcome to change the subject.

CARLYLE: If Ted were a homosexual, he wouldn't be Christian. It says so in the Book of Leviticus. He'd be struck dead, and his blood would be upon him. Do lots of people know about him?

WHITNEY: All the guys at school suspect. I don't think his parents know.

CARLYLE: If I were his mother, I'd do whatever I could to keep from finding out.

WHITNEY: He always stops and talks to me in the hall. People think he's my friend just because I'm not mean to him. He asked if he could borrow my World History notes right when Arthur Horrishill walked by, and I said yes. Suicide.

CARLYLE: Can't you be just a little mean?

WHITNEY: What am I supposed to do?

CARLYLE: If he's really homosexual, don't talk to him.

WHITNEY: I'm supposed to just stand there after he's said "Hello" and is looking all expectant? One time he really got me in trouble. We had lockers right next to each other in gym and we were getting undressed and he bumped into me. I felt him. Part of him was touching me.

CARLYLE: Which part?

WHITNEY: I couldn't move. I just stood there. I froze. Then he started…

CARLYLE: What?

WHITNEY: Horrishill saw, I know he did, because later the coach had to assign me to a team. No one would take me. No one would talk to me. All because of that fucking fairy.
(*Silence. Whitney slaps a mosquito.*)

CARLYLE: Have you been reading that book for English?

WHITNEY: On and off. It's boring.

CARLYLE: My Mama threw it out. Is it really obscene?

WHITNEY: If it was, it'd go faster.

CARLYLE: It doesn't tell the details, does it?

WHITNEY: About what?

CARLYLE: It just tells she's pregnant, right? And that she has to wear the "A." It doesn't tell how she got pregnant …

WHITNEY: I don't think she did it some new or unusual way.

CARLYLE: Marcia Stunt says no one even kisses in the book.

WHITNEY: Are you still failing?

CARLYLE: Of course, if I can't read any of the books! Stories about unwed mothers. Naked boys on islands who slice up pigs. Plays where men sleep with their mothers. If I didn't know Mrs. Ratchet on the textbook committee, I'd swear it was a dirty book club. Mama says they might as well hand out copies of *Hustler* magazine. Have you ever seen one of those magazines?

(*Whitney picks at his shoe.*)

CARLYLE: Oh, Whitney, you have.

WHITNEY: Everybody has. Except you.

CARLYLE: You're the new president.

WHITNEY: I didn't look by choice.

CARLYLE: I'm so disappointed.

WHITNEY: It wasn't my fault. Arthur Horrishill cut out a bunch of pictures and taped them on the inside of my gym locker while I was in the shower.

CARLYLE: Why'd he do that?

WHITNEY: So when I came back and saw the pictures they could rip off my towel.

CARLYLE: Why?

WHITNEY: It was a test.

CARLYLE: For what?

WHITNEY: Never mind, but it worked. (*Silence.*) It was a joke. I laughed.

CARLYLE: What were the pictures like?

WHITNEY: Pictures.

CARLYLE: Ladies?

WHITNEY: No, sports cars.

CARLYLE: Men, too?

WHITNEY: No.

CARLYLE: Just ladies?

WHITNEY: One. One had men.

CARLYLE: That's so disgusting. They were just lying there?

WHITNEY: The pictures?

CARLYLE: The men.

WHITNEY: Yeah. Or standing by pools. Or bending over to pick up footballs. One of them was riding a motorcycle. I don't want to talk about it.

CARLYLE: I couldn't live with myself if I saw one of those pictures. I'd want to stab myself.

WHITNEY: They're just paper.

CARLYLE: Looking at them must feel so lonely.

WHITNEY: When I was looking at them, I felt a hell of a lot more like they were all looking at me.

CARLYLE: It must be like looking at the Shriner's posters with the burn victims on them. You've never bought one of those magazines, have you? You don't have one lying under your bed or sitting somewhere in your house?

WHITNEY: I don't have the courage.

CARLYLE: Those men must've had something on.

WHITNEY: Some did.

CARLYLE: Like what?

WHITNEY: Hats mostly. One had a motorcycle helmet.

CARLYLE: Mama said most of the people who would pose for that trash are ugly anyway. I bet they all looked half-deformed.

WHITNEY: They seemed pretty healthy.

CARLYLE: They weren't just standing there, facing the camera?

WHITNEY: Yes.

CARLYLE: But you couldn't see … you know …

WHITNEY: That's the whole point.

CARLYLE: You could? All of it?

WHITNEY: Stop asking questions.

CARLYLE: That's so sad. People can be so gross. It's what makes us so imperfect and unworthy. People looking at those pictures when they're lonely or bored when there are so many beautiful and inspiring things to see. I saw this huge book on Michelangelo in the library, with color plates. Now he was a genius. I could look at that book all day. There's this one statue of Christ, right after they tore him from the cross. He's all stretched out on Mary's knees, and he's naked except for a little cloth, looking so beautiful, twisting on the folds of his mother's dress. He's smooth and angled at the same time. But he's bleeding from all these horrible wounds. You look at those wounds, not at the angles. And he just lies there while you stare away. Or the slaves Michelangelo carved. They're naked, too, and tied up with ropes, and their muscles are rippling and snapping like rubber bands, but if you look real close you can almost see tears on their stone faces. I look at them, and my heart beats, hard. They're beautiful.

WHITNEY: My mosquito bites need stitches. Can't we go inside?

CARLYLE: Only if you keep the front door open.

WHITNEY: Why? I promise. I won't rape you.

CARLYLE: It's appearances, smarty.

WHITNEY: So if I do rape you, we should close it?

CARLYLE: Whitney!

(*They go inside.*)

CARLYLE: How long are your folks going to be gone?

WHITNEY: Eleven.

CARLYLE: That class lasts four hours?

WHITNEY: They have chips and dip and everybody mingles.

CARLYLE: We're losing all the air conditioning. Close the door.

WHITNEY: I thought ...

CARLYLE: It's a sin to waste.

(*Whitney closes the door.*)

CARLYLE: Look at this. You left the hall light on and the porch light on.

(*Whitney turns out all but one small living room lamp.*)

CARLYLE: That's nicer.

WHITNEY: I can't even see you.

CARLYLE: Course not. You're way over there

(*Whitney sits by Carlyle on the couch.*)

WHITNEY: Hello, Carlyle.

CARLYLE: Hi, Whitney. Do you think I'm pretty?

WHITNEY: Oh yes.

CARLYLE: Damn. Mama says the ugly girls are the lucky ones because they don't have to worry. I was at the nursing home visiting Miss Willoughby and she showed me a picture of herself when she was my age. She was perfect—like an old-fashioned china doll. And she never got married, her whole life through. She was never together with a man. Now, as sweet as she is, her face looks like a road map and her teeth are all pushed out and yellow. And all I thought was, boy, is her chance over now. If I were as gorgeous as Miss

Willoughby was, I'd always be worried that time was running out. I wouldn't want to waste being pretty by being good. So I don't want to be all that pretty.

WHITNEY: Are we going out together or what?

CARLYLE: What do you mean?

WHITNEY: You're here every night, or I'm at your house, we study together, now we're on the Youth Ministry, and we've never even kissed.

CARLYLE: Whitney …

WHITNEY: That makes us abnormal by most standards.

CARLYLE: But I …

WHITNEY: Sort of reverse perverted.

CARLYLE: You can kiss me. (*She offers her cheek.*)

WHITNEY: You're not my grandmother.

CARLYLE: You can kiss me on the lips if you'll sit on your hands.

WHITNEY: What?

CARLYLE: Or go hungry.

(*Whitney sits on his hands and kisses Carlyle. She submits for a moment, then pulls back suddenly.*)

CARLYLE: Mrs. Maxwell found out I made all A's in art, so she put me in charge of all the decorations for the pep rallies and football parties. Arthur Horrishill's having a party at his father's barn tomorrow night but it's not school sponsored and there may not be chaperones. He wants me to do the decorations, and it sure would be good practice. But I'm not sure I should go if there aren't going to be chaperones. What do you think?

WHITNEY: Can I kiss you again?

CARLYLE: Yes.

(*They do.*)

CARLYLE: You moved your hand.

WHITNEY: I know.

CARLYLE: Take it off.

WHITNEY: Move it.

CARLYLE: Please.

WHITNEY: If you really like me, you'll do me a big favor.

CARLYLE: I said take it off, not move it up.

WHITNEY: I think it has a mind of its own!

CARLYLE: *No!*

WHITNEY: It's no different than when someone brushes up against you in the grocery store. That's not sinful. Pretend I'm reaching for the canned peaches only I miss. Excuse me. In which aisle will I find the canned peaches? Seven? Ooh, thank you. Canned apples, canned pears, canned cherries—ah, here we are—peaches!

CARLYLE: (*Laughing.*) Stop it. No more.

WHITNEY: I want to make a whole fruit salad.

CARLYLE: Order out.

WHITNEY: Please, Carlyle. I need this.

CARLYLE: Nobody needs it, Whitney.

WHITNEY: Oh yeah? It's all I've been thinking about. For weeks. Years. Ever since sixth grade. I've lost sleep some nights because there isn't any blood to go to my brain. I can't concentrate on anything. I look at cars, and I think of backseats. I look at people crossing the street, and they're all naked. I look at this couch, and I know it folds out. It's driving me crazy.

CARLYLE: Mama lets me see you because she knows I'll be safe. You're not like Arthur Horrishill and Michael MaCaffey.

WHITNEY: I'm just like them, only not as brave.

CARLYLE: If Mama knew I let you kiss me, she'd kill me.

WHITNEY: We don't have to do anything. Just let me put my hand there. Just once. For five seconds. You can time it.

CARLYLE: I don't have a watch.

WHITNEY: You're not twelve years old! We're both eighteen and we've never done a thing. Don't you think that's a bit weird?

CARLYLE: "It is good for a man not to touch a woman." First Corinthians, chapter seven, verse one.

WHITNEY: Don't be such a prude! I'm dead serious. This is hard for me. Unless I make a move soon, it's all gonna dry up and my chance will be over.

CARLYLE: Whitney...

WHITNEY: People make fun of me for it. Please. You're the only who even likes me. The others are all so eerie. When I'm around them, my whole mouth turns into Jell-O. I can talk to you. Sometimes I think you're my only friend.

CARLYLE: Well, you don't make it very easy. Sometimes they give me a pretty hard time about you.

WHITNEY: Who does?

CARLYLE: The girls. Saying all you do is make wisecracks and that sometimes you try too hard because you're nervous.

WHITNEY: They talk about me like that?

CARLYLE: So it's pretty nice of me to even be here. (*Silence*) Aw, Whitney. I don't care what they say. They're silly. But don't do this to me.

WHITNEY: You're the only person I've ever gone out with. You know that. And I always pay for everything. We've never dutched. I think of how old I am and I get scared.

CARLYLE: Five seconds. No more. (*Whitney places his hand on Carlyle's breast.*) One. Two. Three. Four... (*She jerks away.*) I said you could put it there, I didn't say you could flex it!

WHITNEY: My palm itched.

CARLYLE: Try again. (*Whitney replaces his hand.*) One thousand. Two thousand. Three thousand. Four thousand. Five thousand. (*Whitney removes his hand.*) Was I counting fast?

WHITNEY: I'm not sure.

CARLYLE: You count.

(*Whitney replaces his hand.*)

WHITNEY: One, one thousand...two, one thousand...three, one thousand... four, one thousand...five, one thousand...six, one thousand...seven, one thousand...eight, one thousand...nine, one thousand...ten, one thousand...eleven, one thousand... (*Whitney has pushed her down on the couch and with his free hand he has opened his fly and is guiding her hand to his crotch. She runs her hand in and out across his thigh. Suddenly, she pulls back fiercely.*)

CARLYLE: DON'T ! DON'T YOU DARE! (*Carlyle bolts off the couch.*) GOD IS NOT READY FOR ME TO FORNICATE!

WHITNEY: ...What?

CARLYLE: I'd never say that unless I was very serious.

WHITNEY: Who said anything about... What's wrong with just groping?

CARLYLE: I can't go to bed with you or anybody else. No matter how much I'd like to, which may be very, very much. So please don't think it's you. You're very cute and sweet.

WHITNEY: Even in the Bible sometimes people made it when they weren't supposed to and God forgave them.

CARLYLE: Don't torture me. You don't understand.

WHITNEY: No, I don't.

CARLYLE: I had a celestial vision.

WHITNEY: Huh?

CARLYLE: A revelation. I was sleeping one night, and I heard this soft chorus of bells from upstairs. Only my room is on the top floor.

WHITNEY: Look, Carlyle, you don't have to…

CARLYLE: I have to tell you. I trust you. The bells got louder and louder and I woke up. The ceiling of my room was glowing. We just had the room painted cream and now it was white with heat. I thought I was dreaming so I went to the kitchen to get a Tab 'cause I thought the caffeine would wake me up more and I'd stop hearing the bells and seeing the fire…

WHITNEY: Carlyle…

CARLYLE: Listen to me! When I got back, it was all still there. I crawled up on my bed, and my sheets turned into clouds and I looked down at the carpet and it was whirling like water. For some reason, I wasn't scared, even though my whole bedroom was a vortex. My closet doors turned golden and all these angels flew out and landed on my cloud. And they were all boy angels and they were all naked. Not like Christmas display angels, more like Sistine ceiling angels. I was really embarrassed 'cause I'd never seen a naked man before, and they didn't look at all like Mama said men's bodies should look. They were beautiful and majestic and clean. And they were smooth. Like plastic baby dolls are smooth. There was nothing there. And I knew I was safe, because they were angels and it wasn't dirty. Only naked mortal men are dirty. Only mortal men slice you open and leave you a baby and then run away. And then the angels told me that I was being preserved for the heavenly host. Then I saw that I was naked, too. And beautiful. And they all crawled closer together and I was really nervous but they said they'd give me strength. So we sat together naked and abstained and read Bible verses. We read the Rites of Purification from the Book of Leviticus and sacrificed a lamb right over my pillow. And two turtle doves. When I woke the next morning, everything was normal. So you see, Whitney, there's a real reason.

WHITNEY: All you had to say was "no."

CARLYLE: I'm not lying! Lying would be sacrilegious! I remember right before junior high school, Mama said to me, "Whenever you start thinking nasty sinful thoughts about boys' bodies, just think of your Heavenly Father and your obligation to love and be true to Him."

WHITNEY: Please say you're joking.

CARLYLE: Not about this.

WHITNEY: We can't do anything because I'm not from heaven?

CARLYLE: I'm sorry.

WHITNEY: When do you think all this happened?

CARLYLE: Late July the night after the Youth Ministry Swimming Party—Michael MaCaffey's bathing suit came off in the water and somebody hid it in the bushes. You remember.

WHITNEY: What was all that stuff about being beautiful and not wanting to waste it?

CARLYLE: You don't know how hard it is for me. It drives me crazy sometimes, all right. I want to so bad and I can't. I think about Miss Willoughby and how it might get too late for me, too, and I panic. But I can't. If I could, you'd be the person I'd choose. I love you, Whitney. But I'm being saved. Look at it this way. If God and I went to the same college, and he were in a fraternity, I'd be wearing his pin. That's a stupid way of putting it, but that's how serious it is.

WHITNEY: You had a sex dream.

CARLYLE: I'm going to pretend I didn't hear that.

WHITNEY: Maybe you should read some of those books for English. You might loosen up. Or learn something. Or you should go out and buy one of those magazines you're so curious about.

CARLYLE: You're being mean.

WHITNEY: That's about the dumbest story I've ever heard. I'm desperate, and you're telling me about all these naked Holy Rollers. And I'm sorry, but I think your mother is just a little fried!

CARLYLE: You don't know a thing about my mother.

WHITNEY: And you are so fucking holier-than-thou! Do you want to know something? Katey Whitmore, vice president of the Student Council, screws Arthur Horrishill. And Barbara Mercy gives head to the entire defensive line …

CARLYLE: And Thelma Peeler slept with Michael MaCaffey! Look what happened to her!

WHITNEY: Arthur, Michael, all the guys at school, they're all making fun of me. They know I've never done anything with a girl. They even told the coach and he moved me to an empty locker bank. And somebody took a black marker and wrote "FAG" on every page in my calculus textbook. Even the index. I went to lunch, and I opened my lunch bag, and instead of a banana, there was a dildo. I just can't take it anymore.

CARLYLE: Girls who sin wind up all alone.

WHITNEY: What about Miss Willoughby? She's all alone. (*Short silence.*) Carlyle, you have to help me. They don't let virgins on the team.
(*Carlyle slaps Whitney, hard.*)
CARLYLE: You'll wind up going to hell.
WHITNEY: I'm already there.
CARLYLE: Whitney, you're way ahead of those boys. You don't need the same things they do. You're chosen.
(*Whitney picks up the seminary application.*)
CARLYLE: What are you doing?
(*Whitney starts shredding the papers.*)
CARLYLE: You can't do that.
WHITNEY: I'm not such a great person, Carlyle. All I want right now are two things. To get on the team, and to get laid.
CARLYLE: Your father's going to kill you.
WHITNEY: Fuck him.
CARLYLE: Whitney, you're turning your back on God.
WHITNEY: Fuck Him, too. (*Carlyle gasps and her eyes fill with tears*) And you are one hell of a prick tease.
CARLYLE: Please, Whitney, I'm not! Every night I pray for strength to get through the next day without thinking about it. Pray with me. You can take back what you said. It's frustrated people like us who fall from His Grace and become rapists and prostitutes. Our God is a jealous God.
WHITNEY: You're not being lusted after by God. God doesn't lust! (*Carlyle starts to leave*) If you were normal, you'd want it, too.
CARLYLE: I am not a pervert!
WHITNEY: Fooling around doesn't make you a pervert. It makes you a part of the Animal Kingdom.
CARLYLE: Blasphemer. (*She stares at him.*) I'm going to pray so hard for you tonight.
(*Carlyle exits onto the porch. Whitney looks after her. She turns and reenters the living room. She sits beside him on the couch and tries to kiss him on the cheek. He resists, and she grabs his face and plants an urgent kiss on his lips. He begins to pull her down onto the couch. She wrests herself away and storms out again. She stops for a moment and wipes her lips.*)
CARLYLE: I'm going to pray real hard for both of us.
(*Night overwhelms them both.*)

SCENE TWO

A cool night three weeks later. The far-off moaning of wind. Whitney is alone in the house. Carlyle comes to the door

CARLYLE: Anybody home?

WHITNEY: Hi. Haven't seen you in a while.

CARLYLE: Well, I'm here now. Can I come in?

WHITNEY: Sure.

CARLYLE: Are your parents home?

WHITNEY: The singles seminar was losing money so they started a new one. "God's Role in Divorce." We can sit outside again.

CARLYLE: That's all right. Tonight it's better if they aren't home.

WHITNEY: Why are you so dressed up?

CARLYLE: I just came from Miss Willoughby's funeral. There were three people there. Me, her first cousin once removed, and this old man who didn't know he was at the wrong funeral until it was over. He thought Miss Willoughby was someone else. It was very depressing.

WHITNEY: I'm sorry.

CARLYLE: Oh, it was time for God to take her. I liked visiting her and taking her magazines and her dental floss, but she knew I was only a church volunteer. I think she was lonely for a real relative. Half the time she called me Carmine instead of Carlyle. How are you?

WHITNEY: Fine.

CARLYLE: I just came for a quick visit. How are you feeling?

WHITNEY: You just asked me that.

CARLYLE: Sometimes people say "fine" when they're really not. Miss Willoughby told the doctors "fine" and she had cancer. (*Short silence.*) I heard about the team. I'm sorry.

WHITNEY: I wasn't good enough, that's all.

CARLYLE: I heard Arthur Horrishill told the coach things about you that weren't true and kept you off the team.

WHITNEY: You heard wrong.

CARLYLE: I'm glad. Because the stories were awful.

WHITNEY: What were they?

CARLYLE: They were horrible. All about you and Ted Pewter staying after school in the locker room. Alone.

WHITNEY: That's bullshit, Carlyle. Bullshit.

CARLYLE: I know. It's just what I heard.

WHITNEY: From who?

CARLYLE: Marcia Stunt.

WHITNEY: Who told her?

CARLYLE: Barbara Mercy. Or somebody. I don't know.

WHITNEY: Arthur wouldn't do that to me. He and Michael MaCaffey both told me I had a great tryout. They said I was faster and better than half the other guys. I'm underweight, that's all. Arthur just said I should eat more. Then he and Michael invited me out for a few beers, to start fattening me up, but I had to go. I promised them another time.

CARLYLE: They only talk to you to call you names.

WHITNEY: You're wrong. You're so wrong. They're great guys.

CARLYLE: Did you get the car repainted?

WHITNEY: What?

CARLYLE: I saw what they did to the car. (*Whitney is silent.*) They smashed the windshield with rocks and wrote "Queer" in black spray-paint on the hood. I saw it, Whitney. The whole school saw it. It was in the middle of the football field. That's your father's car.

WHITNEY: It wasn't them. I don't know who it was, but it wasn't them.

CARLYLE: Was your father mad?

WHITNEY: He and I aren't talking much. It wasn't those guys.

CARLYLE: Then who?

WHITNEY: Probably the little faggot, that's who. He's jealous because I've got friends and he doesn't. You should've seen him in the locker room. All spindly and naked, flopping around beside me, never leaving me alone, making people think things. Whiny shit. He did it.

CARLYLE: Whoever did it had no right.

WHITNEY: What do you expect? He tries to pick up grammar school kids … It wasn't Arthur and it wasn't Michael. You should be ashamed of being so suspicious. That's not Christian. It's small-minded and mean.

CARLYLE: They've done things to you before.

WHITNEY: Jokes. Never slander. Sounds to me like your girl friends are the guilty ones. Be careful how you accuse other people. "Thou shalt not bear false witness."

CARLYLE: Just remember. Michael MaCaffey ruined Thelma Peeler's life.

WHITNEY: How do you know it was his fault? How do you know she didn't beg him for it? She was an ugly girl. Probably horny as hell. She probably slept with a lot of guys, then just blamed him because he's captain of the team. She just wanted a good catch. But he was too smart for that. That's the trouble with you. You're so judgmental. You're the one who's so quick to call names. You sling your Bible around like it was a machete.

CARLYLE: I wish you'd told me you were going to quit the Youth Ministry. I just started coming to the meetings and you weren't there. I felt pretty stupid, making up stories about why the president didn't show.

WHITNEY: I've been busy.

CARLYLE: You could've called if you weren't coming. We would've elected a new president, instead of just sitting there like dumb bunnies, waiting. (*Short silence.*) You've been skipping a lot of school. Marcia said you were too ashamed. I don't think you should be ashamed of lies other people tell, or damage other people do.

WHITNEY: Carlyle, will you get off my fucking back?

CARLYLE: You're so much sweeter than all those boys, I don't know why you try so hard to be like them. There are a lot of big-time football players. I don't think there're so many sincere preachers. Your father must be so disappointed.

WHITNEY: Why did you come over here?

CARLYLE: To see you.

WHITNEY: Well, I wish to God you'd stop picking on me.

CARLYLE: I came to ask your help.

WHITNEY: You're doing a pretty piss-poor job.

CARLYLE: I just wanted to see how you were, first, before I asked.

WHITNEY: What do you want?

CARLYLE: Remember the last time I was here and after you kissed me I told you about the party Arthur Horrishill was having at his father's barn? The one without chaperones? And he asked me to do the decorations?

WHITNEY: I missed it.

CARLYLE: Well, I did the decorations. A lot happened at that party.

WHITNEY: Like what?

CARLYLE: Oh, they loved the decorations. I know it's a sin to brag, but I outdid myself. I made goal posts out of wrapping paper tubes and I spray-painted them all gold. And I had this purply tissue left over from the Hallelujah Alliance, so I used it for African violets. The whole barn was goal posts and African violets. I guess it sounds kinda peculiar, but it looked real good.

WHITNEY: They must've lost my invitation.

CARLYLE: Arthur set up the refreshments. An old aquarium filled with punch. I guess it was all he had. And there wasn't any food, which I thought was rude. And then Michael MaCaffey came and Tony Feldman came and Monk Harris and Howard Ritchie and Dude Hawthorne and Fred Stovall and Martin McBride and Runt Adams and pretty soon the whole football team was there.

WHITNEY: Was Marcia there? Or Barbara?

CARLYLE: I was the only girl.

WHITNEY: Huh?

CARLYLE: Oh, Arthur explained it. All the girls were invited for later, and I was early 'cause I'd done all the decorating. And they said how pretty the decorations were, and they toasted me with this grape punch. I couldn't be rude.

WHITNEY: Was it spiked?

CARLYLE: It was tangy.

WHITNEY: But was it spiked …

CARLYLE: What?

WHITNEY: Go on.

CARLYLE: They toasted each other. And then they toasted me. And then they toasted Jesus because I asked them to. They just kept filling my glass and thinking up toasts. And there still weren't any girls, so I got nervous. And Arthur kept talking to me in this low voice, telling me how beautiful I was. Everybody was watching. And then Arthur said the only thing that kept me from being the most popular girl in school was that I was too religious. Then, all of a sudden, Michael MaCaffey got real angry and tried to slug Arthur for no reason, calling him all kinds of names and saying he was pulling out and wanted his money back. The other guys all ganged up and threw Michael out. Then Arthur moved in closer and said I had soft eyes. You'd probably enjoy the seminary, Whitney, if you gave it a chance. You don't have to run around some stony field and get all black and blue.

WHITNEY: Tell me what happened.

CARLYLE: We were at that old barn. You know how far away it is from anywhere. And I wished I had a Daddy I could call, who would drive over and get me. But even if I had, there wasn't a phone. And Arthur wouldn't take me home. And I was so dizzy.

WHITNEY: They didn't try to make you do anything you didn't want to do, did they?

CARLYLE: No! Only you've done that, they never once ... Yes! I don't know. They were breathing all over me.

WHITNEY: Did they touch you at all ...

CARLYLE: They asked me to ... they ripped ... they lifted my ... I don't remember. It was too hot.

WHITNEY: They lifted what?

CARLYLE: Me. My legs. Whitney, I have to go.

WHITNEY: You have to tell me.

CARLYLE: I know what you're thinking. How can you think that about me?

WHITNEY: It's not about you, it's about them. Those guys ... they ... they don't know what they do sometimes. Was it just Arthur? Who else?

CARLYLE: It was nobody!

WHITNEY: I'm calling the police. They should be locked up. Fucking sons-of-bitches.

CARLYLE: Nobody did anything to me!

(*Whitney lifts the phone.*)

WHITNEY: Tell me the truth.

CARLYLE: Whitney, I screamed. I screamed so loud. But no one heard me. Everybody has to know that I screamed.

(*Whitney dials.*)

CARLYLE: No! (*Carlyle grabs the phone away from Whitney.*) I didn't scream! There wasn't anything to scream about.

WHITNEY: You're making things harder. You're going to be O.K., I promise. Give that to me. What you can't tell me you'll have to tell the officer. You shouldn't have waited to tell me. Now give it here...

CARLYLE: You weren't there. You don't know. Who are you trying to hurt?

WHITNEY: They hurt you.

CARLYLE: You said it was my fault. They're good people.

WHITNEY: They're not. I lied. They trashed Dad's car. I sat in the bushes and watched them do it. And Arthur told the coach not to let me on the team because they didn't think I should be allowed in the locker room. They said I was abnormal. And I haven't been going to school because I can't face them. They call me names in class, and they leave dead things in my locker and one day after gym they made me drink from the urinal. And I haven't been going to church because I couldn't face you. Those guys are shitheads and I hate them and they hurt you, so they're going to pay.

CARLYLE: It wasn't the football team.

WHITNEY: Carlyle, please.

CARLYLE: It was the heavenly host in disguise.

WHITNEY: Give me the phone.

CARLYLE: It was wonderful. Really. They ladled more and more of the punch and they poured it right into my mouth, fresh.

WHITNEY: They forced you to drink it.

CARLYLE: I asked them to. And it wasn't grape juice like they serve at Communion. It was the blood. I was drinking that life's blood. It was running down my throat and down my back and down my chest. It made me cry, but I kept drinking.

WHITNEY: It was a bunch of drunken assholes ...

CARLYLE: But I didn't know for sure it was the heavenly host, and this is where it gets kind of embarrassing, until their jeans and their rugby shirts just kind of melted away. They were all big and majestic and naked, and I remembered where I'd seen their bodies before. In the Michelangelo book, the chapter on the Sistine ceiling. Not some grubby athletic field. And I didn't feel ashamed because it wasn't like they were just naked boys in magazines or anything. They were huge and beautiful, more like horses than boys.

WHITNEY: Didn't you say they ripped something? What did they rip? Do you still have it?

CARLYLE: They tore my clothes off me because I wanted them to. I mean, God created Adam and Eve naked and that wasn't dirty. Michelangelo's naked sculptures aren't dirty either. It made me feel as glorious as one of them. They were preparing me. They lay me gently on the table and with their belts they bound my limbs just as Christ was positioned on the cross ...

WHITNEY: Carlyle, stop ...

CARLYLE: I felt the splinters sticking into my back! And then ... Oh, Whitney ... God touched me with his divine light while his angels held me down.

WHITNEY: Who? Was it Arthur?

CARLYLE: It was my vision come true!

WHITNEY: I want a list of everyone at the party. Can you do that for me?

CARLYLE: They were all angels! The angel who looked like Arthur Horrishill had been standing on a barrel, higher up, away from everybody else, casting the reflection of his skin all over the room, like marble. He had the most beautiful smile I'd ever seen. And I knew who He really was. And, as the angels pressed their hands

down hard on my limbs, He alone came into me. And He pushed Himself all through me. And I'd never felt the same special way before. All hot, and my skin was shooting electricity so bright I could see it. I haven't felt so good since I was a baby and Mama gave me backrubs on her knee. I was the sun. And I never screamed. Oh, no. I didn't make a single sound except to say "Yes."

WHITNEY: Fucking bastards.

CARLYLE: I'm telling you I was chosen, and it was the most spiritual night of my life.

WHITNEY: How can people do this to people?

CARLYLE: That's blaspheming God, Whitney! Beg forgiveness.

WHITNEY: Wait. Wait a minute. Was this like your first vision? In your bedroom?

CARLYLE: Exactly.

WHITNEY: Oh, thank God. You woke up the next morning, and you were safe and everything was normal.

CARLYLE: Except my head was aching and I was sore.

WHITNEY: But you were in your own bed.

CARLYLE: No. After God came to me I fell into a deep sleep. When I woke up I was lying on my own front lawn, as if I'd fallen from a cloud in the sky. And when I saw the sun rise, I knew it was carrying a little lost piece of me. I went inside, crawled into bed, and nobody knew it had all happened but me.

(*Whitney embraces her.*)

CARLYLE: You believe in the infallible truth of our Lord, don't you, Whitney? He'd never play a joke or anything. Say he saw the Russians making bombs and the Americans making bombs and overcrowded cities and forest fires and unmarried people fornicating and homosexuals and He got real mad at the world. Or even just bored. Would He ever play a joke and take it all out on one person?

WHITNEY: God wouldn't.

CARLYLE: Because I'm pregnant.

WHITNEY: What?

CARLYLE: I haven't bled for five weeks.

WHITNEY: Oh, hell. Oh, Jesus. Have you seen a doctor?

CARLYLE: I've never been late.

WHITNEY: Does Arthur know?

CARLYLE: It was not Arthur! If it was, I never would've stayed at the party. I would've walked home even. If it was just Arthur, what would that make me?

WHITNEY: Nothing. Anything that happened isn't your fault.

CARLYLE: A football whore. A Thelma Peeler with normal feet. Somebody someone took a pool and won money over. Is that what you think of me?

WHITNEY: No.

CARLYLE: That's how you're treating me.

WHITNEY: I want to help you in the best way. But you can't make up stories and believe them …

CARLYLE: I don't have a choice! I'm not the kind of girl who gets knocked up at a football party. But I'm also not the type who grows ugly and dies lonely. If you want to help me, you'll believe it with me and you won't call anybody.

WHITNEY: Have you told your mother?

CARLYLE: I can't.

WHITNEY: Someone should.

CARLYLE: No. Mary had a Joseph so her mother didn't mind. And God let them all in on the secret. Well, God's only talked to me. Not Mama. I don't have a Joseph. Mama would never question the Lord, but she might question me.

WHITNEY: But it's not your fault.

CARLYLE: Don't keep saying that.

WHITNEY: You don't have to have a baby.

CARLYLE: *I'm not going to murder God's baby!*

WHITNEY: You're not going to have …

CARLYLE: Shut up! I'm not listening to you. Please, Whitney. I'm all alone. You have to be on my side.

WHITNEY: I am.

CARLYLE: You see, Whitney, you're the only one who can be my Joseph. You're sensitive and you can make me laugh. And your Dad's a minister and he'd understand. God would talk to him. And that night three weeks ago you touched me like maybe you'd like it if we were married. We'd never have to count to five thousand.

WHITNEY: We have to get you some help.

CARLYLE: Please marry me.

WHITNEY: I can't.

CARLYLE: Why not? You said you wanted to help.

WHITNEY: I do.

CARLYLE: You think I'm a bad person.

WHITNEY: No, I love you.

CARLYLE: So save me.

WHITNEY: I'm the wrong person to ask.

CARLYLE: You won't marry me because you think I'm a football whore. I thought you'd stick by me. Please, Whitney. I haven't done evil.

WHITNEY: I'm not good enough for you.

CARLYLE: No, you're too good. You got elected president of the Youth Ministry and your best buddies are on the football team and your Daddy's a minister and he's sending you to seminary school, so you don't want to speak to me or touch me or anything ever again.

WHITNEY: Carlyle, I'm the one that's bad.

CARLYLE: I can take a lot, Whitney, but I can't take your hating me.

WHITNEY: It's me, Carlyle. Sometimes I have to be with people even more than I have to be with God. Any person. I think that's the reason I didn't move when Ted brushed up against me in gym class, even though I knew people were looking.

CARLYLE: What?

WHITNEY: Oh, I ran home straight after class and took another shower just to get rid of the locker room stink. Then I put on two pairs of Jockey shorts and walked around the house hating myself because this lonely kid touched me. I lay awake some nights worrying, thinking God must hate me and something horrible is wrong with me. Maybe Arthur's right. Maybe I'm abnormal. But I do know one thing. It's normal to want to be held. And sometimes, skin is just skin no matter who's wearing it. It feels good next to itself for a reason.

CARLYLE: Just tell me. Will you marry me or won't you? I need to know.

WHITNEY: I won't go to hell for just standing there and not moving. And you won't go to hell for not screaming.

(*Carlyle starts to leave. Whitney follows her outside.*)

WHITNEY: Don't go. I never told anyone those things before.

CARLYLE: I can't stay here. It's not good for me.

WHITNEY: Don't. I want to help you.

CARLYLE: I don't see how you can.

WHITNEY: I'm going to call the police and tell them about Horrishill.

CARLYLE: I'll deny anything you tell them.

WHITNEY: Don't do this.

CARLYLE: All the time I thought they were being cruel to you. Now I find out they were just telling the truth. I don't blame the team. Even God hates fags.

WHITNEY: I didn't do anything wrong.

CARLYLE: No, you just stood there. Did he touch you more than once?

WHITNEY: Stop it.

CARLYLE: Were you hoping for more? Most people do it with girls, Whitney. Maybe you can't. Maybe it's impossible for you to do it, now that you're polluted. Faggot.

WHITNEY: I'd say fuck you, but somebody already did.

(*Carlyle lunges at Whitney's chest and begins to pound him with her fists. He doesn't resist. Her arms grow weaker and she begins to sob. Whitney holds her.*)

WHITNEY: It's not fair. It's just not fair. He has no right to be this hard on us. Just us. Other people don't have these problems.

CARLYLE: Other people don't have His grace and His love either. We couldn't know pleasure if we didn't know pain.

WHITNEY: Which is which?

CARLYLE: I don't know.

WHITNEY: I don't want to be a bad person. But I just don't know what else to do.

CARLYLE: God will forgive us.

WHITNEY: How?

CARLYLE: If you said you'd be my Joseph.

WHITNEY: But why would you want …

CARLYLE: Who else would I want?

WHITNEY: You're sure you're pregnant?

CARLYLE: I think so.

WHITNEY: All your visions were just very exciting dreams.

CARLYLE: You don't get pregnant by dreaming. I'm a girl, Whitney. If you were my Joseph, you could do it with me.

WHITNEY: I won't be able to stand myself. I'd be like one of them.

CARLYLE: You should prove to yourself that you can do it. Here.

(*She takes his hand and places it on her breast.*)

WHITNEY: No.

CARLYLE: Shhh …

WHITNEY: I can't marry you.

CARLYLE: Shhh …

WHITNEY: I can't. What would you tell your Mama?

CARLYLE: She loves you.

WHITNEY: What would I tell my parents?

CARLYLE: I don't know. I guess I haven't been promised a star or wise men.

WHITNEY: Carlyle, if we do this, we'd have to tell people I made you pregnant, so we're getting married.

CARLYLE: Whitney, I hoped you say that.

WHITNEY: Then it will have to be my baby. It will have to be my baby and not God's. Do you hear me?

CARLYLE: It would sure show the guys at school. You'll be a husband. A father, while they'll still be a sad group of guys who have to place bets and get a girl drunk before …

WHITNEY: Don't.

CARLYLE: We'll have the most extraordinary life together.

WHITNEY: We can't.

CARLYLE: You need to know.

(*She places his other hand on her second breast.*)

CARLYLE: Now don't talk so much. This is how you'll become my Joseph.

WHITNEY: Jesus. My parents'll be home in an hour.

CARLYLE: A whole hour?

WHITNEY: Can't we at least go inside? It's freezing.

CARLYLE: We're safe. There are trees. And the stars are so pretty. We can pretend we're on one of those clouds, way up there.

WHITNEY: Can I kiss you?

(*They do.*)

WHITNEY: This is so wrong.

CARLYLE: You need to know if you can.

WHITNEY: I need to know.

CARLYLE: You can kiss me again.

(*She strokes his thigh. They slowly sink to the ground.*)

CARLYLE: Oh, look, Whitney! It's so beautiful. And calm. Look at your hair. In the moonlight it shines.

(*She unbuttons his shirt and slips it off his shoulders. She kisses his chest.*)

CARLYLE: Your skin is glowing like marble. It's radiating light. You look like something Michelangelo might paint somewhere high on a ceiling.

(*She runs her hands down his sides and kisses him on the forehead.*)

CARLYLE: You look like an angel. Just like an angel.

(*Tableau.*)

END OF PLAY